United States Military Justice
in the Civil War

ALSO BY R. GREGORY LANDE
AND FROM MCFARLAND

Spiritualism in the American Civil War (2020)
Psychological Consequences of the American Civil War (2017)

United States Military Justice in the Civil War

Court-Martial Practices and Administration

R. Gregory Lande

McFarland & Company, Inc., Publishers
Jefferson, North Carolina

ISBN (print) 978-1-4766-9584-6
ISBN (ebook) 978-1-4766-5387-7

Library of Congress and British Library
cataloguing data are available

Library of Congress Control Number 2024038814

© 2024 R. Gregory Lande. All rights reserved

No part of this book may be reproduced or transmitted in any form or by any means, electronic or mechanical, including photocopying or recording, or by any information storage and retrieval system, without permission in writing from the publisher.

Front cover image: Drumming a thief out of camp with the "Rogue's March." The thief wears the placard "THIEF—This man stole … money from a wounded friend." Morris Island, South Carolina. [LC-B8156-89 Library of Congress Prints and Photographs Division, Washington, D.C.]

Printed in the United States of America

*McFarland & Company, Inc., Publishers
Box 611, Jefferson, North Carolina 28640
www.mcfarlandpub.com*

To my wife, Brenda Lande, whose understanding
fills these pages, and to our son, Galen Lande,
who gives purpose to every word.

Acknowledgments

The author extends sincere gratitude for their critical review of the present work to William Bograkos, DO, Colonel (Retired), Medical Corps, USA; Sawsan Ghurani, MD, Captain (Retired), Medical Corps, USN; and Jack Pierce, MD, Captain (Retired), Medical Corps, USN.

Table of Contents

Acknowledgments vi
Preface 1
Introduction 5

ONE
Court-Martial Law in the Civil War 11

TWO
Unauthorized Absences 27

THREE
Alcohol and Misconduct 68

FOUR
Violent Misconduct 129

Five
Subordinate Military Crimes 186

Bibliography 221
Index 237

Preface

United States Military Justice in the Civil War: Court-Martial Practices and Administration is the result of my three intersecting interests: medicine, the military, and history. After completing a military psychiatry residency, my first assignment was to an Army division in Germany. A few months later, I became involved in my first Army court-martial, where I served as an expert witness in a trial centered around the sanity of a service member. Throughout this process, I discovered a fascination with medical jurisprudence, yet I simultaneously realized my significant lack of knowledge in the field. To address this gap, I undertook a year-long fellowship in forensic psychiatry. In the following years, I used my growing expertise to help establish the Army's first forensic psychiatry fellowship. Additionally, I testified in a wide range of administrative, civil, and criminal cases.

The historical underpinnings of medical jurisprudence increasingly engaged my curiosity. This led me to undertake earnest research on the topic, culminating in the publication of various articles, chapters, and books. The beginning of my journey in that direction started with "The History of Forensic Psychiatry in the U.S. Military," a chapter in *Principles and Practice of Military Forensic Psychiatry* (Lande 1997). I gradually restricted my research to focus on the American Civil War. *Madness, Malingering, and Malfeasance: The Transformation* of *Psychiatry and the Law in the Civil War Era* was my first book devoted to that subject (Lande 2005), followed by *The Abraham Man: Madness, Malingering, and the Development of Medical Testimony* (Lande 2012), *Psychological Consequences of the American Civil War* (Lande 2017), and *Spiritualism in the American Civil War* (Lande 2020).

United States Military Justice in the Civil War furthers my historical research and offers readers a scholarly examination of the principles and practices of military law as it existed in the Union Army, Navy, and Marine Corps. It became evident to me that a patchwork quilt of publications addresses the subject, but *United States Military Justice in the Civil War* fills a niche for readers interested in a comprehensive overview.

An analysis of American Civil War legal policy, procedures, and practices must include the Army, Navy, and Marine Corps. This is a unique contribution that *United States Military Justice in the Civil War* brings to the subject. By broadening the research to include the three services, *United States Military Justice in the Civil War* compares the customs, traditions, and approaches implemented by the Union force's different services.

United States Military Justice in the Civil War provides comparative insights into the practice of military law from which readers will discover both similarities and differences among the three services. For example, although Navy general courts-martial sentenced a few service members to death, none were ever executed, in stark contrast to the 267 executed in the Army. The Navy and Marine Corps had no convictions for rape, a revelation and understudied area. Post-trial reviews mitigated, remitted, or reversed many courts-martial, another under-studied subject.

Historians who limit their examinations of Civil War justice to soldiers who were officially executed by military authorities run the risk of oversimplifying their conclusions based on a small sample size. While the courts-martial of executed soldiers offered a compelling window into the complexities of military justice during the period, they represent only a fraction of the legal proceedings that occurred during the conflict. To fully understand the nature and impact of military justice during the Civil War, historians must examine a wider range of cases and legal issues.

A more comprehensive approach to studying the administration of military justice during the Civil War would involve identifying cases that authorities mitigated before reaching President Lincoln, examining the incidence of acquittals, describing the factors that could reverse a trial's outcome, and exploring the common issues that contributed to criminal behavior among service members. Of particular importance is the often-overlooked role of alcohol in such behaviors, which has been largely ignored by many researchers. Through a more comprehensive and nuanced study of military justice during the Civil War, historians can gain a fuller appreciation of how law, politics, and social dynamics intersected during this pivotal period in American history. *United States Military Justice in the Civil War* adopted this approach by including research that looked at an extensive group of courts-martial and the many factors that altered a trial's outcome.

United States Military Justice in the Civil War highlights the unmistakable relationship between alcohol misuse and misconduct, how the prosecutions of sexual misconduct differed between the services, and how the application of military law was at times uneven, even unfair, but overall, adequately addressed the balance between discipline and the service member's legal protections.

The principal sources of data collection were reports published in the *General Orders of the War Department 1861–1865*; *General Court Martial Orders from the Departments of the South, Middle, Pacific, Gulf, and Missouri*, among others; *Proceedings of US Army Courts-Martial and Military Commissions of Union Soldiers Executed by US Military Authorities 1861–1866*; *Records of General Courts-Martial and Courts of Inquiry of the Navy Department, 1799–1867*; state regimental rosters; adjutant general reports; pertinent military personnel records; legal treatises; and contributions from modern historians. I cataloged and statistically analyzed the verdicts from 5,000 courts-martial and courts of inquiry and I also analyzed a list of Navy officers from 1775 to 1900 and identified 698 surgeons who served varying amounts of time between the dates from April 12, 1861, to April 9, 1865.

Let me remind readers that the representational database of 5,000 military trial verdicts is a sample, albeit an exceptionally large one, in *United States Military Justice in the Civil War*. It would be impossible to accurately identify every Civil War service member's disciplinary history; records are too often incomplete, the use of aliases surprisingly common, and crimes such as desertion never adjudicated for lack of apprehension. At the same time, *United States Military Justice in the Civil War* primarily focused on trial verdicts, although in some cases readers will discover how post-trial reviews affected the outcomes. I also need to mention that my research only examined Union military trials.

The Introduction describes the representational database in detail. The author believes readers will benefit from a basic understanding of military law as it applied to service members during the Civil War, and a chapter in *United States Military Justice in the Civil War* reviews that subject. This is not a complete analysis of military justice, which lies outside the scope of this book. However, understanding the elementary aspects will enhance the readers' experience of the subsequent chapters. Readers interested in a comprehensive education on court-martial rules and regulations during the Civil War will find helpful references in the chapter devoted to that subject.

The remaining chapters discuss the alleged military crimes through a three-part, integrated discussion that includes pertinent data from the representational database, the thoughts of modern historians, and an extensive presentation of courts-martial allowing the reader "to witness the legal proceedings." This collective approach provides readers with a balanced, comprehensive, and nuanced understanding of *United States Military Justice in the Civil War*.

United States Military Justice in the Civil War may surprise some readers with its revelations. Casual readers of the subject may be familiar with Union soldiers executed during the war, a subject that historians have dealt with extensively. This key area of historical research is dramatic and riveting but by itself may lead a casual reader to conclude that Civil War military justice was capricious and cruel.

The research on *United States Military Justice in the Civil War* provides the basis for a different argument, one that suggests a more nuanced opinion. In most cases, court-martial verdicts and their subsequent punishments were swift and certain and if left unchanged would have sustained the casual reader's conviction. But that was not the case, as *United States Military Justice in the Civil War* revealed echelons of review that amended a substantial number of the original punishments and, to a lesser degree, the verdicts.

Far from being rigidly uncompromising and devoid of benevolence, *United States Military Justice in the Civil War* chronicles a system in evolution, straddling the imperatives of discipline and legal protections for service members while simultaneously engaging Southern forces on the battlefields. Through the process, military law gradually adapted to meet the changing needs of the war effort and contributed to the foundation of modern military justice.

Introduction

Military forces routinely fight two battles. One is against a determined physical enemy, and the other is a psychological fight within the service member. Military commanders rely on weapons and strategy to defeat a determined physical enemy, but the psychological battlefield is on a different terrain, dominated by the peaks and valleys of human behavior that must yield to hierarchical authority, subjugation of self, and discipline. An effective force traverses this landscape by aligning the interests of the military personnel with the mission, crafting a unified response with minimal dissension and maximum motivation. In the broadest sense, obedience captures the essence of the psychological battle.

Training is the touchstone for honing obedience. Military instruction provides the foundation built on the customs, traditions, and obligations expected of service personnel. More specific training adds the framework that differentiates the various military roles. Obedience requires more than training. Motivational factors such as pay, patriotism, and a leader's character shape a service member's willingness to follow a military commander's directives. Those same factors when inverted can also undermine discipline. Military organizations enforce obedience through a system that delegates increasing levels of authority based on rank: a time-tested structure that permits the use of rewards and punishments to influence behaviors.

Punishment can be a two-edged sword. When deftly dispensed it supports equity, but when applied unfairly it bleeds injustice, and like a hemorrhaging wound it can be disastrous unless staunched. Staunching the flow falls within the province of military law, which aims to balance the military's need for discipline with procedural safeguards for service members.

Military laws proved to be a valuable ally for commanders facing the daunting challenge of transforming an untrained and undisciplined civilian force into a proficient fighting unit capable of withstanding the rigors of battle during the Civil War. The implementation of strict rules and regulations was crucial to achieving this goal, and military laws provided commanders with the necessary tools to enforce discipline and ensure the effectiveness of their troops.

During the Civil War, political debates and battlefield conflicts overshadowed the public's awareness of the day-to-day enforcement of command authority, making it a relatively mundane and unremarkable aspect of military life. While high-profile trials or military executions occasionally captured the public's attention, the routine administration of military justice rarely surfaced as a topic of newsworthy discussion. This lack of public scrutiny, however, should not be taken to mean that command authority was not taken seriously by military leaders or that the enforcement of discipline was not a critical factor in the success of military operations. The ability of commanders to maintain order and ensure the obedience of their troops was essential to the functioning of the military hierarchy and the effective execution of military strategy.

Despite its relative invisibility to the public, the administration of military justice was a central feature of military life during the Civil War, and it played a vital role in maintaining the discipline necessary for military success. Over time, historians have turned their attention to the practice of military justice during the Civil War and have arrived at different conclusions regarding its fairness and integrity. While some scholars have criticized the military justice system for being arbitrary and excessively harsh, others have defended it as a necessary means of maintaining discipline and order in the face of the unprecedented challenges posed by the conflict.

Analyzing the courts-martial of soldiers executed by Union authorities is one of the most dramatic ways to study the administration of military justice during the Civil War. These cases offer a unique perspective on the challenges and complexities of military justice, as well as how it intersected with broader political and social issues of the time. A valuable resource in that regard is *All Were Not Heroes: A Study of the List of U.S. Soldiers Executed by U.S. Military Authorities During the Late War* (Johnson, E., Johnson, and Williams 1997, 132–133). Another important study of military legal practices on this subject is *Civil War Justice: Union Army Executions Under Lincoln* (Alotta 1989). Additionally, President Abraham Lincoln was a staunch bulwark standing firmly between a soldier's death sentence and his execution, which offers researchers another avenue to explore military justice. *Merciful Lincoln* did just that with a comprehensive study of the President's intercession in capital cases (Lowry 2010).

In *Civil War Justice: Union Army Executions Under Lincoln* the author pointed out that the speed with which military authorities handled execution cases during the period was a cause for concern (Alotta 1989, 18).

However, to fully appreciate the strengths and weaknesses of the military justice system during the Civil War, it is necessary to examine not only the speed with which cases were handled but also the incidence of acquittals, mitigations, and reversals in a larger group of courts-martial.

This volume, *United States Military Justice in the Civil War*, has achieved a more comprehensive analysis through the author's creation of a representative database of 5,000 trial verdicts. These data include trials involving 786 Navy, 136 Marine Corps, and 4,078 Army service members. One-third of this representative database included courts-martial involving officers (n = 1,655, 33.1%), and the remainder enlisted service members (n = 3,345, 66.9%). Except for thirty-nine courts of inquiry and five military commissions, general courts-martial issued the remaining decisions. The combined Army, Navy, and Marine Corps databases provide a more complete picture of Civil War legal practices while additionally enabling detailed analyses of each service's similarities and differences.

The earliest court-martial included in the representative database began on August 1, 1861. The author continued adding military trial data until mid–June 1865, an admittedly arbitrary extension two months after the Civil War ended, for the sole purpose of capturing crimes committed during the war. These data included 538 trials from 1861, 1,277 in 1862, 1,379 in 1863, 1,452 in 1864, and 354 in the Civil War's truncated last year.

The author cross-referenced service members' names with other demographics such as rank, regimental unit, and date of the court-martial to eliminate duplicates. Identical names that remained in the representative database were either unique individuals or courts-martial of the same service members at separate times.

In terms of rank distribution, enlisted personnel furnished most of these data. The Army data included 2,725 enlisted soldiers (n = 4,078, 66.8%). The lowest Army rank furnished most of the soldiers for these courts-martial, with privates constituting nearly the entire group (n = 2432/2725, 89.2%). Noncommissioned officers added 131 soldiers to the tally, a number that included ten first sergeants and three sergeant majors.

In a pattern like that of the Army, two-thirds of the Navy data incorporated 496 enlisted service members (n = 786, 63.1%). The lowest Navy enlisted rates contributed the lion's share of data. Over one-third of the navy courts-martial involved seamen (n = 197/496, 39.7%). Landsmen added 96 courts-martial to the total (n = 496, 19.4%). Higher up the ladder were 81 master's mates (n = 496, 16.3%).

The Marine Corps data included a greater proportion of enlisted personnel (n = 124/136, 91.2%) as compared to the Army and Navy. Even so, the percentage of privates in the Marine Corps sample was like the Army data (n = 110/136, 80.9%).

To provide a more complete picture of military justice during the Civil War, the representative database included examples of officers' courts-martial. One-third of the total Army database includes 1,353 officers (n = 4078, 33.2%). As was the case with enlisted service members, lower-ranking officers constituted most of the database. Lieutenants composed just over half of the officer sample (n = 764/1353, 56.5%), which included 446 first lieutenants (n = 764, 58.4%). Captains composed nearly one-third of the group (n = 401/1353, 29.6%). Perhaps surprisingly, the next most frequently represented officers in the database were Army surgeons, with a total of 50 (n = 1353, 3.7%).

The Navy data included 290 officers (n = 786, 36.9%). Engineers contributed most of the officers in the Navy courts-martial (n = 114/290, 39.3%), followed by ensigns, who added another 59 to the data (n = 290, 20.3%). There were 10 Navy surgeons (n = 290, 3.5%).

Marine Corps data included 12 officers (n = 136, 8.8%). As with the Army and Navy, lower-ranking officers comprised the group. Lieutenants accounted for one-half of the Marine Corps officers' courts-martial (n = 6/12, 50.0%). Captains added five (n = 12, 41.7%) and there was one lieutenant colonel.

The Army, Navy, and Marine Corps have similar percentages of enlisted and officer service members. As a representative database, this balance facilitates a more accurate comparative analysis of the three military services.

Courts-martial typically charged service members with multiple crimes. The 5,000 trials in the representative database documented the first five individual charges per service member. Extending the analysis beyond the first charge, such as murder, to include desertion or drunkenness, for example, provides a more complete view of the alleged unlawful behaviors.

This study grouped various allegations in terms of similarity. Desertion, absence without leave (AWOL), quitting guard, and leaving post are examples of crimes collected under the general heading of unauthorized absences. The alcohol group comprised military charges that alleged drunkenness and intoxication. A violence group integrated murder, mutiny, assault, and rape.

When allegations are grouped in this manner, military authorities predominantly prosecuted unauthorized absences, followed by alcohol-related offenses. Some less common crimes in the representative database did not fit neatly into a broad category, and specific examples of these offenses will illustrate sections in a subsequent chapter.

Regardless of the crime, a guilty verdict was the overwhelming outcome of these courts-martial. When examining the 5,000 trials, 88.2

percent ended with a guilty verdict (n = 4410/5000). By service, Army courts-martial concluded with an 87.7 percent conviction rate (n = 3576/4078), the Navy a bit higher with 91.0 percent of their trials ending with guilty verdicts (n = 715/786), and the Marine Corps slightly less with an 83.8 percent conviction rate (n = 114/136).

Officers did not fare much better. Army courts-martial convicted 84.3 percent of their charged officers (n = 1140/1353), the Navy 88.0 percent of their charged officers (n = 255/290), and the Marine Corps found 91.7 percent of their charged officers guilty (n = 11/12).

Punishments varied for convicted service members, with just over one in ten cases resulting in the death penalty (n = 559/5,000, 11.2%). Given the dates studied, this database included 243 enlisted service members who suffered capital punishment. Another one-fifth of the sentences combined hard labor with varying lengths of confinement (n = 1,010/5,000, 20.2%). Ignominious discharges were common among the officers in this representative database, with 883 officers dismissed (n = 1,655, 53.4%) and another 311 cashiered (n = 1,655, 18.8%).

The authoritative database included service members from all the Union states that participated in the Civil War, as well as members of the United States Regular Army units. New York supplied the largest contingent of service members from a state (n = 1,003), followed by Pennsylvania (n = 521) and Massachusetts (n = 234). Service members assigned to infantry units comprised most of the entries (n = 3,271), followed by cavalry (n = 407), artillery (n = 320), and engineers (n = 80).

ONE

Court-Martial Law in the Civil War

South Carolina's secession from the Union unleashed passions and patriotism that propelled the divided nation into a cataclysmic abyss. Political leaders from the newly constituted Confederate States of America and the states remaining loyal to the Union exhorted men to rally for their respective causes. Those nationalistic winds fanned animosities, blew doubts aside, and inflated dogma, the basic ingredients for expanding military units.

Citizen soldiers heeded the call to arms, long on enthusiasm but short on military proficiencies. Military leaders, some of whom suffered the same deficiencies, struggled to train and contain their recruits. One of their principal allies in the quest for a cohesive and effective fighting force was a legal structure that regulated the conduct of all military service members.

This legal structure, otherwise known as military law or military justice, ideally served two broad goals: promoting military authority, and simultaneously providing every service member with certain legal protections. Tension existed between these two imperatives, but when they were balanced, equity was dominant, whereas a lack of equipoise could threaten a military unit's integrity and combat capabilities.

Many factors can tilt the scales of justice and undermine a system's probity, one of the more powerful of which is the degradation of rules and regulations during times of existential crises such as occurred during the Civil War. Exigencies of conflict may amplify and support arguments that favor authority over individual rights, but chronic, cavalier dismissal of service members' interests can erode command influence.

Military law seeks to maintain a balance between authority and protection that respects both, while remaining adaptive to amendments that may change the calculus. One pertinent example of military law's malleability was President Lincoln's directive in General Orders Number 206, published February 26, 1864, "that the sentences of all deserters, who have been condemned by Court Martial to death, and that have not been otherwise acted upon by him, be mitigated to imprisonment during the war, at the Dry Tortugas, Florida" (General Orders Number 206, 1864).

As a starting point, military law can be defined as "that part of the law of the land relating to the government of the military forces, and having for its object military discipline" (Ives 1879, 16). The United States Constitution provides the authority for military law by expressly directing Congress "to make rules for the government and regulation of the land and naval forces" (Ives 1879, 16).

The United States Congress did not start with a blank slate when developing military law. When the thirteen American colonies declared their independence, our founding fathers understood that words alone would not achieve that outcome; instead, this led to the creation of the Continental Army. The rules and regulations of the Continental Army closely mirrored the English Mutiny Act and Articles of War, a familiar and easily replicable template adopted by the dissident colonials. Sixty-nine articles subsequently governed the Continental Army. A major revision resulted in the sixty-nine articles increasing to 101 articles when the United States Congress approved the additions in 1806. With just a few subsequent changes, the 101 articles remained in force until 1874, spanning the Civil War years (Ives 1879, 18).

Supplementing the articles are regulations that since 1813 have been the province of succeeding Secretaries of War, subject to the review and approval of the United States President. General regulations provide a timely and responsive mechanism for the administration of the military (Ives 1879, 18–20).

The Articles of War enshrined military authority by declaring "that any officer or soldier, who disobeys any lawful command of his superior officer, shall suffer death, or such other punishment as a court-martial may direct" (Ives 1879, 20). This directive included both general orders and verbal orders.

An example of a general order "published for the information and government of the Army" was President Lincoln's Emancipation Proclamation, which in part stated "That, on the first day of January, in the year of our Lord one thousand eight hundred and sixty-three, all persons held as slaves within any State or designated part of a State, the people whereof shall then be in rebellion against the United States, shall be then, thenceforward, and forever, free ... and that the Executive government of the United States, including the military and naval authorities thereof, will recognize and maintain the freedom of said persons" (General Orders Number 1, 1864).

Military law primarily consists of Articles of War, regulations, and orders but does not operate in a vacuum ignoring civilian court decisions, particularly those issued by the United States Supreme Court. Lesser courts and executive officers with legal expertise, such as an attorney general, may also influence the practice of military law (Ives 1879, 22–23).

The uneven performance of military justice during the Civil War could be attributed in part to a lack of familiarity with military law. The complexity of military law was a foreign subject for many enlisted service members and officers. Seasoned members of the ranks had more experience, but it seems reasonable to suggest that some uneven performance of military justice could be attributed to a lack of familiarity with the governing rules. Strict procedures defining the conduct of military trials and both formal and informal avenues for appeal lessened the burden of learning and the potential for injudicious harm.

Approximately one year before the Civil War, a court-martial in the soon-to-secede state of South Carolina offered a detailed examination of military legal practices. Special Order Number 41 directed the formation of a court-martial at Fort Moultrie for the trial of Surgeon Bernard M. Byrne, assigned to the United States Army Medical Department. Eight officers, including Brevet Brigadier General Sylvester Churchill, assembled on March 26, 1859, to consider "Neglect of duty, to the prejudice of good order and military discipline ... when a fatal and epidemic disease, known as yellow fever, prevailed among the troops ... said Byrne did then and there neglect and abandon his duty, to attend the sick of said post." The court-martial also considered "Conduct unbecoming a gentleman." [Byrne] falsely state[d] as follows: "At the time I was taken ill, the health of the command ... was better than it had been at any time for several months previously ... whereas, in truth and in fact, at the time when the said Byrne alleges that he was taken ill ... the health of the command at Fort Moultrie, South Carolina, was worse than it had been for several months previously. Epidemic yellow fever was on the increase, and there were eight sick men in hospital at said post" (General Orders Number 9, 1859).

Byrne was not a stranger to infectious diseases, having published his second edition of *An Essay to Prove the Contagious Character of Malignant Cholera* in 1855 (Byrne 1855). His enlightened treatise derisively denounced "non-contagionists" as physicians who tenaciously clung to preventive strategies that for decades had failed to arrest the spread of the dreaded disease. Unaware of the bacterial basis for the disease, Byrne argued that human contact transmitted cholera and prevention required effective quarantine (Byrne 1855, 124–133).

Byrne pleaded not guilty to the charges, and after hearing the testimony, members of his court-martial agreed and acquitted the surgeon.

Unfortunately for Byrne, that verdict did not please Secretary of War John B. Floyd, who disagreed with the doctor's claim that lumbago and sciatica prevented his care of the sick soldiers. Adding weight to Floyd's argument was the testimony of an assistant surgeon who disputed Byrne's disability. While reluctantly sustaining the court-martial's verdict, Floyd appended a critical postscript: "It was an error in the ruling of the Court on the law of evidence, to reject testimony offered by the prosecution, in rebutting the defence of sickness, to show fear of contagion ... a chief motive of feigned sickness" (General Orders Number 9, 1859).

The published rebuke no doubt motivated Byrne to counter the Secretary of War's opinion, which he did by "publishing the proceedings of this Court Martial in full ... that all the facts relating to the unfounded slander on which this trial was based, may be spread before the public, to enable it to make its own deductions, and to form its own judgment on the subject." The transcript included Byrne's lengthy defense read to the court by his attorney, William E. Martin (Byrne 1859, 1).

Byrne's rebuttal and efforts at reputation rehabilitation ended abruptly with his death at Fort Moultrie on September 6, 1860. In an ironic twist, the 46-year-old physician died from a fulminant case of typhoid fever ("News Summary" 1860).

The court-martial of Army Surgeon Bernard M. Byrne followed procedures that typified military trials, but the rapid mobilization of men in the Civil War threatened legal consistency and equality. Military authorities could not ignore discipline given the innumerable infractions, although in most cases nonjudicial actions sufficed to maintain order, but more egregious offenses demanded the constitution of a court-martial.

William Martin, Byrne's defense counsel, referenced William C. De Hart as a legal authority based on his 1846 publication of *Observations on Military Law and the Constitution and Practice of Courts Martial*. De Hart prefaced his book by noting that no previous work exclusively devoted to the administration of American military justice existed. As an acting judge advocate of the Army, De Hart observed the inconsistent application of military laws and he sought to rectify that deficiency with his primer on the subject. The book's publisher provided reprints of his book throughout the Civil War (De Hart 1863, 1).

In contrast to civilian courts, the military only convenes a trial when a senior officer orders the constitution of a court-martial. The gravity of the preferred charge determines the type of court-martial convened, and military law during the Civil War recognized three types of courts-martial: general, regimental, and garrison. General courts-martial prosecuted the most serious infractions of military law and wielded the broadest range of punishments, including the death penalty. Regimental and garrison courts-martial had a more restricted role in terms of both the infractions prosecuted and the sentences imposed (De Hart 1863, 4).

Courts-martial members were always officers, and military law required a minimum of five and a maximum of thirteen for a general court-martial. The law added the stipulation that "as many members shall be summoned, not to exceed thirteen, on every such court, as can be convened without injury to the service" (De Hart 1863, 5). The senior officer summoning the court-martial, otherwise referred to as the convening authority, determined the particulars including the number of officers, their ranks, and when the trial would commence. President of the court-martial was a title awarded to the highest-ranking member (De Hart 1863, 46). De Hart extensively discussed the legal impropriety of permitting officers without a rank, such as chaplains, assistant surgeons, and surgeons, to serve as court-martial members (De Hart 1863, 41). Officers suspected of any offense were tried by a general court-martial (De Hart 1863, 37).

To guard against errors or abuse, the procedures and findings of a general court-martial were subject to review or revision by the convening

Court-martial, Army of the Cumberland, Chattanooga, Tennessee (LC-DIG-ppmsca-34060 Library of Congress Prints and Photographs Division, Washington, D.C.).

authority. As De Hart noted, "every officer authorized to order a general court-martial shall have power to pardon or mitigate any punishment ordered by such court, except the sentence of death, or of cashiering an officer." There were instances where senior military commanders had the authority but would defer solemn decisions to the President of the United States (De Hart 1863, 47).

Military law defined regimental and garrison courts-martial as lesser or inferior courts that functioned within a restricted scope and authority. The convening authority assigned three officers for these trials and, like the general court-martial, could pardon or mitigate punishment. Regimental and garrison courts-martial excluded capital offenses punishable by imposition of a death penalty and the trial of officers. While it may seem excessively burdensome in terms of personnel appointed, general courts-martial could preside over any legal case, even those where a lesser court had authority. When a general court-martial assumed province over the lesser court, the members of the general court-martial could not increase the offender's punishment beyond what the lesser court could have imposed (De Hart 1863, 48).

General courts-martial members could impose a wide variety of punishments extending from monetary fines to the death penalty: a flexibility that permitted adjusting the sentence based on mitigating or aggravating factors. In some cases, military law prevented or restricted sentencing discretion. A notable example was the prohibition of the death penalty for desertion during peace—a cap lifted during the war. Flogging, otherwise known as stripes, was only permitted for desertion, and court-martial members were limited to punishing offenders with fifty lashes, although subsequent legislation eliminated this practice. General courts-martial sentenced service members to varying types of confinement, with hard labor often added to the punishment (De Hart 1863, 195, 246). Although military courts had significant discretion, the United States Constitution required that "excessive fines shall not be imposed, nor cruel and unusual punishments inflicted" (De Hart 1863, 68).

Military law defined specific crimes that required a general court-martial, such as mutiny, violence directed toward a superior officer, desertion, disobedience of an order, a sentinel sleeping on post, misbehavior before the enemy, unauthorized disclosure of a watch word, and forcing a safeguard (De Hart 1863, 61–64). Once assembled, a court-martial continued until dissolved by the convening authority. Urgent wartime responsibilities and sickness sapped court-martial membership and often delayed the trial's onset. If the member could not return after a reasonable delay in the proceedings, the trial would resume if the minimum number of officers were still present (De Hart 1863, 87–88).

De Hart counseled prospective officers to carefully consider the type and degree of punishment to ensure it was equitable. Inconsistent punishment undermined the legitimacy of military law—remedied when court-martial members understand that "the path before them, is not intuitively derived. A habit of reflection, and study of the laws by which they are governed, can alone place it within their reach" (De Hart 1863, 70).

John O'Brien authored *American Military Laws and the Practice of Courts-Martial* in 1846, the same year that De Hart's book debuted. O'Brien was an Army lawyer whose experience with courts-martial exposed a cogent observation: Adjudicating officers needed a comprehensive resource detailing the legal principles and precedents, and he concluded that "there is no work on American military law which even aims at the supply of this want" (O'Brien 1846, 1).

Part of O'Brien's interest in educating prospective court-martial officers evolved from a personal encounter. While stationed at Fort Monroe, Virginia, O'Brien received orders to march a group of soldiers "to a Protestant church on Sunday." He obeyed the directive as far as escorting the soldiers to the church's door but then allowed each man the option to enter the building. O'Brien believed that forcing men to attend religious services was unconstitutional: an opinion not shared by a commanding officer, who promptly arrested the disobedient man. Incipient court-martial proceedings raised the specter of an accomplished Army attorney debating a contentious constitutional matter, an unseemly performance prevented when the War Department quashed the trial (Shea 1890, 579).

O'Brien organized *American Military Laws and the Practice of Courts-Martial* as a practical tool for officers, with the book's first part devoted to specific crimes such as insubordination, desertion, cowardice, and general offenses. The second part instructed officers on the rules of evidence, findings, sentencing, avenues of review, and appeal. As a forward-thinking Army lawyer, O'Brien concluded his treatise with arguments for improving military law. Striking at the core of indiscipline, he noted that "one great cause of irregularity and vice arises from the want of what may be called home comforts, and of means of amusement or employment, in hours of idleness. By removing these wants temptations of the most irresistible kind would disappear." His proposals included small, comfortable barracks housing squad-sized units, physical competitions to hone combat skills, and readily available books promoting a moral, military lifestyle (O'Brien 1846, 556–557).

In the years preceding the Civil War, the books by De Hart and O'Brien were the foremost resources on military law. Both respectfully referenced Alexander Macomb, a military lawyer, and Major in the United States Corps of Engineers, whose 1809 *A Treatise on Martial Law and*

Courts-martial bridged an earlier gap between British military law and the practices in her former colonies (Macomb 1809).

Stephen Vincent Benét added to the meager library of books on the subject with his authorship of *A Treatise on Military Law and the Practice of Courts-Martial* (Benét 1862). His 1862 publication was both timely and comprehensive, and supported De Hart's recommendation that officers should study military law.

Benét was born in St. Augustine, Florida, in 1827 and later graduated from West Point Military Academy. During the Civil War, he served in successive roles in the Ordnance Department. He authored *A Treatise on Military Law and the Practice of Courts-Martial* while serving as a captain in the Union Army. In 1874 Brigadier General Benét became the Chief of the Ordnance Department (*Library of Universal Knowledge* 1880, 249).

A Treatise on Military Law and the Practice of Courts-Martial was a practical resource outlining the authority, rules, and procedures governing courts-martial. Officers appointed to a court-martial could review titled chapters devoted to military charges, challenges and oaths, formation, adjournment, and dissolution of the court, the trial and its incidents, and sentencing. Throughout the text, Benét addressed differences in military law as it applied to officers, noncommissioned officers, and enlisted personnel (Benét 1862).

Senior military commanders preferred charges against accused service members. The military charge consisted of two parts: a charge and one or more specifications. The charge identified the crime, and military commanders could list the specific Article of War that defined the offense and associated punishment, or in more general cases "where the offence alleged is a mere disorder or neglect, not specifically provided for, it must be charged under the general article as conduct to the prejudice of good order and military discipline." Specifications added detail to the charge and were carefully written by military commanders to briefly describe the facts, attendant circumstances, and, for crimes requiring it, the accused's mental state in terms of criminal intent (Benét 1862, 232–233).

Courts-martial required the judge advocate as the prosecutor to identify an accused service member by his rank, first and last names, and assigned unit designation. Procedural rules recognized that service members sometimes used different names, and the term "otherwise called" separated the various appellations. The judge advocate added the date and location for crimes of commission with reasonable precision, but for crimes of omission, the judge advocate only added those details if they were available (Benét 1862, 233–234). Before the commencement of the court-martial, accused service members received a copy of the military charges to prepare their defense, except that "extreme cases, where the necessity of immediate example is imminent, may justify a departure from this well-established custom" (Benét 1862, 78).

As a customary practice in the military, the accused received not only a copy of the military charges but also a list of the court-martial members. Military law prohibited peremptory challenges of court-martial members, but the accused could challenge a member for cause, citing specific reasons that would prejudice the member. The court-martial would consider the challenge and decide the matter before proceeding with the trial (Benét 1862, 239). In another customary practice, the judge advocate would provide the accused with the names of the prosecution's witnesses (Benét 1862, 73). The judge advocate's authority extended to defense witnesses as far as deciding if the requested person's "testimony is material and necessary to the ends of justice" (Benét 1862, 250). The accused could appeal to the court-martial if the judge advocate denied a request for a defense witness. Neither side was bound by the witness lists and could request additional witnesses at any point (Benét 1862, 74).

Before the trial began, the judge advocate administered the oath to each member: "You ... do swear, that you will well and truly try and determine, according to evidence, the matter now before you, between the United States of America, and the prisoner to be tried, and that you will duly administer justice ... without partiality, favor, or affection; and if any doubt shall arise, not explained by said articles, according to your conscience, the best of your understanding, and the custom of war in like cases" (Benét 1862, 89). The president of the court-martial administered an oath to the judge advocate (Benét 1862, 91). A legally valid court-martial required that the trial's proceedings document that the accused was present when the members and judge advocate swore their oaths. All witnesses testified under oath, and refusing to do so exposed the service member to possible arrest (Benét 1862, 92).

The judge advocate inquired whether the accused had counsel and after receiving the answer proceeded to the arraignment, with "you have heard the charges and specifications preferred against you; how say you—guilty or not guilty?" (Benét 1862, 107). In most cases, the accused pleaded guilty or not guilty, but on some occasions the service member would not respond. Standing mute instead of pleading derailed the trial as far as requiring the court-martial to decide the cause: whether willfully silent, insane, or incompetent. Each determination resulted in a different outcome, with deliberate muteness proceeding as if the accused pleaded not guilty; insanity barred further trial proceedings, and incompetency mandated that the accused have "competent intelligence, and can be made to understand the proceedings and evidence, and can also communicate" (Benét 1862, 107–108).

The judge advocate was responsible for the prosecution of military charges and for transcribing the trial proceedings. All questions to witnesses, whether by the judge advocate, court-martial members, or the accused, were "reduced to writing" and read aloud (Benét 1862, 128). The trial then commenced with the direct examination of witnesses, cross-examinations, and optionally their reexamination. An important procedural safeguard mandated that "all the testimony in substantiation of the charges and specifications must be produced, and no further evidence shall be permitted in proof of the facts specified, after the prosecution is closed" (Benét 1862, 131).

After the prosecution's case closed, the accused could respond to the charges by presenting testimony from defense witnesses, followed by a defense statement. Court-martial rules allowed the accused to read the defense statement to the members after the examination of witnesses. In constructing the document, the accused had the "right to construe the evidence adduced in any way, to draw any deductions from it, and to explain all that may seem to bear against him," including the impeachment of prosecution witnesses if it was respectful and free of profanity (Benét 1862, 133).

Military law recognized the accused's right to legal counsel, although in practice it closely resembled amicus curiae, or friend of the court, in a role solely confined to providing guidance. "The assistance is strictly restricted to giving advice, framing questions which are handed by the accused to the judge advocate on separate slips of paper, or offering, in writing, through the same channel, any legal objections that may be rendered necessary by the course of the proceedings" (Benét 1862, 75).

The concept of defense counsel did not exclusively apply to attorneys since the accused could request the assistance of friends or willing officers subject to the judge advocate's approval. In any case, military law denied the counsel's direct participation in the trial such as addressing court-martial members or objecting to any aspect of the proceedings. An exception to this iron-clad rule allowed the accused's written defense statement to be "read to the court by his professional counsel, or by a military friend" (Benét 1862, 133). As might be imagined, artful attorneys exploited this concession to defend their clients.

Judge advocates could reply to the defense statement, countering arguments supporting the accused. Unless the defense introduced new material the prosecution could not add charges or additional evidence. On the other hand, if the defense statement plowed new ground this allowed the judge advocate to call witnesses who then were subject to examination by the accused. Once both sides closed their respective cases court-martial members began their deliberations. During a court-martial proceeding, the members had the authority to independently call back any previous witnesses before reaching a verdict. However, legal procedures prohibited the court-martial from introducing new witnesses, as the rules of evidence required that all witnesses be subject to examination by both the prosecution and the accused (Benét 1862, 139–142).

Court-martial members openly and fully discussed the evidence concerning the military charges and with their judicial oaths in mind either acquitted or convicted the accused. When the court-martial concluded its deliberations the judge advocate recorded the vote of each member. The judge advocate also confirmed the number of votes required for a valid verdict and then destroyed the tally that reported the individual member's vote. The judicial oath preserved the voter's anonymity by admonishing the judge advocate and court-martial members not to "disclose or discover the vote or opinion of any particular member of the court-martial, unless required to give evidence thereof, as a witness, by a court of justice" (Benét 1862, 145).

Conviction or acquittal required a simple majority vote except in capital cases that exposed the accused to the death penalty. Capitol cases required agreement by two-thirds of the court-martial members and the vote's explicit documentation as such in the official transcript. The Articles of War allowed a general court-martial to consider the death penalty for many military crimes but removed that discretion and imposed the death penalty upon conviction for two crimes, "as is declared by the 55th article of war, for forcing a safeguard in foreign parts, and by the 2d section, concerning spies" (Benét 1862, 128). Except for the two mandatory death sentences, convictions requiring either a majority or two-thirds consensus among the voting members helped ensure the secrecy of individual decisions (Benét 1862, 146–147).

Courts-martial had discretion in determining verdicts and could, for example, find the service member guilty of a crime based on judging the accused guilty of some, but not all, of the listed specifications. The court could also find the accused guilty of some of the specifications but then acquit the man of the military charge. In another example, the court-martial could decide that the evidence supports the malfeasance but "attach no criminality thereto" (Benét 1862, 147). In cases of desertion, the members could substitute "absence without leave" as a lesser crime (Benét 1862, 132–133).

Accused service members could employ various defense maneuvers beyond simply refuting the judge advocate's assertions. Military law recognized absolute insanity, which barred guilt and punishment, but if the accused had "lucid intervals" free of mental aberration and if the court-martial could distinguish such periods, then the accused could be held accountable (Benét 1862, 135).

Compulsion was akin to insanity in the sense that it required a special mental state that removed the accused's free will, albeit temporary and related to certain circumstances. Mutiny was a serious military crime, and one of the possible defenses involved compulsion. In such cases, the accused might argue that participation in the uprising was involuntary, his freedom of choice vitiated through fear of the angry mob's violence. To succeed, the accused needed to prove "actual force or fear, and not the resultant of an excited imagination" (Benét 1862, 136–138).

An accused service member could also argue that his criminal behavior flowed from an illegal order from an officer. If this was sufficiently persuasive, the court-martial could accept the justification and render a verdict in the accused's favor. Such a strategy was fraught with risk since obedience was a core element of military law. If the accused pursued a defense postulated on the receipt of an illegal command, it would not succeed unless an order was "decidedly and flagrantly in opposition to, or in violation of, the laws of the land or the established customs of war." The perils even extended to hesitation, during which time the service member presumably considered the order's validity: a pause in compliance conceivably construed as disobedience (Benét 1862, 137).

Military law took a dim view of accused service members claiming ignorance of the rules and regulations that governed their behavior. In terms of officers, it was an entirely antithetical approach since their duties required such knowledge. Enlisted service members, many of whom were illiterate, depended on officers to provide this information and could submit a commander's dereliction as a defense to a military charge (Benét 1862, 136).

During the Civil War, alcohol assumed prominence as a medicinal agent, through its widespread recreational use, and with its corrosive effect on discipline. Benét astutely concluded that "drunkenness is the prolific source of most of the serious offences committed in the military." Given its ubiquitous presence, accused service members frequently emphasized alcohol in their defense, hoping for exculpation or at least mitigation but not realizing that military law weighed intoxication as aggravating and not ameliorating the crime. By adopting this approach, military law discouraged drunkenness and its artful dissimulation (Benét 1862, 135).

Benét's *A Treatise on Military Law and the Practice of Courts-Martial* offered the reader a comprehensive resource, but Henry Coppée authored a simpler and more convenient alternative. *Field Manual of Courts-Martial*, revised in 1864 to reflect changes in military law, was Coppée's contribution to "the unskilled, a pocket manual for immediate use at any moment; so that an officer, recently appointed, being unexpectedly ordered to act as member, recorder or judge advocate of a court, may, by consulting it, know how to proceed at once." Even while emphasizing expedience, Coppée respectfully acknowledged Benét and De Hart and advised officers not to ignore their subject matter expertise (Coppée 1864, 5–6).

Henry Coppée was born in Savannah, Georgia, in 1821, and twenty years later attended West Point Military Academy, graduating in 1845. Coppée served with distinction during the Mexican War and received a brevet promotion to captain. At the war's end he returned to West Point, educating cadets in French, English, and ethics until 1855. After this period, his career turned to successive academic responsibilities at the University of Pennsylvania and later at Lehigh University in Bethlehem, Pennsylvania. Coppée was a prolific writer, with books spanning historical, military, and philosophical subjects (Duyckinck 1866, 141).

Coppée's *Field Manual of Courts-Martial* provided officers with concise guidance on punishment. Although certain crimes such as spying assigned the death penalty on conviction, most military charges permitted court-martial members a limited degree of discretion. The Articles of War outlined the range of punishments based on the crime and the type of court-martial and broadly included "death; confinement; confinement on bread and water diet; solitary confinement; hard labor; ball and chain; forfeiture of pay and allowances; discharges from service; and reprimands, and, when non-commissioned officers, reduction to the ranks" (Coppée 1864, 96–97).

Military law permitted flogging for desertion until an Act of Congress dated August 5, 1861, banned it (Coppée 1864, 98). Courts-martial legally inflicted the punishment only for a narrow period during the Civil War. Solitary confinement or confinement on bread and water could not exceed 84 days in a year or fourteen continuous days without a successive period free of that punishment (Coppée 1864, 97). Executions by firing squad and hanging or being drummed out of the service included specific ceremonies emphasizing the prisoner's ignominious conduct. These public ceremonies served as a stark warning to deter misconduct among the ranks of soldiers who were required to observe them (Coppée 1864, 101–103).

Courts-martial proceedings were subject to review and approval by the convening military authority. The convening authority's review helped maintain legal consistency and ensured the senior military leader's involvement in the outcomes. The same authority could also pardon or mitigate a sentence, except in the case of an officer's dismissal or a death sentence. As the commander-in-chief of the armed forces, President Lincoln had the authority to grant clemency, including cases involving an officer's dismissal or a service member's death penalty. An officer senior in rank to the convening authority could suspend a court-martial sentence, recommend clemency or cite legal deficiencies, and defer final judgment to the President of the United States (Coppée 1864, 93–94).

At the beginning of the Civil War, Navy military justice relied on rules promulgated in the *Act for the Better Government of the Navy of the United States*, which took effect on June 1, 1800. Referred to as the 1800 Act, its rules authorized two tribunals, a court of inquiry that ascertained facts but could not penalize those under its purview, and general courts-martial. The 1800 Act provided little guidance in the conduct of either (Siegel 1997, 35).

The Navy relied on civilian attorneys, United States district attorneys, and Navy or Marine Corps officers to prosecute cases on shore. Courts-martial convened on ships at sea relied on Navy and Marine Corps officers to promptly adjudicate criminal behavior. In the Army, uniformed officers were responsible for prosecuting all trials, despite often having limited experience or training in legal matters (Siegel 1997, 37). The Navy's practice of hiring civilian attorneys for the prosecution of cases onshore presumably brought a higher level of legal expertise to military trials. It is possible to make the case that the Navy's adoption of civilian attorneys to prosecute cases onshore was an important evolutionary step in the development of the military justice system.

Changes in the 1800 Act that affected the Civil War included the eradication of flogging as a punishment and the institution of a summary court-martial to prosecute lesser offenses (Siegel 1997, 99). On the surface, both changes favored a more humane disposition of disobedience, but "because of the abolition of flogging and consequent degradation of discipline, the better qualified and reliable class of seaman refused to reenlist" (Siegel 1997, 101).

Secretary of the Navy Gideon Welles presided over 7,600 men and 42 commissioned ships when the Civil War began. Through the succeeding years, the roster of Navy personnel expanded to 51,500 by the war's end, an increase that inevitably magnified disciplinary problems and stressed the Navy's meager judicial capacity (Siegel 1997, 102).

The *Naval Appropriations Act of 1862* expanded the Secretary of the Navy's rule-making authority, and detailed the practices involving prize proceedings, but offered little guidance beyond the 1800 Act and the intervening changes such as the abolition of flogging and the creation of summary courts-martial. Importantly, the *Naval Appropriations Act of 1862* was the first military statute briefly recognizing a right to full legal defense counsel, including the cross-examination of witnesses in courts of inquiry (Siegel 1997, 105–106).

The practical administration of Navy justice during the Civil War suffered from limited guidance and confusing rules. Although conspicuously

Navy court-martial held on a ship's quarter deck (From *Iconographic Encyclopedia* [1851], Volume III, NH 71124, courtesy Naval History & Heritage Command).

absent as legal authority from the *Naval Appropriations Act of 1862*, the "customs of the sea" still influenced legal proceedings (Siegel 1997, 106–107). "As a practical matter, just like in the Army, the Navy principally relied on DeHart's *Observations on Military Law, and the Constitution and Practice of Courts Martial*" (Siegel 1997, 83–84).

In a manner like the Navy, on the eve of the Civil War, the Marine Corps was ill-equipped to deal with the coming conflict. At the outset of the Civil War, the Marine Corps counted 63 officers, 20 of whom "either resigned or were dismissed from the service" in 1861 (Field 2004, 5). The Marine Corps struggled to attract recruits and retain officers and by the war's end had only grown to 3,882 men (Field 2004, 5). Marine Corps officers routinely contributed to courts of inquiry and courts-martial.

On April 24, 1863, President Lincoln promulgated the *Instructions for the Government of Armies of the United States in the Field* prepared by Francis Lieber. Lieber "sought a military code of conduct which preserved the Union, achieved peace quickly, and applied to biracial armies" (Mindrup 2021, 7). Articles 42 and 43 addressed slavery by declaring that "if a person held in bondage by that belligerent be captured by or come as a fugitive under the protection of the military forces of the United States, such person is immediately entitled to the rights and privileges of a freeman" (Lieber 1863, 13). Articles 44 and 47 addressed the illegality of wartime rape (Lieber 1863, 14). Article 48 justified the death penalty for desertion during wartime (Lieber 1863, 15).

Two

Unauthorized Absences

During the Civil War, desertion was a significant concern within the military justice system, and countless courts-martial were convened to address this issue. Despite the emphasis on using severe punishments as a general deterrent, such efforts proved largely ineffective in curbing the number of desertions.

An exhaustive review of the subject reported roughly 200,000 Union soldiers deserted during the Civil War (Lonn 1928, 154). Another author pegged the number at 125,000 but then subtracted 21,056 deserters who returned to active service (Livermore 1901, 48). A less precise calculation suggested that Union desertion rates exceeded ten percent throughout the Civil War, but averaged 7,300 per month in 1864 (Gallagher et al. 2003, 84, 211).

Authorities apprehended only a small proportion of the military deserters, with many service members evading capture and avoiding punishment. Those who were caught were often treated as legal cannon fodder, being made an example of in a futile attempt to deter others from desertion. This approach placed a heavy burden on those who were arrested, who were seen as morally expendable and subjected to harsh punishments. Unfortunately, this approach did little to address the underlying causes of desertion, which were often complex and deeply personal.

Desertion impacted not only the Army but also the Navy and Marine Corps, and while the Army has been extensively studied, the same cannot be said for the Navy and Marine Corps. According to one account, there were 2,210 desertions from the Marine Corps in the period from April 12, 1861, through April 15, 1865. A quarter of that group either voluntarily returned or were arrested (n = 573/2210, 25.9%). The lack of Marine Corps recruits influenced punishment. A particularly severe manpower shortage in 1862 forced Marine Corps authorities to return deserters to active duty minus the cost of their apprehension. By 1863 the drought had deepened, and President Lincoln issued an amnesty proclamation to deserters on March 10, 1863: an offer accepted by an estimated 15,000 mostly Army soldiers. Only six service members from the Marine Corps accepted President Lincoln's amnesty proclamation and returned to duty (Sullivan 1997, 281–287).

Unfortunately, there is a lack of reliable estimates regarding the number of desertions from the Union Navy during the Civil War. Anecdotal reports suggest that desertion was a significant challenge for the Navy, as it was for the Army, and that efforts were made to address the issue through various means. For example, in a letter dated August 19, 1863, to Acting Master Bowen, Commanding Naval Rendezvous, Cincinnati, Ohio, Rear Admiral David D. Porter commented on the recruits, "it will be the duty of the commander of the receiving ship to reject all persons improperly shipped ... brought on board drunk, persons deserting from Army or Navy ... Men come here expecting prize money, and claim that they have been misled ... the consequence is continued desertion" (Stewart 1912, 374).

The official records contain redundant examples of Navy officers citing losses from desertions and seeking replacements. A letter from Commodore Andrew A. Harwood, Commanding, Potomac Flotilla, to the Assistant Secretary of the Navy, dated September 29, 1862, requested additional seamen, as "in consequence of sickness and desertion, we shall be short of men for the vessel fitting out, as well as to fill vacancies in the flotilla" (Rush and Woods 1894, 103). A report from Commander Christopher Raymond Perry Rodgers, Commanding, USS *Iroquois*, January 9, 1865, said that "the allurements of the large bounties now paid to [Army] recruits at home and their little hope of prize money ... render them anxious for their discharge. We have already lost some men by desertion, and need sixteen sailors, marines, and firemen to fill our complement" (Rush and Woods 1896, 406).

To address the problem of desertion, Rear Admiral David D. Porter implored Secretary of the Navy Gideon Welles to grant him the authority to convene courts-martial without having to await permission from higher headquarters. Porter complained that "I can only keep [deserters] in confinement until such time as the vessels to which they are attached come into port, and when ordered by the Department to try them ... Officers can desert ... and hope to escape by the law's delay." Porter emphasized the importance of timely, summary justice and concluded by declaring that once given the authority, "I will promise the Department that not another act of treachery, desertion, or insubordination shall occur in this squadron" (Stewart 1911, 433–434).

For purposes of analysis, the present volume included desertion, absence without leave (AWOL), leaving a duty area without permission, overstaying a pass, failure to repair, and straggling as instances of

Civil War U.S. Navy Recruiting Poster (NH 45-X-10, courtesy Naval History & Heritage Command).

unauthorized absences. Taken together, this collection of military charges provides a broader view of the scope of unauthorized absences prosecuted by courts-martial. The representative database identified 2,048 examples of unauthorized absences. The Army contributed the vast majority with 1,723 charges, followed by the Navy with 285, and the Marine Corps added 40 to the total.

In terms of each service, courts-martial in this sample prosecuted 505 Army officers with unauthorized absences, with AWOL the predominant crime (n = 358/505, 70.1%), followed by desertion (n = 59/505, 11.7%). The representative database for Navy officers included 136 unauthorized absences, but in contrast with the Army, desertion led the list (90/136, 66.2%), followed by AWOL (46/136, 33.8%). Military prosecutors charged only two Marine Corps officers with unauthorized absences, both for being AWOL.

Army enlisted soldiers specifically accused of desertion accounted for two-thirds of all unauthorized absence military charges (n = 822/1,218, 67.5%) and another 291 for AWOL (n = 291/1,218, 23.9%). Desertion among Navy enlisted personnel was the most common unauthorized absence (107/149, 72.0%) followed by AWOL (34/149, 22.8%). Among the enlisted members of the Marine Corps, desertion was most common (n = 30/38, 78.9%), followed by AWOL (n = 6/38, 15.8%).

Military authorities executed 267 soldiers between 1861 and 1866, a period that exceeds the numbers collected in the representative database for this volume (*Proceedings of U.S. Army Courts-Martial and Military Commissions of Union Soldiers Executed by U.S. Military Authorities, 1861–1866*, Rolls 1–8, M-1523). The official tally only documented court-martial sentences that resulted in an execution, but many more service members received a death sentence. In the representative database, courts-martial sentenced 343 service members guilty of desertion to death, but post-trial reviews reversed many of those decisions. For example, military authorities mitigated the sentences of 96 soldiers to imprisonment at the Dry Tortugas in Florida, instead of execution. Convening authorities voided 43 courts-martial death sentences based on various mistakes in the trial proceedings.

Desertion was a serious military charge, but when weighing the evidence, general courts-martial returned 55 not guilty verdicts in the representative database. Another 136 verdicts found the service members not guilty of desertion but guilty of AWOL. In terms of mitigation, 206 service members guilty of desertion but not facing death had their sentences mitigated based on influences such as the service member's character, youth, and bravery in combat.

Throughout the Civil War military commanders unevenly punished unauthorized absences even though it depleted regiments and military law permitted severe penalties for the offense. The typical punishments for desertion in 1861 were mixtures of incarceration, forfeiture of pay, and branding the offender with the letter D. In contrast, Private William H. Johnson, Company D, 1st Regiment, New York Cavalry, was the first soldier executed for desertion on December 13, 1861 (Johnson, W.H., 1861).

Military authorities also executed Private Richard Gatewood, Company C, 1st Regiment, Kentucky Infantry, on December 20, 1861, for desertion and assault (Gatewood 1861). As the war progressed the number of executions in the succeeding years increased but so did acts of clemency and procedural errors that spared many men.

One of the earliest Civil War courts-martial for desertion involved Private Bryan Fahey, Company D, 3rd Regiment, United States Infantry. Fahey deserted his unit on August 3, 1861, while in Washington, D.C., and remained absent for five days. He pleaded not guilty, and after the short trial concluded, the court-martial members agreed with his pleading and acquitted the man (Fahey 1862).

Military authorities charged Second Lieutenant J. Albert Holden, 2nd Regiment, Excelsior Brigade, as absent without proper authority spanning four days beginning on September 12, 1861. Holden pleaded guilty, but contrary to his admission, court-martial members weighed the prisoner's good character and returned the officer to duty without suffering any punishment (Holden 1862).

Marine Corps First Lieutenant Eugene A. Smalley faced a court-martial at the Navy Yard in Norfolk, Virginia, on September 6, 1862, for being AWOL. The prisoner pleaded not guilty to the charge and relied on his attorney, Thomas Smith, who vigorously supported his client during the three-day trial (Smalley 1862).

Smalley's commander admitted approving a day pass for the prisoner; however, when he failed to return by nine o'clock that evening, as per standing orders for all officers, a group of two officers was dispatched to apprehend him. Smalley insisted that the commanding officer did not include that time limit in the pass. Another point of contention involved Smalley's excuse for tardiness. The commander claimed that the errant officer offered no excuse for the tardiness, but Smalley countered by claiming that he missed the evening boat. Complicating Smalley's defense was his side trip to Fort Monroe, to visit his brother. After weighing all the evidence, the court-martial members returned a guilty verdict and punished the man with an official reprimand (Smalley 1862).

A Navy general court-martial convened at the Navy Yard in New York City on September 17, 1861, in the case of Seaman William Lamb. Navy authorities charged Lamb with desertion from the USS *Saratoga* in Philadelphia around mid–November 1860. Lamb's trial took place following his reenlistment on August 8, 1861, just a few months after the Civil War began (Lamb 1861).

Lamb had no sooner set foot on the Receiving Ship *Princeton* when Corporal Jacob Trout recognized the man as a deserter from the USS *Saratoga*, a discovery that thwarted Lamb's "advance" payment and led to his arrest. The court-martial members affirmed Lamb's guilty pleading and with no testimony from the accused, sentenced the man to "thirty days solitary confinement ... [and] to forfeit three months' pay" and added the time absent from the USS *Saratoga* to his current enlistment (Lamb 1861).

Court-martial members could submit recommendations to the convening authority urging clemency in certain cases. Such was the case with Private Elbin L. Hamlin, Company G, 5th Regiment, Maine Infantry, charged with desertion. Hamlin admitted deserting his unit around July 27, 1861. Authorities arrested the man on November 24, 1861, and after the short trial sentenced Hamlin "to forfeit all pay and allowances ... and to be confined at hard labor ... during the remaining period of his enlistment." Immediately after pronouncing the sentence, the court-martial members implored Major General George B. McClellan to remit the punishment "in view of the utterly disorganized state of the Regiment, the total want of discipline therein, and the good character of the accused" (Hamlin 1863).

The indictment of regimental indiscipline might have irked McClellan, who responded by noting that "it must have cost the Court a strong effort to allege, in extenuation of the offence of one man, that fact that he was ... merely a fair representative of a large class ... [and] it was the especial duty of some of the Court to teach and enforce." Miffed by the lenient sentence for a capital crime and the recommendation for mercy, McClellan nonetheless presumed that "the record gives imperfect evidence, but which were properly weighed and considered by the Court." With that tone of deference, McClellan ordered the prisoner back to duty (Hamlin 1863).

Marine Corps Private Patrick McMenamin suffered one of the more ignominious deterrents handed down by court-martial members for his desertion from the Marine Corps Barracks, Washington, D.C., around July 27, 1861. Five Navy officers listened as Judge Advocate Captain James H. Jones read the charges and then awaited the accused's pleading. McMenamin pleaded guilty and offered no evidence, after which the court-martial members briefly deliberated and decided to punish the man, "to be marked on each hip with the letter D, in India Ink, in the presence of the troops at this Post and to be drummed out of the Corps as worthless" (McMenamin 1861).

Desertion did not go unnoticed by the press. *Frank Leslie's Illustrated Newspaper* attacked the problem in 1862, lamenting that "the streets of our cities and the whole country swarm with men in uniform, irresponsible and beyond the ken of the police or citizen to detect. For all proof to the contrary, one-half these men may be deserters" ("Desertion" 1862).

From the newspaper's viewpoint, the crux of the problem was the absence of swift detection and punishment. Leslie's solution envisioned

Two. Unauthorized Absences   33

Drumming out a soldier of the federal army through the streets of Washington, D.C. (LC-USZ62-99839, Library of Congress Prints and Photographs Division, Washington, D.C.).

regionally positioned military boards that would receive notice of deserters from Army regiments. Once equipped with that information, the military boards would coordinate with local officials to apprehend the men. The military boards would then return the arrested deserters to their regiments for the appropriate military punishment ("Desertion" 1862).

Leslie upped the ante with a follow-up article bemoaning the lack of action. He chided the lackadaisical response to "the most heinous crime known in time of war" by ticking off the professed reasons that "they desert to show their independence or reenlist in other regiments ... to go home during harvest ... go on a 'spree' ...the work was too hard ... their officers were 'stuck up' ...the clothing was not suitable" ("What shall be Done with Deserters?" 1862).

Until authorities apprehended and punished the soldiers, Leslie feared the moral depravity would tempt others and further decimate the war effort. In a prophetic note, the newspaper reminded readers that military service was the man's voluntary choice and that had "this occur[ed] at a time of drafting there would be some mitigation for the act" ("What shall be Done with Deserters?" 1862).

The first full year of the Civil War in 1862 produced a stronger trend toward more severe punishment for desertion, driven in part by the growing exodus. As Leslie noted, multiple factors accounted for a man's decision to desert, but the realities of war, which included the hardships, deprivations, loneliness, and fear of death, surely added weight. Homesickness or nostalgia was another potent factor (Lande 2017, 4-20).

Spirit of the Age, an influential North Carolina temperance-oriented newspaper, published "A Solemn Warning to Wives," denouncing letters to soldiers that undermined their morale. Referencing a soldier who deserted and was pending execution, the newspaper pointed to the wife's letter brimming with grievances and an earnest plea for her husband's return home. "He became restless, disconnected, unhappy. He ceased to take any interest in the discharge of his military duties and thought of only how he could get home" ("A Solemn Warning to Wives" 1863).

Dark humor occasionally lightened the subject of desertion and execution, as described in an amusing anecdote: A group of soldiers was discussing the recent execution of a deserter and, on a lark, dared James Lansing to visit the man's nearby grave. As proof of his visit, the challengers required Lansing to carve three notches in the wooded stake memorializing the dead man's grave. Unbeknownst to Lansing, one of the revelers lay in wait near the grave equipped with a large piece of white canvas in the shape of a ghost attached to a pole. Upon approaching the grave, the simulated ghost rose high in the air, terrorizing the nighttime visitor. Lansing recovered from the fright and expressed no ill will toward the prankster ("Seeing a Ghost" 1863).

Military authorities at the Naval Yard, Charleston, Massachusetts, court-martialed Seaman James Martin, Seaman George Harris, and Seaman Richard Boyd in May 1862, for desertion. Their trials exemplified a trend toward harsher punishments for desertion. Boyd's trial was representative of the lot (Boyd 1862).

Judge Advocate Harvey Jewell read the military charge to Richard Boyd and the six officers comprising the court-martial that assembled on May 5, 1862. The judge advocate charged Boyd with desertion around April 16, 1862, from Westfield, New York. After hearing the charge, Boyd pleaded not guilty and hoped the officers would fairly consider his case (Boyd 1862).

The first witness to testify was Commander Louis C. Sartori, Commanding, Receiving Ship USS *Ohio*, Charleston Navy Yard. Boyd left the USS *Ohio* on April 16, 1862, after Sartori assigned the recruit to the Western Flotilla. The next day a police officer arrested Boyd and four others for desertion. Sartori promptly placed the deserters in confinement, where they awaited their subsequent courts-martial (Boyd 1862).

Lieutenant William F. Spicer provided details about Boyd's arrest. Spicer testified that "I took them [Boyd and others] from the Receiving Ship 'Ohio' to the Worcester Rail Road and by the Worcester and Western Rail Road to Albany and by the Central Rail Road from Albany to Buffalo and so on by Rail Road to Cairo" (Boyd 1862).

Spicer expected problems along the journey and implemented prudent steps to avoid trouble, with his efforts devoted to preventing desertions. He implemented a plan to thwart such efforts with the help of seven officers who monitored the recruits and prevented them from leaving the railroad cars, except to get water. During transit, the officers locked the train doors in a determined effort to prevent the more intrepid recruits from jumping out. Despite his best efforts, Spicer testified that "men were missed from time to time. The first I missed I found had deserted at Westfield, Massachusetts" (Boyd 1862).

Boyd lacked legal counsel and decided not to interrogate the prosecution witnesses, but he did request that Sick Bay Steward Patrick H. Driscoll testify as a defense witness. Driscoll recalled a conversation where "Boyd told me if any letters came to him to keep them till I got a letter from him stating what ship he would be in." Driscoll agreed to Boyd's request (Boyd 1862).

Boyd's strategy involved using Driscoll's testimony to blunt the desertion charge by demonstrating his intent to join the Western Flotilla. With no further witnesses, the judge advocate transcribed Boyd's oral defense statement and read it to the court-martial members. His statement began with an admission that "a great deal of liquor passed into the cars ... I am sorry to say I got my share as well as the rest" (Boyd 1862).

Boyd arrived in Westfield in the afternoon and promptly left the train of his own accord. He proceeded straight to a nearby grocer for food and liquor. Unfortunately, while he was enjoying a meal and drink, the train departed the station, leaving Boyd behind. Upon his discovery of being stranded, he raced back to the store in an attempt to explain his dilemma, but only a brief time passed before the local police arrested the man. At several points in Boyd's defense statement, he reiterated his innocence, proclaiming, "I can say with a clear conscience that I had no thought of deserting ... I didn't think of it at the time having liquor in me" (Boyd 1862).

In rendering the verdict, the court-martial members first amended the transcript's original military charge by replacing Boyd's elopement from New York with the precise location in Massachusetts. With that housekeeping detail corrected, the court-martial found Boyd guilty of desertion and sentenced the man to two years in prison (Boyd 1862).

Bounty jumpers derisively took advantage of recruiting inducements and, like a revolving door, would enter and exit their service obligations with the explicit objective of collecting lucrative monetary rewards. William Lamb's desertion and subsequent reenlistment for an "advance" payment foreshadowed this growing problem, indirectly hinted at in *Frank Leslie's Illustrated Newspaper*. The practice grew in tandem with the imposition of the Union draft through the *Enrollment Act in 1863*. The law permitted draft-eligible men to avoid conscription by hiring a substitute, but northern communities could sidestep that requirement by filling their military quotas with volunteers. Local draft boards, joined by sympathetic politicians and well-heeled citizens, enticed men with cash incentives, popularly known as bounties (Varhola 2011, 204).

Entrepreneurial agents known as bounty brokers scoured communities for substitutes, offering a range of inducements. Prospective volunteers could scan local newspapers' competing advertisements. A typical notice in 1864 offered $400 to Army recruits, as well as to Navy landsmen, seamen, and firemen, and confidently proclaimed that "men coming to this office to enlist can rely upon the most honorable treatment, upon receiving the money offered in full, upon choice of regiment and arm, without humbug or imposition" ("Military and Naval" 1864).

Exploitations of recruits through unfettered schemes taking advantage of the competition for men and the pressure to fill the ranks ultimately robbed military units of qualified men and drained the nation's coffers. Bounty brokers colluded with bounty jumpers, facilitating their enlistments and desertions: a lucrative practice that lined the conspirators' pockets and subsidized the broker's war-supporting charade.

In his autobiography, Colonel Isaac Jones Wistar, 71st Regiment, Pennsylvania Infantry, criticized a practice that supplied recruits "drugged and kidnapped in New York, there purchased by the 'quota agents' ... their musters papers regularly made out ... confined in box cars, and shipped like cattle, to his regiment" (Wistar 1914, 98). Wistar was of two minds: He sympathized with the recruits' plights but not with their epidemic desertions that "must at last be stopped at any cost, even by wholesale executions, if required" (Wistar 1914, 99).

The fraud was extensive, and authorities rarely captured the culprits, which emboldened the actors. Reports of systemic abuse surfaced a year after the passage of the *Enrollment Act of 1863*, and while the practice was widespread throughout the Union States, New York was at the epicenter. In New York City, "there is hardly a recruiting officer in the city which is not haunted by brokers with their experienced jumpers some of whom have been through the sham enlistment process upward of twenty times, and few of those fellows, if they are adepts, will ever go so near actual service" ("Startling Disclosures in New York in Regard to Bounty Jumping" 1865).

Two. Unauthorized Absences 37

THE RECRUITING BUSINESS.
VOLUNTEER-BROKER (*to Barber*) "Look a-here—I want you to trim up this old chap with a flaxen wig and a light mustache, so as to make him look like twenty; and as I shall probably clear three hundred dollars on him, I sha'n't mind giving you fifty for the job."

The recruiting business: A well-dressed man "Volunteer-Broker" with an old man, the volunteer, in a barbershop talking to the barber: "Look a-here—I want you to trim up this old chap with a flaxen wig and a light mustache, so as to make him look like twenty" (LC-USZ62-132935, Library of Congress Prints and Photographs Division, Washington, D.C.).

With impunity, "hundreds of men daily walk the streets of New York who are deserters, and who have been enlisted upwards of a dozen times." Many were criminals and ne'er-do-wells who quickly dissipated their ill-gotten gains and then turned their steps to a receptive broker, replenishing their wallets. Estimates suggested that only ten percent of recruited soldiers from New York City ever joined a regiment. As proof of the profit, a pair of corrupt bounty brokers netted a quarter-million dollars in three months ("Startling Disclosures in New York in Regard to Bounty Jumping" 1865).

In his autobiography, controversial Lafayette C. Baker, the self-styled "First Chief of the Secret Service of the United States," devoted four chapters to bounty jumpers and brokers. Baker decried the moral depravity of bounty brokers and the feckless military officers and civilians who ignored the practice. In the same breath, he denounced the lenient treatment of desertion, citing as evidence the infrequent arrests, rare imposition of the death penalty, and the excessive use of presidential pardons mitigating punishment (Baker, L. 1894).

Pressured by the War Department, but needing more permission than encouragement, Baker settled on a plan to thwart the cheats and swindlers. Baker believed corruption was rampant and that any plan involving military and civilian officers involved in the draft would fail. Admitting the unconventional nature of his plan, Baker concluded, "I must select for my service some bounty broker who had been connected with the business a considerable length of time, and who was, consequently, familiar with all its details" (Baker, L. 1894, 252).

Commentators of the time dubbed Baker's plan the Hoboken Raid. It was a carefully concocted plot to ensnare bogus brokers. Baker recalled that "on a certain day I requested nine brokers, with whom I had business, to come to my room at the same hour, bringing their papers. I had concealed, in an adjoining room, a number of my assistants. I instructed them [on] the signal I should use to bring them to my aid" (Baker, L. 1894, 254).

Baker's plans succeeded in nabbing scores of bounty brokers and bounty jumpers but earned the man more disapproval than praise. While lauding him for capturing the scoundrels, critics condemned Baker's tactics, variously denounced as harsh or illegal. In one publicized account, Baker and his minions devised a cruel trick on 193 incarcerated brokers and jumpers. In the courtyard adjoining their cells, prominently placed gallows confronted the inmates. Whatever curiosity this invited was satisfied when an official read a phony order to the inmates, purportedly from the War Department, declaring that "the evils of bounty jumping was widespread, and that the most vigorous measures were now to be taken to suppress it; and further, that it had been decided to select twenty names out of the number ... who should be hung the following day as an example." The next morning officials marched the horrified inmates to the gallows and only after a suitable amount of terror did they return the men to their cells ("Recent Execution at Fort Lafayette" 1865).

Baker's arrests made headlines but little else. The captures came in the closing months of the Civil War, which precluded any deterrent benefit, and as Baker documented, the practice was common in the

Union States and the practitioners were skillful operators who thwarted detection.

The Marine Corps' experience with the bounty system was similar in some respects to that of the Army, but government policies added to the malaise. One of the principal problems centered on the four-year Marine Corps enlistment. Government bounties paid a maximum of $300 for a three-year enlistment, a disparity that hobbled Marine Corps recruiting efforts. Attempts to correct the financial discrepancies to entice Marine Corps recruits had a perverse effect. Bounty jumpers flourished, and just like with the Army, they deserted shortly after securing a bonus, but the Marine Corps had a self-inflicted wound because the law "excluded from the bounty cornucopia by reason of already being in the service, [and] many absconded" (Sullivan 1997, 162).

Federal bounties peaked at four hundred dollars in 1864 for the new Army and Navy recruits, with the men receiving twenty-five dollars when mustered and the remainder with an honorable discharge. States added to the federal bounty, with Connecticut most generously providing a three-hundred-dollar incentive. Bounty jumpers were adept at exploiting the financial rewards and would hop from one service to another. Union policies tackling the arrest and punishment of deserters were also subverted through uneven enforcement, such as an 1865 requirement that deserters had to make up in service the time lost during their absence (Fantina 2006, 81–82).

The trial of Private William Miller, alias James Craig, Company F, 5th Regiment, New Hampshire Infantry, was an exception. Nine officers convened on December 14, 1864, at City Point, Virginia, to consider the military charge of deserting the enemy. Miller pleaded guilty to desertion but denied joining the enemy's ranks. Captain Paul Whitehead, 68th Regiment, Pennsylvania Infantry, served as the judge advocate, and he presented two prosecution witnesses (Miller, W., alias J. Craig 1864).

Both prosecution witnesses addressed Miller's recruitment and desertion. According to the first witness, Miller was among a group of recruits joining the regiment as a substitute, in consideration of which he received a bounty. Miller left the regiment without permission near Petersburg, Virginia, around October 10, 1864. The second prosecution witness provided more damaging testimony. This officer heard Miller proclaim his support of the Confederate cause (Miller, W, alias J. Craig 1864).

Miller had no witnesses and relied on his defense statement, a one-page appeal that began, "I was boarding with a man in Quebec, who brought me to this country, for the purpose of joining the Navy, at least that was the promise ... I was told to ask two hundred dollars for bounty, and I found out afterwards that some got eleven hundred dollars" (Miller, W., alias J. Craig 1864).

To make matters worse, Miller maintained that authorities had made repeated promises to assign him to the Navy, but sent him to an Army regiment near Petersburg, Virginia, instead. Miller implicitly conceded his unauthorized absence from the regiment, but he offered an alternative explanation that "after leaving camp I was picked up by two Rebel Scouts. It was useless to try to get away from them." Miller's pleading did not convince the officers in attendance. The 90-minute court-martial concluded with the prisoner's conviction and sentence "to be hung by the neck until dead" (Miller, W., alias J. Craig 1864).

Private William Kane, alias William Carter, Company A, 8th Regiment, Maryland Infantry, had a different grievance. The 25-year-old man hailed from Montreal, Canada, and after arriving in Baltimore, Maryland, he agreed to substitute for another man. The muster roll described the man as a former sailor, standing five feet seven inches tall, with auburn hair and gray eyes. On June 1, 1864, he enlisted for a three-year term. Less than a month later, Kane deserted near Petersburg, Virginia (Kane, W., 1864).

Eight officers assembled at City Point, Virginia, on the morning of December 6, 1864, to hear the testimony in Private Kane's trial. The judge advocate read the military charge of desertion to the enemy based on the accused's unauthorized absence on June 28, 1864, near Petersburg, Virginia. The military specification accused Kane of entering the enemy's lines and remaining absent until arrested at Lexington, Kentucky, in November 1864. Kane pleaded not guilty (Kane, W., alias W. Carter, 1864).

The prosecution's first witness was Captain Lewis Cassard, Kane's company commander. Cassard provided testimony indicating that Kane had been a substitute and had deserted the regiment only two days after joining. While in custody after his arrest, two witnesses recalled a conversation where Kane declared that he was a British citizen apprehended in a blockade runner and was never in the Union Army (Kane, W., alias W. Carter, 1864).

Kane's only defense was a statement read to the court-martial members. "When I first enlisted in Baltimore I was sent to camp—when I got there what little bounty I got was taken from me, also a silver watch ... I thought it was too hard to lose my money and stay in the service ... I was trying to escape north and was picked up by 6 Rebel scouts—I did not intend going to the enemy at all—they took my uniform ... I gave myself up as having come in a blockade runner" (Kane, W., alias W. Carter, 1864).

The court-martial found Kane guilty and sentenced the prisoner "to be hung by the neck until dead." Major General George G. Meade approved the proceedings, findings, and sentence. Military authorities executed Private Kane on December 16, 1864. Chaplain William O'Neill received the man's last will and testament, which included a request for information regarding the whereabouts of his money and watch (Kane, W. 1864).

Two. Unauthorized Absences   41

Brigadier General Robert S. Foster ordered a court-martial convened in the case of Private James F. Brown, Company G, 3rd Regiment, New Hampshire Infantry. Seven officers assembled on December 20, 1864, "in the field" in Virginia, to weigh the evidence in Brown's trial. Captain George Waddle, the judge advocate, charged the prisoner with desertion. According to the specifications, Brown deserted at Wilcox Landing, Virginia, on June 25, 1864, and remained absent until authorities arrested him on December 18, 1864, near Laurel Hill, Virginia. During the interlude, the man enlisted as a substitute in the 47th Regiment, New York Infantry (Brown, J. 1864).

Brown pleaded not guilty and listened as William H. Trickey, his company commander, testified. According to Trickey's testimony, Brown left the camp to fill canteens with water and never returned. Nothing more was known of Brown's whereabouts until a quirk of fate alerted the commander (Brown, J. 1864).

An unknown soldier with the 47th Regiment, New York Infantry, identified Brown as a former member of the 3rd Regiment, New Hampshire Infantry, and alerted Trickey. Brown joined the 47th Regiment, New York Infantry, as a substitute around December 6, 1864, using the name James Barrett. Seizing on the intelligence, Trickey went to the 47th Regiment's camp, but the elusive man was missing. Surely disappointed, Trickey returned to his regiment empty-handed. The next morning, a soldier sighted Brown in a nearby field and quickly notified Trickey, who "took my horse ... and arrested him" (Brown, J. 1864).

Brown responded to the prosecution's case with a short defense statement that began, "In the first place I knew nothing about enlisting in the N.H. Regt, another young man besides me was told how we were drugged, and our bounty taken from us. The Brokers of the city must have done it." The accused soldier then pivoted to explaining his absence from the 3rd

Wilcox Landing, James River, Virginia (LC-DIG-ppmsca-33265, Library of Congress Prints and Photographs Division, Washington, D.C.).

Regiment, New Hampshire Infantry, by explaining that "we had leave to go after water. In search of it we lost our way ... we traveled around until it got to be about dark and I told this fellow we had better lay down and not try to find it until morning" (Brown, J. 1864).

Brown furtively escaped later that night fearing for his safety when he heard nearby horses and guessed that the horses belonged to a small Rebel scouting party. Over the next day, he crossed thickets and streams before arriving at the York River in Virginia, where "a schooner [was] laying in the river." After some finagling, Brown managed to get onboard and return to Boston (Brown, J. 1864).

Brown's comments concluded without any reference to his subsequent presence in the New York regiment. Court-martial members, "after mature deliberation on the evidence adduced," found Brown guilty of desertion and sentenced the man "to be shot to death with musketry" (Brown, J. 1864).

Five Navy officers gathered on the USS *Potomac* in the waters off Pensacola Bay, Florida, on September 14, 1864, for the trial of Landsman Samuel G. Scovill. The judge advocate read the charge of desertion preferred by Rear Admiral David G. Farragut: "on or about the Third day of September, one thousand eight hundred and sixty four ... did desert from said vessel, and did attempt to swim to the shore on the North side of the Bayou Grande, where a force of the enemy was said to be stationed, and did swim in the said direction until exhausted." Authorities arrested the man as he floundered in the narrow protected inlet adjoining Pensacola Bay (Scovill 1864).

Scovill pleaded guilty, apparently not appreciating the gravity of the military charge. His escape from the ship lasted mere minutes, but what sank the man's defense was his alleged desertion to the enemy. The prosecution presented no evidence considering the prisoner's guilty pleading. In deference to Scovill's request to prepare a defense statement, the court-martial briefly adjourned, allowing him the time he needed to gather his thoughts and present his case (Scovill 1864).

Scovill's defense began with a less than favorable admission: "I had been in the rebel service and was captured by U.S. forces in May [1864]." While imprisoned, Scovill claimed that a government official offered to release him if he enlisted in the Union Navy. Scovill hesitated: "I told him I did not want to join the service to fight," but he agreed after being "promised that I would get a situation as a carpenter in some Navy Yard and that I would receive a Bounty of $100." As it turned out, Scovill ended up on the USS *William G. Anderson* and bitterly complained, "I thought I had been enticed under false pretenses, and I thought I would try and go home to my family" (Scovill 1864).

The guilty verdict was inevitable, given the prisoner's pleading. If the man harbored any thoughts that his admission of guilt or his defense statement would lessen the punishment, the court-martial members dispelled that by sentencing Scovill "to imprisonment for life in such prison or penitentiary as the Honorable Secretary of the Navy shall select" (Scovill 1864).

The mere accusation of desertion sometimes became a legal cudgel, defying common sense, as illustrated by the indictment of Marine Corps Private Edmund McVaugh on February 3, 1863, for a nine-hour absence from the Marine Corps Barracks at Norfolk, Virginia. First Lieutenant Joseph F. Baker, acting as the judge advocate, read the military charge to the five officers sitting in judgment. McVaugh pleaded not guilty and listened as Baker presented the prosecution's case (McVaugh 1863).

Four witnesses testified for the prosecution, each describing the January 26, 1863, "absence of Private McVaugh ... from his guard." The chance discovery of McVaugh's absence occurred when another Marine Corps private scheduled for guard duty fell ill, prompting the need for a replacement. Sergeant of the Barrack Guard John Hoban reported the incident to the officer of the day, resulting in McVaugh's selection to fill the opening (McVaugh 1863).

Hobart took the necessary steps to alert the intended replacement of the assignment around "a quarter past nine at night," but after a careful search, McVaugh was missing from the guard room. Hobart ordered McVaugh's confinement once authorities found the man. Early the next morning Hobart discovered McVaugh in bed in the guard room (McVaugh 1863).

McVaugh presented two witnesses in his defense, with both addressing the pivotal point posed by the court-martial, "did you know of an order against the Guard leaving the Guard Room without permission from the Sergeant or Corporal of the Guard?" Private James A. Blaney said "No," undermining the prosecution's claim of desertion (McVaugh 1863).

The two defense witnesses completed the trial except for the accused's defense statement. McVaugh explained that "to account for my absence from my guard I was taken sudden Sick with Diarrhea and was Compelled to remain at the rear until 10 o'clock that night after which I came back to my quarters and went to sleep, there was no person awake in the room when I returned" (McVaugh 1863).

McVaugh's nine-hour absence and subsequent trial for desertion concluded with the court-martial finding the man not guilty of desertion but instead guilty of being AWOL. Given the severe punishments for desertion, perhaps McVaugh was content with "six weeks solitary confinement on bread and water with one full ration one day in each week. At the expiration of that time to be put at hard labor with a ball and chain attached to his left leg for six months and the loss of all pay while undergoing sentence" (McVaugh 1863).

James Devlin, a substitute with Company E, 43rd Regiment, New York Infantry, otherwise known as Pat Diamond and Frank Tully, personified one of the more brazen examples of bounty jumping. Major General John Dix, from his Headquarters, Department of the East, ordered Devlin's court-martial to meet on December 28, 1864, in New York City. Despite the order, assembling the minimum of five officers for Devlin's trial repeatedly fell short and delayed the trial until January 30, 1865 (Devlin 1865).

The judge advocate charged the prisoner for desertion, "in this that he James Devlin, alias Pat Diamond alias Frank Tully Substitute assigned to the 43rd Regiment New York Vols … did absent himself … desert the service … and remain absent … until arrested." The prosecutor also charged Devlin with enlisting as a substitute with the 1st Regiment, Connecticut Cavalry, and deserting that unit in September 1864. Devlin pleaded guilty to both specifications of desertion, following which the judge advocate closed the prosecution. Devlin's subsequent defense statement relied on a remarkably candid commentary to the court-martial members, part biography, confession, and perhaps a naive expectation of a sympathetic reception (Devlin 1865).

Devlin opened his defense statement with a quick disclosure: "I am a native of Ireland, am 29 years of age, and by profession a Butcher." He then pivoted to his exploits in the military, beginning with his enlistment as a substitute at Tarrytown, New York, on May 31, 1864, under the alias of Pat Diamond. One week later, Devlin was in City Point, Virginia, with the 43rd Regiment, New York Infantry, a unit joining in the siege of Petersburg, Virginia (Devlin 1865).

Nine days after the Petersburg field assignment, Devlin's commander transferred him to City Point Hospital after the man developed a bout of diarrhea. It was a short hospital admission, and after one day "I was then sent to Camp Distribution, Alexandria, Va, to be forwarded to my Regiment" (Devlin 1865).

Devlin had no desire to return to the regiment and while en route he deserted, scrapping his uniform for civilian clothes. He stayed in Washington, D.C., for five days and then traveled to Baltimore, Maryland, where authorities arrested him. Devlin's incarceration lasted a mere two days after convincing his captors that he was a sutler. Following his release, Devlin spent one month in New York City and then returned to Washington, D.C., working as an assistant wagon master "for three (3) months at $43 per month, I then came to New York" (Devlin 1865).

The allure of a large bounty motivated the man, and "I went to New Haven and then enlisted under the name of Frank Tully. I received $600 Bounty." Authorities expected Devlin to join the 1st Regiment, Connecticut Cavalry, but thoughts of desertion were uppermost in the man's mind. While traveling through Washington, D.C., ostensibly to join his new regiment, Devlin recognized his former wagon master (Devlin 1865).

According to Devlin's defense statement, he asked the wagon master where he could buy civilian clothes. The wagon master suggested Devlin visit a rum shop and "the man who kept the rum shop ... sold me the citizens clothes ... I did desert, and I came to New York, and I enlisted in the Navy." Authorities arrested Devlin on January 20, 1865, probably thwarting another desertion (Devlin 1865).

The court-martial members confirmed Devlin's guilty pleading and sentenced the prisoner to be shot to death at Fort Columbus, New York Harbor, on February 3, 1865. Major General Dix "is thus prompt in the execution of the sentence ... Within eight months he enlisted twice in the Army, and once in the Navy, having deserted twice during the same period ... His case is one of those in which bad men, tempted by enormous bounties, enlist into the service for the sake of making money, with the deliberate purpose of deserting." Dix offered no mercy, insisting that the man's moral depravity demanded swift punishment (Devlin 1865).

Military authorities also brought charges against Army officers for unauthorized absences, often for the crime of AWOL rather than desertion. Although the numbers of AWOL charges may have been somewhat inflated when court-martial verdicts reduced the more severe charge of desertion to AWOL, such cases were still a major concern within the military justice system.

First Lieutenant B.J. Ashley, 7th Regiment, New York Heavy Artillery, was AWOL for one week, commencing on September 2, 1864. Ashley was an artillery instructor "to the troops garrisoning Fort No. 4, N.W. Defences, Baltimore" when he left the unit. Ashley's general court-martial took place at Camp Carroll, Baltimore, Maryland, on October 8, 1864. The officer pleaded guilty to the charge, which the court-martial members affirmed before sentencing Ashley's dismissal from the service. Court-martial members recommended mercy, but Brigadier General Henry H. Lockwood, the convening authority, rejected that request because "in breaking his arrest and absenting himself without leave, [Ashley] rendered such a course now impossible" (Ashley 1864).

Major General George B. McClellan spared no verbiage in denouncing First Lieutenant William Strachan, 9th Regiment, Massachusetts Infantry. Strachan's court-martial convened at the Camp of Fitz John Porter's Division, and charged the man with desertion "at Minor's Hill Virginia, on or

Major General George B. McClellan (LC-DIG-pga-05571, Library of Congress Prints and Photographs Division, Washington, D.C.).

about the 9th day of January 1862, and did remain absent from said service till the 14th day of January 1862." By means not described, the officer was returned under arrest to his regiment along with a bill for 50 dollars that ostensibly covered the costs of the apprehension (Strachan 1863).

Strachan pleaded not guilty to desertion, but the court-martial disagreed and affixed a penalty that cashiered the officer and deducted 50 dollars from his pay. In reviewing the trial, McClellan icily remarked, "It is rather unusual for a commissioned officer to be guilty of desertion, since the door for the withdrawal from the service of those commissioned officers who unworthily wear its uniform is so invitingly open as to leave no excuse for this crime. But when it does occur, it is to be regretted that a penalty so trivial should be inflicted by sentence of a court-martial" (Strachan 1863).

McClellan criticized the trial's proceedings that provided no mitigating evidence that justified the lenient sentence. Lacking extenuation, McClellan favored "the extreme penalty," an implied reference to the Articles of War that permitted the imposition of the death penalty for desertion during war. In a further thought on the matter, McClellan commented, "In the opinion of the Major General Commanding, its extraction in this instance would, at a cheap rate, have promoted the good of the service." Despite his caustic commentary, McClellan accepted the court-martial sentence (Strachan 1863).

First Lieutenant Richard F. Tighe, Company G, 73rd Regiment, New York Infantry, fared little better than First Lieutenant Strachan. A general court-martial convened in the field to hear evidence in Tighe's trial of desertion. The court-martial found the officer not guilty of desertion but guilty of the lesser offense of AWOL. Even so, the court-martial dismissed the man from Army service along "with loss of all pay and allowances now due or that may become due him" (Tighe 1864).

Courts-martial rarely sentenced officers to prison, but Major General George Meade approved such a punishment for First Lieutenant Elbridge W. Guilford, 1st Regiment, Massachusetts Heavy Artillery, following his conviction for desertion. The court-martial members also convicted Guilford of forgery and sentenced the man "to be dismissed ... forfeit all pay ... and to be confined in such a penitentiary as the proper authorities may direct, for the term of one year." In reviewing the case, Meade disapproved the forgery charge as not "triable by a Court Martial," a dispensation that otherwise left the sentence intact (Guilford 1864).

Union authorities did not execute any officers, but Second Lieutenant John Boyle, Company K, 82nd Regiment, New York Infantry, came uncomfortably close. At a trial held near Falmouth, Virginia, on April 5, 1862, court-martial members found Boyle guilty of desertion and sentenced the man to be shot to death. The division commander reversed the findings and Major General Joseph Hooker agreed when details emerged that "he was tried by mistake after having been released from arrest and returned to duty" (Boyle 1863).

First Lieutenant Henry C. Overin had the misfortune of suffering a different fate. A court-martial at City Point, Virginia, met on November

14, 1864, and charged the officer with desertion. After hearing the evidence, the court-martial found the man not guilty of desertion but guilty of AWOL and sentenced Overin "to be reduced to the ranks, and to serve as an enlisted man" (Overin 1865).

Overin's punishment had an escape clause that permitted promotion subject to his commander's approval. In reviewing the case, Major General George G. Meade approved the court-martial's sentence and directed that "Henry C. Overin will be taken up as an enlisted man upon the rolls of such a company of the 40th New York Volunteers, as the commanding officer thereof may designate" (Overin 1865).

Third Assistant Engineer Anthony French faced a Navy general court-martial convened on board the USS *Rhode Island*, Key West, Florida, on February 19, 1863. Five Navy officers and one Marine Corps officer listened as Judge Advocate Francis Bowman detailed the military charge. Bowman charged the officer with AWOL, citing two specifications alleging French's unauthorized absence from the USS *Rhode Island* on or about February 13, 1863, "for several hours" and two days later again when the man went ashore at Key West after his commander refused his request for leave (French 1863).

French pleaded not guilty, setting in motion the prosecution's case. Acting Chief Engineer John F. McCutcheon, attached to the USS *Rhode Island*, recalled being surprised that French was on the boat going ashore with him and commented, "You are doing very wrong, and you must not let this occur again." French directly challenged McCutcheon's testimony by pointedly asking, "Did he [French] not offer to leave the boat and remain on board ship?" McCutcheon replied, "He made some reply about getting permission after he was out of the ship." While on shore McCutcheon admitted the pair chatted amiably while walking to a liquor store. Two days later, French again asked for permission to go ashore, but McCutcheon denied the request, based on the need to retain a complement of officers on the ship. Despite the refusal, French went ashore sometime in the early evening (French 1863).

Acting Master William Williams, Lieutenant Norman H. Farquhar, Acting Ensign Albert Taylor, and Commander Stephen D. Trenchard, all attached to the USS *Rhode Island*, completed the prosecution's case, with each testifying to the accused's absence without authority (French 1863).

With the prosecution's case closed, French called his first witness, Third Assistant Engineer George H. Rutter, attached to the USS *Rhode Island*, who denied receiving any instructions from the senior officers regarding the policy for requesting leave. Rutter believed that requesting permission from the chief engineer was sufficient, not from the executive officer as the prosecution's witnesses claimed (French 1863).

Acting Third Assistant Engineer Joseph Lewis and Acting Master's Mate Samuel Pope echoed Rutter's testimony, while Acting Master Mate Daniel R. Brown, a crewmember on the boat ferrying the occupants ashore, recalled McCutcheon telling French, "Never mind now, you can go ashore but do not let this thing occur again." Seaman Charles Lewis supported Brown's version of the events (French 1863).

The prosecution recalled witnesses including Lieutenant Farquhar to rebut French's witnesses and reassert the policy that authorized leaves required his permission. French countered with one additional supportive witness, and a lengthy defense statement brought the factual phase of the court-martial to a conclusion. After a brief recess, the court-martial found French not guilty of the first specification, guilty of the second, and guilty of the military charge of AWOL (French 1863).

The court-martial sentenced French "to be publicly reprimanded on board the USS Rhode Island ... and be suspended from duty for six months with the loss of all pay." Yet the court-martial members went further, and recommended French receive clemency, considering the unspecified "various extenuating circumstances." Rear Admiral Theodorus Bailey, Commanding, East Gulf Blockading Squadron, supported the clemency and remitted the suspension and loss of pay (French 1863).

A court-martial convened on board the USS *Portsmouth* on November 26, 1864, in the matter involving Third Assistant Engineer Morgan Lutton. Rear Admiral David G. Farragut, Commanding the Gulf Coast Squadron, preferred the military charge of AWOL. According to the charge's specification, Lutton left the USS *Milwaukee* near Mound City, Illinois, on or about October 9, 1864, without permission. In what was a common scenario, the military charge also included a second specification accusing the man of drunkenness while on shore in Mound City (Lutton 1864).

The prosecution offered no witnesses or testimony after Lutton pleaded guilty to the military charge. Lutton also had no witnesses, but he did submit a written defense. Despite his pleading, Lutton's defense statement was mostly conciliatory with one exception (Lutton 1864).

Lutton's defense statement opened by noting, "I entered the U.S. Navy on the 26th day of July 1864," an obvious appeal emphasizing his status as a military novice. He refuted the AWOL charge, contending that he received permission to go ashore during the refurbishment of the USS *Milwaukee*'s boilers but once on land, "I ... frankly acknowledge that I did drink too much and to that course alone I attribute my absence from the vessel" (Lutton 1864).

The man circled back to his youth and inexperience and in asking for mercy, "promise[d] that in the future I will conform to the Rules and

Regulations of the U.S. Navy." The trial closed with the defense statement, and following a short deliberation the court-martial members confirmed the man's guilty pleading and sentenced him "to be dismissed from the navy of the United States" (Lutton 1864).

Ship's Writer James E. Rooney typified an amplification of the military charge of desertion with the addition of language "in time of war" or similar connotations that magnified the moral turpitude. Rooney was a ship's writer, a petty officer assigned to the ship's executive officer, and "does the writing and keeps the watch muster, conduct and other books of the ship" ("Clerk" 1891).

A ship's writer commanded considerable authority when the officer "relegate[d] to that individual everything concerning the internal economy of the ship which he does not care to be bothered with himself. The men have to be stationed at the battery, crews for the different boats selected, a fire bill arranged and every man of the crew informed as to what is his special duty at every evolution" ("The Ship's Writer" 1893).

Rear Admiral George F. Pearson, Commanding, Pacific Squadron, preferred two charges against Rooney and ordered the formation of the Navy general court-martial on board the USS *Fredonia*. Acting Assistant Paymaster Leander Chamberlain, detailed as the judge advocate, read the two military charges to the six officers assigned to the trial. Chamberlain charged the accused with desertion in time of war from the USS *Lancaster* around January 12, 1865, while the ship was in the Bay of Callao, Peru. Rooney remained absent until arrested on February 16, 1865. The second military charge of "scandalous conduct tending to the destruction of good morals" specified that the accused misappropriated ninety-three dollars entrusted to his care by several crewmembers. Rooney pleaded not guilty to desertion but admitted his culpability to the second charge (Rooney 1865).

The evidentiary phase of the trial commenced on February 23, 1865, after Rooney declined the assistance of legal counsel. Since Rooney pleaded guilty to the second charge, the prosecution's case focused on desertion. Lieutenant Commander Edward P. McCrea testified first, "I gave the accused permission to go on shore in a market boat, return in her. He did not return." McCrea offered several rewards for Rooney's apprehension, but a chance encounter with the accused led to his arrest (Rooney 1865).

Coxswain Hugh Jones, USS *Lancaster*, testified, "I saw him [Rooney] walking in the street ... When I saw him and called his name he did not run away ... told him I wanted him to come on board the ship with me ... He said he had been away a good while and was ashamed to go back again" (Rooney 1865).

Quartermaster William Chadwick, USS *Lancaster*, echoed much of Jones's testimony. Both men were searching for Rooney, but Chadwick recalled, "I was told he was caught by Jones and put in the Calaboose." Jones and Chadwick returned their prisoner to the USS *Lancaster* (Rooney 1865).

Rooney called three witnesses in his defense, each declaring that the accused had multiple opportunities to escape while in the custody of his captors. They also agreed with the prosecution's witnesses who considered Rooney's general behavior as reliable, fair, and honest (Rooney 1865).

The prosecution's case consisted solely of proving the man's unauthorized absence and subsequent arrest. Rooney provided the explanatory details in his defense statement, beginning with an oblique admission confessing to the pilfered money, followed by a statement reporting where some of the funds went: "I went to several saloons, I got intoxicated, for I remember nothing more until the next morning; when I awoke I found myself in a strange place with a suit of citizen's clothes" (Rooney 1865).

Rooney's debauch severely depleted his cash but the man somehow managed to survive for a month. Stricken with shame, Rooney refused to return to the USS *Lancaster*, "but exposed myself in the most public places … hoping each day that I would be arrested." The remainder of Rooney's final words to the court-martial emphasized his docile capitulation when arrested, and with a looming promotion to master's mate the accused man rhetorically posed, "Would any man under these circumstances willfully desert his ship?" (Rooney 1865).

The court-martial concluded with Rooney's expected conviction on the second charge, but the man dodged the most serious accusation when the members found him not guilty of desertion but guilty of AWOL. Even so, the man received a stiff sentence, "to be confined at the Tortugas or any other place the Secretary of the Navy may designate for the space of two years." The court-martial also demanded Rooney provide restitution for the stolen money (Rooney 1865).

Landsman Edward Eagan, USS *Wyandank*, appeared at a court-martial on March 14, 1865, for desertion. According to the specification, Eagan received a leave of absence for a few hours from the St. Inigoes Navy Yard in Maryland, but he did not return until arrested six days later. Following the arrest, Acting Ensign Ambrose Felix, the ship's executive officer, confined Eagan in double irons. Attorney Charles Jack assisted Eagan during the trial, and under cross-examination, Felix admitted, "He [Eagan] was the last man that I thought would run away. I thought so because he was a very good man and never gave any trouble" (Eagan 1865).

Lucius Fisher testified next for the prosecution and described Eagan's arrest. Fisher spotted the man about five miles from St. Inigoes and approached him asking "where he had been, and he said he had been on a spree." According to further testimony, Eagan was traveling by foot from Point Lookout, Maryland, back to the Navy Yard, presumably following the spree (Eagan 1865).

The court-martial members deliberated and returned with an interesting decision, acknowledging the prisoner's unauthorized absence but insisting that "it has not been proved that he was forcibly brought back, but on the contrary thereof it appears that he returned voluntarily." With that in mind, the court-martial found Eagan guilty of AWOL but extracted only three months' pay as punishment (Eagan 1865).

Another form of unauthorized absence embroiled Captain Francis V. Randall, 2nd Regiment, Vermont Infantry, in a court-martial. Just a few months after armed conflict splintered the United States, Captain Randall appeared before a general court-martial convened on October 22, 1861, at the "Camp of Smith's Division." The court-martial accused the officer of three military crimes, "shamefully abandoning his post," "leaving the regiment without permission of his commanding officer," and "conduct prejudicial to good order and military discipline" (Randall 1861).

Colonel H. Whiting, Commanding the 2nd Regiment, Vermont Infantry, ordered Randall as the commander of Company F, on September 29, 1861, to post his soldiers as skirmishers in a wooded area near Falls Church, Virginia. Randall moved his troops as directed but two hours later "withdrew his company back into the road without leave or permission of his commanding officer." Following this, Randall left his company and regiment and returned to the rear encampment around Fort Marcy, Virginia (Randall 1861).

Captain Randall pleaded not guilty to all three military charges. The court-martial, with Colonel H. Whiting acting as president of the tribunal, issued confusing verdicts. In terms of "shamefully abandoning his post" and "conduct prejudicial to good order and military discipline," the court-martial found the man guilty of the specifications describing the two crimes but attached no criminality to his behavior and then rendered the man not guilty of the military charges. There was no similar equivocation when the court-martial declared Randall guilty of "leaving the regiment without permission of his commanding officer" and consequently sentenced the officer to a thirty-day suspension from command along with an official reprimand (Randall 1861).

After reviewing the transcript, Major General George B. McClellan censured the conclusions and with apparent exasperation was "at a loss to understand how it is possible for a Court to verify the specification ... and yet to attach no criminality thereto." Compounding McClellan's ire was testimony impugning Randall. According to Colonel Whiting's recollections, the accused soldier justified the unauthorized absence as "self-preservation." Another witness testified that Randall explained his premature arrival at Fort Marcy because he "was sick; feared that if he stayed he would be sick" (Randall 1861).

McClellan shredded Randall's behavior for "leaving his company in presence of the enemy, expos[ing] himself to the worst interpretation of his conduct. He proved, by way of repelling this interpretation, that he had been slightly unwell ... Of course, no illness that did not absolutely incapacitate him for service would be regarded by a good soldier as a cause for absence at such a critical time" (Randall 1861).

Randall's lenient thirty-day suspension and reprimand earned further scorn from McClellan since "such punishments fall very short of what the good of the service requires." While leaving the verdicts and punishments unchanged, McClellan obliquely castigated Randall's honor and implied that the court-martial should have dismissed the officer (Randall 1861).

Review of court-martial proceedings by the convening authority provided an opportunity to correct judicial errors, return the case for reconsideration, or rebuke the findings. In the case of First Lieutenant William H. Harrison, 107th Regiment, Ohio Infantry, the post-trial review favored the accused soldier (Harrison 1864b).

First Lieutenant Harrison appeared before a general court-martial at Jacksonville, Florida, on March 2, 1864. The judge advocate presented the officer with three military charges: misbehavior before the enemy, disobedience of orders, and conduct unbecoming an officer and a gentleman. In describing the offenses, the specifications alleged that Harrison left his company and regiment without permission after receiving orders to advance against the enemy at John's Island, South Carolina, on or about February 7, 1864. At the time of the incident, a senior officer approached the man and questioned his absence. Harrison replied "that he was excused, because he had been on three days' picket." The judge advocate alleged that this was a false statement that justified the third military charge of conduct unbecoming an officer and a gentleman (Harrison 1864b).

Harrison pleaded not guilty to all three military charges, but the court-martial members decided otherwise and returned three guilty verdicts. His punishment was "to be cashiered, and that his crime, name, place of abode, and punishment, be published in the newspapers about the camp, and in those of the State of Ohio" (Harrison 1864b).

Major General John G. Foster reviewed the transcript and spotted an error. "The record, in this case, shows that a member of the Court, who was absent from its sitting on the first day of the trial, attended and participated in the proceedings of the second day. This inexcusable irregularity vitiates the action of the Court." Foster conceded that the "irregularity" might simply reflect a clerical mistake, but with the attending officers reassigned to other duties, reconstituting the court-martial was impossible. Despite Foster's misgivings, he disapproved of the verdicts and sentence and returned Harrison to duty (Harrison 1864b).

Harrison's good fortune was fleeting. Just a few months later the officer once again faced a general court-martial at Jacksonville, Florida, on June 22, 1864, with Lieutenant Colonel Ulysses Doubleday presiding at the trial. The judge advocate charged Harrison with three crimes: neglect of duty, conduct prejudicial to good order and military discipline, and breaking his arrest (Harrison 1864a).

Harrison was the provost guard's commanding officer when Private John Aleck Williams, Company D, 35th Regiment, United States Colored Troops, escaped. A court-martial at Jacksonville, Florida, on March 3, 1864, previously convicted the 19-year-old man of three military crimes: disobedience, mutiny, and assault upon his senior officer. Williams pleaded not guilty, but the court-martial found the man guilty on all three charges and sentenced him to be "shot to death with musketry" at Jacksonville (Williams, A. 1864).

In addition to permitting Williams to escape, the court-martial prosecuted Harrison for not removing the sidearms of several soldiers in confinement, arresting an officer without cause, and "having been placed in arrest ... [Harrison] did leave his quarters and the limits of his camp and proceed ... [to] the City of Jacksonville" (Harrison 1864a).

Contrary to his pleadings of innocence, the court-martial found Harrison guilty of the first two military charges but not guilty of breaking arrest and sentenced him "to be suspended from rank and pay for one year." In a pyrrhic victory, Major General Foster disapproved of the military charge of conduct prejudicial to good order and military discipline, citing insufficient evidence, but he left the sentence intact (Harrison 1864a).

Second Lieutenant Charles H. Forshay (Forshey), Company A, 126th Regiment, New York Infantry, benefited from a judicial review of his trial. Forshay's court-martial decided the man's fate regarding three military crimes: misbehavior in the face of the enemy, cowardice, and absence without leave. The court-martial found Forshay guilty on all counts and sentenced the officer "to be cashiered, and that his crime, name, place of abode, and punishment of the said Charles H. Forshay, Second Lieutenant Company A, 126th New York Volunteers, be published in the State of New York, in one or more newspapers, as the Secretary of War may direct" (Forshay 1863).

A curious anomaly vacated the court-martial's findings. From the record, it became known that Forshay had "not been discharged from the service as a Sergeant or mustered into it as a commissioned officer." As such, Forshay was not an officer and could not be cashiered. The remedy directed by Major General George B. Meade returned Forshay to active duty as a sergeant and, without special dispensation from the War Department, barred the man from a future commission (Forshay 1863).

Interestingly, not every officer dishonorably dismissed received that outcome from a court-martial. Second Lieutenant Donald Gillies, 125th Regiment, New York Infantry, submitted his resignation "on the ground that a wound received in the battle of Gettysburg has so intimidated him, that he has become constitutionally a coward and unfit to lead his company into action" (Gillies 1864).

Straggling was an ordinary form of absence from duty, but one that courts-martial rarely invoked. Even so, military leaders understood the damage and issued strict orders "to watch the conduct and behavior of officers and men, on the march as well as in battle. Regiments not moving promptly, as ordered, permitting straggling, or where the officers show a lack of capacity and zeal in pushing forward ... must be specially reported for neglect" (General Orders Number 40, 1863).

The rare prosecution of straggling by a general court-martial was not an indication of tolerance, but instead partly reflected the imprecise legal definition that failed to distinguish the crime from desertion, misbehavior before the enemy, or even AWOL. Another factor limiting straggling's prosecution was the sheer volume, with most soldiers receiving summary punishment such as loss of pay or trial by a regimental court-martial (Carmichael 2018, 178–180).

First Lieutenant Walter J. Morgan, Company G, 28th Regiment, Massachusetts Infantry, was a rare example of an officer tried by a general court-martial for straggling. Morgan's general court-martial convened on June 29, 1864, and presented the man with two military charges, straggling and AWOL. A guilty verdict followed, and the court-martial sentenced Morgan "to be reduced to the ranks to serve three years." Major General George B. Meade approved the sentence and further stipulated that Morgan would serve three years as a private with the 28th Regiment, Massachusetts Infantry (Morgan, Walter 1864).

Desertion in time of war was not limited to the Army, as evidenced by a Navy general court-martial convened on board the USS *Tioga*, near Key West, Florida, on August 7, 1863. Rear Admiral Theodorus Bailey preferred the military charge of desertion in time of war against Landsman Jeremiah McCarthy, attached to the USS *Octorara*. According to the specification, around July 22, 1863, the accused abandoned the USS *Octorara* and hid on two successive ships to escape from Key West. McCarthy pleaded guilty, obviating any testimony, and the five Navy officers assigned to the court-martial affirmed the pleading and sentenced the man "to forfeit all pay and prize money ... to be reduced in rating to a 1st Class Boy ... for three years...[and] the first six months of which to be confined in double irons at night while in port" (McCarthy 1863).

If at first you do not succeed, try, try again, was a motto that defined Marine Corps Private James Ford. Nine officers joined a Navy general court-martial on March 2, 1864, to hear the man's exploits. Ford was born in Providence, Rhode Island, and he enlisted in Philadelphia, Pennsylvania, on September 23, 1861, for a period of four years. Ford was 20 years old and stood nearly five feet, eight inches tall, with blue eyes, brown hair, and a ruddy complexion (Ford 1864).

The record is silent until September 8, 1863, when an annotation noted that Ford "joined [the Navy] from the USS Brooklyn 8th Sept 1863." From this time forward, a summary of the man's military service documented his desertion on October 25, 1863, and his subsequent arrest on November 23, 1863. Ford deserted again on December 18, 1863, and authorities arrested him on February 21, 1864. The footloose man deserted yet again on February 24, 1864, and was apprehended four days later (Ford 1864).

Judge Advocate H.H. Goodman read the military charge of desertion in time of war, accusing the man of desertion from the Marine Corps Barracks at Brooklyn, New York, on October 25, 1863, and December 18, 1863. Without explanation, the court-martial did not prosecute the last desertion (Ford 1864). Goodman was a civilian lawyer working for the Navy Department and he frequently prosecuted cases in Brooklyn (Siegel 1997, 115–116).

Private Ford pleaded not guilty to the military charge and received permission from the court-martial for A.R. Cutler, Esquire, to assist his defense. Goodman then proceeded to call Marine Corps Sergeant William Tepley as his first witness. Tepley was a tepid witness who under cross-examination admitted little direct knowledge of the accused's activities (Ford 1864).

New York City police officer Patrick Kenealy arrested the accused on February 19, 1864, after Ford's wife "came to the Station house, and she stated that her husband was a deserter." Two days later, Kenealy surrendered the prisoner to authorities at the Brooklyn Navy Yard and received a ten-dollar reward. Ford's detention at the Navy Yard was brief because he escaped from confinement on February 24, 1864 (Ford 1864).

First Sergeant Samuel W. Deemer testified that Ford voluntarily returned to the Brooklyn Navy Yard after his first desertion and the Navy Yard's commander returned the man to duty without assigning any punishment. Both sides in the contested case vigorously interrogated Deemer, but the defense pointedly inquired whether Ford's return to duty without any penalties constituted absolution. The beleaguered witness conceded, "It was a forgiveness, in my opinion" (Ford 1864).

Sergeant David Barry, a witness for the defense, testified about Ford's character. Barry had close personal contact with the accused in the preceding ten years and at the Brooklyn Navy Yard, where Ford's role as a mess cook ensured continued opportunities to observe him. Barry extolled Ford's good behavior during battles in the war, including Vicksburg and New Orleans. First Lieutenant James Forney considered Ford a disciplined member of the Marine Corps who obeyed all orders (Ford 1864).

Private Ford's legal counsel, A.R. Cutler, submitted a comprehensive defense statement attacking the prosecution's case on multiple points. Cutler assailed inconsistencies between Deemer's testimony and the daily records documenting Ford's presence at the Brooklyn Navy Yard. He dismissed Tepley's narration as hearsay, condemned Kenealy's dogged, illegal wrangling of a confession from Ford, and insinuated that the ten-dollar reward tainted the policeman's testimony. Cutler highlighted the lack of punishment for the first desertion and then ended his oratory on a high note by reminding the court-martial about Ford's good character. Cutler copiously quoted Dehart's authoritative *Observations on Military Law and the Constitution and Practice of Courts Martial* throughout the lengthy legal argument (Ford 1864).

Cutler's robust legal defense partially succeeded. The court-martial found Ford not guilty of desertion on October 25, 1863, but guilty of AWOL. For the second charge of desertion, the court-martial found the accused guilty. The mixed verdicts resulted in the court-martial sentencing Private Ford "to be imprisoned at hard labor ... for the term of fifteen years" (Ford 1864).

Shore duty tempted two Navy landsmen, both of whom took advantage of the respite from ship duties to escape. A Navy general court-martial convened on board the USS *Roanoke* near Newport News, Virginia, to hear the cases of Theodore W. Draper on October 27, 1863, and John Laven on October 28, 1863 (Draper 1863; Laven 1863).

Marine Corps Captain John Schermerhorn functioned as the judge advocate and charged both men with desertion in times of war. The facts were similar in both cases, as explained by Acting Third Assistant Engineer Volney Crank. Crank testified that Draper and Laven were both attached to the ferryboat USS *Commodore Morris* and were members of a shore party ordered to destroy a railroad track. A brief time later the officer discovered the men missing and "I went in search of them. The next I saw...[both] were in a skiff crossing the River. I hailed the men in the skiff and ordered them to return, they paid no attention to my order ... I then

USS *Roanoke* (NH 59548, courtesy Naval History & Heritage Command).

fired my revolver at them and they continued their flight over the river" (Draper 1863; Laven 1863).

Crank reported the matter to his commander, and following a flurry of activity, an armed cutter began patrolling the river for the escapees. The deserters abandoned their skiff and assumed land positions. A volley of bullets greeted the cutter as it approached the deserters, but the boat's return fire failed when "none of them [weapons] would go off." The one-sided skirmish ran aground with the subsequent apprehension of the deserters (Draper 1863; Laven 1863).

The prosecution's witnesses acknowledged both men's good character, but Draper and Laven had no witnesses. The two landsmen relied on their separate defense statements, which proclaimed their innocence and lack of intent to desert. Draper additionally explained that "while walking in the vicinity of that place [work detail], I procured some whiskey, of which I am sorry to say, some of my shipmates and myself drank freely. I got very drunk ... and did not know what I was doing" (Draper 1863; Laven 1863).

The court-martial found both men guilty and sentenced the pair to seven years of confinement, half of which would be hard labor. At the same time, the court-martial recommended mercy for Draper and Laven based on their history of good conduct. Rear Admiral Samuel Phillips Lee accepted the court-martial's recommendation and reduced the sentence to six months of confinement (Draper 1863; Laven 1863).

Intoxication was a central feature in the trial of Seaman John McDonald, attached to the USS *Sacramento*, on August 6, 1863. Rear Admiral

Two. Unauthorized Absences

Samuel Phillips Lee, Commanding, North Atlantic Blockading Squadron, convened the Navy general court-martial on board the USS *Sacramento* and preferred the military charges of desertion in time of war and enticing others to desert. Seven officers formed the tribunal, and Surgeon John S. Kitchen supported the accused's not guilty defense (McDonald 1863),

Acting Master's Mate Daniel C. Harrington testified first and supported the prosecution's case by narrating the incidents that unfolded on board the USS *Sacramento* on July 7, 1863. Toward late afternoon on that day, McDonald was missing and a small group under Harrington's command searched the USS *Sacramento* without avail. The search party next turned their attention to the schooner *Trade Wind* lying nearby (McDonald 1863).

The *Trade Wind* had supplied coal to the USS *Sacramento* earlier in the day and after completing that task moved toward the shore and ran aground. Harrington suspected that McDonald might have escaped to the *Trade Wind* and from there made his way ashore. With that in mind, Harrington and his crew boarded the *Trade Wind* and methodically sought the deserter's whereabouts. Acting on a tip from an unnamed *Trade Wind* crewmember, one of Harrington's men approached the forepeak and demanded that McDonald surrender. Increasingly strident appeals finally forced the hidden McDonald from the cubbyhole (McDonald 1863),

Harrington shackled McDonald with single irons, and together with the other search party members they left the *Trade Wind* in a dinghy and made their way back to the USS *Sacramento*. During the short trip, McDonald pleaded with his captors to release him, but failing to convince them, "he said he wanted to play half drunk" (McDonald 1863).

Lieutenant Commander Andrew Benham testified that "when the accused came out of the boat [dinghy] he appeared to be under the influence of liquor, that is his body was swaying backwards and forwards, but whether this state was assumed, or he was really intoxicated I cannot state." Once on board the USS *Sacramento* and confined in double irons, McDonald requested a meeting with Benham and confessed "that he was under the influence of liquor at the time, and had stowed himself away in the afternoon aboard the Schooner [*Trade Wind*] and had gone to sleep there, and that he had no intention of deserting" (McDonald 1863).

Surgeon Kitchen read the accused's defense statement to the court-martial, an entreaty that began with McDonald's complaint that "I was a shipped man when I came on board the Sacramento. I subsequently received not a rating but a written appointment as Master at Arms." In a more substantive argument, McDonald challenged the second military charge of incitement, pointing to the contradictory testimony of the prosecution's witnesses. Curiously, his defense statement made no mention of alcohol intoxication. Ultimately, McDonald prevailed on the second charge, but the court-martial found him guilty of desertion in time of war and sentenced the man to imprisonment at hard labor for ten years (McDonald 1863).

Private William Southwick had the unenviable distinction of being the only member of the Marine Corps sentenced to death in the representative database for this volume. Rear Admiral David D. Porter, Commanding, Mississippi Squadron, convened a Navy general court-martial at Cairo, Illinois, on board the USS *Clara Dolsen*, on December 4, 1863. Judge Advocate Acting Ensign James M. Alden read the military charge of desertion. Alden accused Southwick of deserting the Marine Corps Barracks at Cairo, Illinois, around October 2, 1863, and remaining absent until arrested on October 26, 1863. Southwick declined counsel, pleaded guilty, and offered no defense to the charge (Southwick 1863).

Without further ado, the court-martial sentenced Southwick to five years of hard labor in prison. The court-martial reconvened on December 5, 1863, and "it was moved by a member of the Court that the vote on the sentence of William Southwick be reconsidered." This was not a plea for clemency, as the members quickly adopted the court-martial member's proposal and substituted for incarceration a sentence condemning the man to be shot to death (Southwick 1863).

Secretary of the Navy Gideon Welles reversed the court-martial's harshly revised sentence and reinstated the original imprisonment, sending the prisoner to the Joliet Illinois Correctional Center on January 8, 1864. Upon his reception, correctional officials described Southwick as a temperate man, standing five feet seven inches tall, with dark hair and gray eyes, and who could read but not write. Southwick's ill health resulted in a pardon on March 10, 1866 (Registry of Prisoners Incarcerated at the Joliet Correctional Center. Image 1–0055 1864).

Reviews of courts-martial by convening authorities served as an important legal safeguard, often altering the outcomes of trials. While most courts-martial decisions were upheld on review and the sentences were imposed, there were exceptions, such as when Colonel John T. Foland, Commanding, 2nd Brigade, 3rd Division, convened a court-martial near Fayetteville, Virginia, on February 16, 1863, for the trials of two officers, three corporals, and five privates (General Orders Number 38, 1863).

Captain James A. Anderson, Company I, 34th Regiment, Ohio Infantry, faced three military charges: uttering disloyal language against the Unites States, encouraging desertion, and assisting men to desert. Anderson's disloyal language consisted of two themes, a wish that the war was over and his dissatisfaction with President Lincoln's Emancipation Proclamation. The officer hoped that "the people at home would raise such a row as to break up the Army, so that we would have to return home." He also virulently opposed the Emancipation Proclamation, with the prosecutor alleging that Anderson "would rather see the South conquer than have such treasonable doctrine sustained." Anderson's lackluster support of the Union's war included suborning desertion. After hearing the evidence, the court-martial found Anderson not guilty of encouraging desertion, but guilty of disloyal language and assisting men to desert and sentenced the man to be dismissed from the Army (General Orders Number 38, 1863).

Second Lieutenant Isaac C. Fair, 1st Regiment, Ohio Light Artillery, voiced sentiments like Captain Anderson's in criticizing "the President's proclamation [as] unconstitutional." His temerity brought two military charges for uttering disloyal language and using contemptuous language against President Lincoln. The court-martial declared Fair guilty of both charges and sentenced the man to be dismissed from the Army. Both officers' behaviors seemingly influenced eight enlisted soldiers, the subject of the subsequent courts-martial (General Orders Number 38, 1863).

Secretary of the Navy Gideon Welles (NH 54641, courtesy of the Naval History & Heritage Command).

The same court-martial that tried the two officers then turned their attention to Private Stephen C. Kent, Company I, 34th Regiment, Ohio Infantry, and charged him with conspiring to mutiny and desertion; charged Private Eli McPherson, Company I, 34th Regiment, Ohio Infantry, with desertion; charged Private John Davidson, Company I, 34th Regiment, Ohio Infantry, with conspiring to mutiny and desertion; charged Private Harrison Hays, Company I, 34th Regiment, Ohio Infantry, with desertion; and charged Private Jacob Fasnacht, Company I, 34th Regiment, Ohio Infantry, with conspiring to mutiny and desertion. In each case, the court-martial found the men guilty of desertion but not conspiring to mutiny and sentenced them "to be shot to death with musketry" (General Orders Number 38, 1863).

Three remaining cases came before the court-martial and charged Corporal George W. Mowry, Company I, 34th Regiment, Ohio Infantry, with desertion; Corporal Richard Davidson, Company I, 34th Regiment, Ohio Infantry with desertion; and Corporal Theodore Handle, Company I, 34th Regiment, Ohio Infantry, with desertion. Yet again, in each case, the court-martial found the men guilty of desertion and sentenced them "to be shot to death with musketry" (General Orders Number 38, 1863).

Major General Robert C. Schenck disapproved and rescinded all ten courts-martial, not by mentioning the spectacle of executing eight men from the same unit, but instead stating that Colonel John T. Foland "was not authorized ... to convene a General Court-martial ... The proceedings of the Court are therefore void." In further comments, Schenck considered the charges and evidence sufficient to convene a new court-martial but "he [Schenck] forbears to take this course however, in the hope that time and the serious condition in which the parties have been placed may have induced reflection and wise resolutions on their part" (General Orders Number 38, 1863).

A judge advocate's error fatally flawed a court-martial. Private Gustav Hoffman, Company B, 6th Regiment, Connecticut Infantry, pleaded not guilty to deserting from his unit at Hilton Head, South Carolina, around February 9, 1864, and remaining absent until arrested on February 21, 1864. The court-martial returned a guilty verdict and sentenced the man "to be shot to death with musketry" (Hoffman, G. 1864).

Major General Quincy A. Gillmore annulled the court-martial and ordered the man restored to duty. For unstated reasons, Gillmore launched an investigation of the court-martial's proceedings and he discovered that Private Gustav Hoofan was the accused's proper name, not Gustav Hoffman. In a withering rebuke, Gillmore castigated the court-martial because "this is a radical and fatal error, and the inexcusable carelessness, upon the part of the Judge advocate ... in recording the proceedings of the Court, and of the Court itself in reviewing the same, merits the severest censure" (General Orders Number 51, 1864).

The general court-martial of Private George Biggs, Company C, 23rd Regiment, Missouri Infantry, violated one of the fundamental tenets of military law. Lieutenant Colonel James Peckman, 29th Regiment, Missouri Infantry, was president of the court-martial that assembled at Cape Girardeau, Missouri, on September 27, 1862, for the trial. The judge advocate charged Biggs with desertion on or about October 21, 1862, and for remaining absent until a special detail arrested the man five days later. Biggs pleaded guilty and the court-martial promptly sentenced him "to be shot." Post-trial review disapproved of the sentence because only four members of the general court-martial decided the case. Military law required a minimum of five members. The legal error sent Biggs back to duty without suffering any punishment (Biggs 1862).

Courts-martial members could weigh a range of factors when considering punishment, as they did in the case of Private Nicholas Shivers, Company G, 2nd Regiment, Maryland Eastern Shore Infantry. According to the military charge, Shivers deserted from the Lafayette Barracks, Baltimore, Maryland, on or about October 24, 1862. Despite finding Shivers guilty, the court-martial did not impose capital punishment, opting instead to revoke his pay along with assigning a dishonorable discharge because "the Court [members] are induced to be thus lenient in the sentence, on account of the feeble and diseased physical condition of the prisoner" (Shivers 1863).

A different type of compassion played out in the case of Private John B. Perdue, Company D, Purnell Legion, Maryland Infantry. A general court-martial convened at Fort Delaware, Maryland, on September 8, 1863, charging Perdue with desertion. Perdue's crime was not uncommon in the Civil War and consisted of "having received a furlough ... [Perdue] did fail to report to his regiment ... at the time his furlough expired." Perdue pleaded not guilty, a verdict partially sustained when the court-martial decided the man was not guilty of desertion but was guilty of being AWOL, justifying as a punishment only a loss of pay during the absence (Perdue 1863).

Major General Robert C. Schenck reviewed Perdue's trial and, while not condoning the unauthorized absence, explained that "much of the prisoner's fault was caused by the illness and death of his wife, and so in view of his excellent character as a soldier, the Commanding General remits the forfeiture of his pay and allowances and directs the prisoner to be released from confinement and restored to duty." At the same time, Schenck warned that "while thus exercising clemency towards this man, the Commanding General feels constrained to remark upon the utter inadequacy of the punishments imposed in the cases of desertion by this Court. In fact, there has been no difference made in the punishment of this man for an absence without leave, under extenuating circumstances, and in the case of actual desertion" (Perdue 1863).

Major General Schenck surely balanced the value furloughs created in terms of improved morale versus the cost in terms of lost battlefield manpower, but he could not support its widespread misuse, as exemplified in Perdue's trial. Even medical furloughs contributed to the systemic abuse of authorized absences and forced the War Department to restrict the practice: "the number allowed to be absent at one time to be limited to five (5) percent and the period not to exceed thirty (30) days, and to be graduated according to the distance of the applicant from his home" (General Orders Number 391, 1863).

A stricter order from the War Department in 1864 demanded "that the furloughs of all regimental officers and enlisted men fit for duty will terminate on the 14th [of November]." To ensure compliance, the order directed the Provost Marshal General to "take measures" to identify and return reluctant service members to active duty (General Orders Number 279, 1864).

One exception to the increasingly limited options rewarded reenlisting service members with a furlough. The Secretary of War enshrined the practice and authorized "volunteers now in service, re-enlisting as Veteran Volunteers ... shall have a furlough of at least thirty days previous to the expiration of their original enlistment" (General Orders Number 376, 1863).

Another case of clemency spared Seaman John Kennedy, attached to the USS *Brilliant*. Seven Navy officers gathered on board the USS *Moose* on July 11, 1864, near Smithland, Kentucky, and constituted a Navy general court-martial to hear Judge Advocate Acting Assistant Paymaster J.W. Clark accuse Kennedy of desertion on or about December 3, 1863. Acting Assistant Paymaster Falcott was Kennedy's counsel and listened as the man pleaded not guilty (Kennedy, J. 1864).

Acting Ensign George D. Little was the prosecution's first witness, and he recalled refusing Kennedy's request for shore leave on December 3, 1863. Little's decision stemmed from "his having come on board drunk the last time he was ashore and being incapacitated for duty for several days." Kennedy protested, insisting he was not previously intoxicated and swearing to avoid alcohol if Little would reconsider. To bolster his argument, Kennedy claimed that his sole motivation was to buy a pair of comfortable boots. The officer relented, granted the man's request, and demanded that he return on time (Kennedy, J. 1864).

At the appointed time Kennedy did not return. Little instructed a gunner's mate to conduct a thorough search for the missing man the following day, but the effort was unsuccessful. Nine days later another shipboard officer arrested Kennedy and brought him back to the ship. According to the arresting officer, Kennedy was not drunk but "he looked as if he had been very sick." The man's ailment preceded his desertion, and Surgeon's Steward William Stephens confirmed that Kennedy suffered from diarrhea and was not fit for duty. Even so, Stephens adamantly denied Kennedy's stated wish to go ashore for medical care (Kennedy, J. 1864).

Several witnesses, including Acting Ensign Little and Acting Master's Mate James H. Meley, observed Kennedy's odd behavior, prompting the judge advocate to inquire, "Do you think his mind was sound at the time?" Meley responded by noting that "he acts strangely sometimes." Judge Advocate Assistant Paymaster Clark pushed back, contending that

Kennedy was frequently intoxicated and suggested that any sickness was due to liquor. Defense witnesses were less certain, and their equivocation dominated their testimony, with none willing to concede the judge advocate's point. Kennedy's defense witnesses did consider the man "a little weak" mentally, determined to get medications while onshore, but always faithful to his duties (Kennedy, J. 1864).

Kennedy's trial revolved around two competing arguments, the prosecution assigning the man's willful desertion to his penchant for alcohol and the defense focused on his chronic illness and "weak mind." The court was then cleared for deliberation "and having maturely considered the evidence adduced find the accused guilty" and then sentenced Kennedy to death by hanging. Having sentenced Kennedy to death, the court fervently requested mercy based on his "apparent weakness of mind, which without amounting to idiocy or insanity, nevertheless, is in the opinion of the court sufficient to render him incapable of justly appreciating the grave consequences of desertion" (Kennedy, J. 1864).

Rear Admiral David D. Porter reviewed the trial proceedings and confirmed the court's compliance with the law. At the same time, Porter acknowledged that Kennedy did not appreciate the criminality of his conduct and in so doing recommended that President Lincoln extend mercy to the man (Kennedy, John 1864). Since the Union Navy did not execute any service members during the Civil War, it is safe to assume that President Lincoln accepted Porter's recommendation (Alotta 1989, 10).

A Navy general court-martial convened on board the USS *Roanoke* on March 19, 1864, for the trial of George E. Smith, "colored, an Ordinary Seaman attached to the U.S. Steamer Frigate Minnesota." Eleven Navy and Marine Corps officers constituted the panel to hear the judge advocate begin the trial, during which Smith

Admiral David G. Farragut, USN (NH 49522, courtesy of the Naval History & Heritage Command).

requested the assistance of Acting Ensign Frederick A. O'Connor as his counsel. Rear Admiral Samuel Phillips Lee, Commanding, North Atlantic Blockading Squadron, preferred the military desertion charge because Smith "did desert [from the USS *Minnesota*] then lying off Newport News in Virginia, on or about the seventeenth day of November 1863." Smith was arrested and returned to the ship on December 26, 1863 (Smith, G. 1864).

Smith pleaded not guilty, after which the judge advocate presented Master-at-Arms John Glynn, USS *Minnesota*, as the first witness. Glynn reported Smith missing on November 17, 1863, and the next day searched nearby Fort Monroe, aided with a twenty-dollar reward. The elusive deserter was not at Fort Monroe and Glynn, now provided with a forty-dollar reward, searched for Smith in Norfolk, Virginia. Glynn's hunt revealed an important clue. Smith had enlisted in the "Second North Carolina Regiment." A Navy officer eventually arrested Smith on December 26, 1863, while "dressed in the uniform of an orderly sergeant in the army" (Smith, G. 1864).

Lieutenant Joseph P. Fyffe, the commanding officer, did not approve of Smith's repeated requests for leave, "for being dirty and not behaving well." Perhaps sensing the inevitable outcome, Smith admitted deserting the USS *Minnesota* "and entering the army, that he did not know but that it was just the same." With no defense witnesses, the accused seaman submitted a letter to the court-martial previously sent to Brigadier General Edward A. Wild on January 4, 1864. In the letter, Smith respectfully began, "You will pardon me for taking the liberty of writing you ... but I am now kept a prisoner ... on board this ship." Smith plaintively asked Wild for help, admitting he deserted "on account of the general treatment men of color receive here" (Smith, G. 1864).

Wild was a sympathetic choice, as an ardent abolitionist who aggressively recruited soldiers for the United States Colored Troops (Casstevens 2015, 52–53). From Norfolk, Virginia, he led the eponymous Wild's African Brigade in numerous battles in South Carolina. In succeeding years, Wild's Black soldiers participated in the Siege of Peterburg and later supported the occupation of Richmond (Casstevens 2015, 204–207).

Upon receiving Smith's letter, Wild drafted a response on January 14, 1864, which he dispatched to the commander of the USS *Minnesota* imploring the officer to extend "your leniency, and if possible, your kind offices in his favor ... in consideration of ... his ignorance of the enormity of the offense, of his earnest desire to take a stand among those of his own race ... that he did not desert from cowardice, or for money ... as he has showed himself anxious to fight for his country" (Smith, G. 1864).

With all the evidence submitted, the court-martial closed for deliberation, subsequently found Smith guilty, and sentenced him to five years of hard labor "in such prison or penitentiary as the Secretary of the Navy may direct." What effect Brigadier General Wild's appeal had is unknown, but Rear Admiral Lee approved the court-martial proceedings on March 29, 1864 (Smith, G. 1864).

Three

Alcohol and Misconduct

The Rules and Articles of War from 1776 clearly stated that "whatever commissioned officer shall be found drunk on his guard, party, or other duty under arms, shall be cashiered for it; any non-commissioned officer or soldier so offending, shall suffer such corporeal punishment as shall be inflicted by the sentence of a court-martial" (Callan 1863, 70). By 1806 the 45th Article of War incorporated the same language (Callan 1863, 183). During the Civil War, the 45th Article of War remained the same as its 1806 predecessor (Coppée 1864, 140).

Army regulations in 1862 empowered the Army of the Potomac's Provost Marshal to enforce the "suppression of drunkenness beyond the limits of the camps ... drinking-houses or bar rooms ... regulation of taverns ... enforcement of orders prohibiting the sale of intoxicating liquors, whether by tradesmen or sutlers" (Butterfield 1862, 65).

The various rules and regulations served notice to the military that drunkenness was intolerable, but the implementation of the policies was ineffective, in large part due to alcohol's socially ambivalent role. Across a continuum existed fervent teetotalers, alcohol's numerous advocates, and the scorned ranks of the dissipated. Military leaders, physicians, politicians, and the public at large all had opinions weighing the value of alcohol versus its undeniable harm.

Military and medical leadership joined forces over the whiskey ration. Special Order Number 152 from the Army of the Potomac, issued on May 19, 1862, authorized "an extra ration of one gill of whiskey daily ... to every officer and soldier in this army" based on the recommendation of the medical director (Hamilton, F. 1865, 71).

William A. Hammond assumed the role of Surgeon General of the Army on April 25, 1862, and was no doubt influential in crafting policies on the value of alcohol in the military. Hammond targeted the growing impact of the prohibitionists and accused the group of demonizing alcohol solely based on its excessive use, a specious argument since the physician himself conceded that "no one can for a moment deny that alcoholic liquors, when used in excessive amount, are not only injurious to the individual but are also in the highest degree pernicious to society" (Hammond 1863, 531).

Hammond railed against partisan persuasions demanding abolition. His reasoned approach acknowledged alcohol's useful attributes even while conceding that immoderate use was dangerous. Chief among alcohol's benefits, Hammond argued, was its propensity to impede the decay of a person's physical energy, just as food regenerated worn muscles and nerves. Alcohol was a stimulant when used in moderation, but Hammond could not proclaim the beverage a food. He instead speculated that unknown physiologic forces accounted for its effects. Hammond adopted the "wear and tear" philosophy in recommending the use of alcohol to combat the strains of arduous exercise and to quickly restore the soldier's vital energies, commenting that "whiskey is an excellent stimulant ... it is issued to troops whenever from exposure or excessive labor it is deemed necessary" (Hammond 1863, 544).

Hammond's views permeated the Civil War Medical Department, but some physicians disagreed. The whiskey ration generated lively debate among Civil War surgeons, with a survey of twenty practitioners suggesting that "the great majority ... are of the opinion that the issuing of a whiskey ration, as a rule, is injurious instead of being useful" (US Sanitary Commission 1867, 113).

Surgeon John E. Sanborn proclaimed that "although a temperance man, I have always used whiskey liberally with my men,—using a barrel in my regiment during a march. My testimony is unequivocally in favor of its judicious use." Surgeon Samuel L. Adams noted that "in bad weather, or when exhausting duties were required, I have observed the very best effects from a toggle of whiskey." Surgeon Samuel Flagg regarded "the ration of whiskey, when regularly served, doubtless beneficial. It acted as an adjuvant to the digestive functions" (US Sanitary Commission 1867, 116–117).

Surgeon John Wright disagreed with his colleagues, and "my opinion, based upon observation, is that the whiskey ration, as used in the army, is always an injury and that the sick list is increased by it." Surgeon Orpheus Everts had a similar thought "respecting the whiskey ration ... that it does not promote the ability of the soldier to endure physical exertion, and that it diminishes the ability to resist disease." Surgeon Henry Z. Gill bluntly declared that "in every instance under my observation the whiskey ration has done more harm than good" (US Sanitary Commission 1867, 114–115).

Despite debating alcohol's restorative and nutritive benefits, the surgeons agreed that excessive use invariably hampered a soldier's fitness to fight. With that in mind, in the early years of the Civil War, the consensus nonetheless promoted alcohol's routine distribution following medical consultation and restricted its use to physically weakened troops.

The United States Sanitary Commission supported that recommendation in 1861 with its *Rules for Preserving the Health of the Soldier*, urging that "spirits should only be issued to the men after unusual exertion, fatigue, or exposure, and on the discretion of the surgeon. Those men who drink spirits habitually, are the first to fail" (Van Buren 1861, 4). The public could view the key findings from the 1861 Sanitary Commission report ("How to Preserve the Health of the Soldier" 1861).

The Union Army's official infatuation with the whiskey ration abruptly ended on June 19, 1862, when Major General George B. McClellan directed that "the extra issue of whiskey heretofore ordered will be immediately discontinued. All commanding officers are enjoined strictly to enforce the existing orders directing that hot coffee be served to the troops immediately after reveille" (General Orders Number 136, 1862). McClellan's order offered no clues for the about-face, but surging disciplinary problems and equivocal health benefits probably played a role.

Troops were not universally happy with McClellan's proclamation, but like a blocked river, alcohol breached the barrier, rendering the edict meaningless. Soldiers' letters from the field mirrored the controversy, with temperance activists sparring with their more liberal comrades. An anonymous soldier stationed near Fredericksburg, Virginia, in mid–December 1862, expressed the views of many when relating the constant bombardment, rifle fire, mounting injuries, death, and then "we lay all night waiting ... to see what might turn up ... the ground was wet and muddy ... cold, wet, hungry, and half-frozen." After describing the miserable conditions, the soldier complained that "the abolishing of the whiskey ration in the army is an absurd, nonsensical, fanatical idea of the ultra, crazy temperance party ... make the commander of the regiment responsible for its proper use, and no evil results can follow" ("Correspondence" 1863).

A Vermont soldier applauded the Temperance Movement, bolstering his argument with a blistering critique of rampant intoxication among officers. Tackling a common argument, he went further by denouncing "the sentiment ... that if men are on fatigue duty or obliged to perform extra duty, they need a ration of whiskey." By way of proof, the soldier pointed to a regiment free of whiskey that "has had less sickness, and fewer deaths by far" ("From the Sixteenth Vermont Regiment" 1863).

The Medical and Surgical History of the War of the Rebellion tabulated instances of inebriation, delirium tremens, and chronic alcoholism under the general heading of alcoholism. Surgeons of the various regiments collectively reported 5,589 inebriated soldiers, 3,744 soldiers with delirium tremens, and 920 cases of chronic alcoholism over "five and one-sixth years" among white troops. Surgeons reported the annual equivalent of one colored soldier per 4,500 men and one white soldier per 220 men who required medical attention because of intemperance. Alcoholism contributed to the mortality statistics, with 605 soldiers' deaths attributed to the beverage. In a telling comment regarding responsibility for alcoholism, *The Medical and Surgical History of the War of the Rebellion* suggested that "preventive measures belong rather to the government and discipline of camps ... more than the medical officer" (Smart 1888, 890–891).

Improvised battlefield brews contributed to the morbidity. In Howell Carter's *A Cavalryman's Reminiscences of the Civil War*, an amusing anecdote provides a hint of that when "some soldiers brought in a bottle of white whiskey that was so vile that only a sip could be taken by anyone, and the smell was enough for most of them ... Someone suggested that if the assistant surgeon could not drink it, it had as well be thrown away. He was induced to try it but failed to drink, so it was destroyed" (Carter 2018, 31).

The Navy followed a trajectory like the Union Army, with the merits of alcohol facing determined resistance from the growing Temperance Movement. Navy Surgeon William M. Wood was among the earliest ardent detractors, summarizing his opposition in an 1842 pamphlet *Practical Reflections upon the Grog Ration of the U.S. Navy* (Steyn 1976, 24). Wood contended that the grog ration promoted disobedience and disability, and the "3,000 gallons of whiskey in the spirit room of a frigate constituted a fire hazard" (Steyn 1976, 25).

Rear Admiral Andrew Hull Foote deserved much of the credit for the Navy's move toward abstinence, a belief molded by his tenure at the Philadelphia Naval Asylum in 1841, saying that when "I came here I found these old sailors dreadful drunkards. Whenever I gave them any privilege, they invariably got drunk. I could do nothing with them. At last, I signed the [temperance] pledge myself, and then they followed me" (Hoppin 1874, 56).

Foote remained faithful to his temperance pledge. An incident on board the USS *Cumberland* in 1843 bolstered Foote's resolve when a group of sailors absconded with a barrel of whiskey and, soon besotted with the beverage, attacked one of the ship's officers. With the approval of the USS *Cumberland*'s Commodore, Foote organized a Temperance Society, and "the movement became popular, and soon all the sailors but one consented to commute their grog-rations for money; and that solitary one, coming up every day to receive his grog, became a laughing-stock, and was soon got rid of" (Hoppin 1874, 58).

In succeeding years Foote ardently pushed the Navy to eliminate the grog ration and replace it with nonaddicting stimulants such as tea or coffee and, in consideration of the loss, add an extra dollar a month to the sailor's pay (Tucker 2000, 44). The 1818 *Rules, Regulations, and Instructions, for the Naval Service of the United States* harbored one stumbling block to Foote's ambitions, indirectly enshrining the ration by limiting a Navy officer's punishment of a wayward sailor by not depriving "them of grog for more than a week" (Siegel 1997, 59).

The Navy's approach of substituting money for grog did little to lessen the demand for alcohol, but it did contribute to additional misconduct, a revelation that invoked a court of inquiry. Commander Samuel Lockwood, Commanding, USS *Daylight*, spearheaded the investigation with a letter dated June 12, 1862, addressed to Flag Officer Louis M. Goldsborough, Commanding, North Atlantic Blockading Squadron. In the letter, Lockwood stated that "it has recently come to my knowledge that several officers of this Ship have been in the habit of taking liquor from the grog tub, and getting paid for it at the same time, thus robbing the Union States" (Wade 1862).

Lockwood accused five officers of double-dipping, with all but one requesting their resignations from "their situations here" or leaving the Navy entirely. One obstinate officer was Second Assistant Engineer Van Rensellaer Terry, described by Lockwood as "an exceedingly insubordinate officer [who] brought to me ... his resignation couched in disrespectful allusions to me." Lockwood refused to forward the officer's resignation and, in its place, recommended his dishonorable dismissal (Wade 1862).

Secretary of the Navy Gideon Welles reviewed Lockwood's allegations and ordered the court of inquiry to investigate the facts and recommend courses of action. The court of inquiry convened at the New York Navy Yard on July 30, 1862, and investigated allegations that took place in November 1861. Acting Third Assistant Engineer Eugene J. Wade was the only officer who did not submit his resignation and consequently remained the sole target of the court of inquiry. H.H. Goodman acted as the recorder and read Lockwood's letter to the court, after which Wade pleaded not guilty (Wade 1862).

Goodman's witnesses collectively testified that despite receiving grog money Wade continued drinking the beverage. After Goodman's investigation, Wade simply relied on the court's judgment, waiving any defense to the allegations. The members of the court briefly deliberated and confirmed Lockwood's allegations and "in accordance with the direction ... to give an opinion ... the court deems that [Wade] deserves punishment, but in consideration of his inexperience and general good conduct the Court recommend him to the merciful consideration of the Honorable Secretary of the Navy" (Wade 1862).

Commander Percival Drayton from the USS *Pawnee* off the coast of Fernandina, Florida, on April 14, 1862, bitterly complained about the Navy's equivalent of a sutler in reporting, "an evil which has already become very great ... that is the trading schooners which come with stores to the squadron ... but which are fast becoming in spite of every precaution more or less floating grogshops. The [schooner] R.R. Higgins carried on a most disgraceful trade in almost poisonous liquors, retailed at most exorbitant prices to the sailors, until detected and sent off, but not until considerable mischief had been produced both ashore and afloat" (Stewart 1901, 741).

Navy surgeons, like their Army colleagues, vigorously debated the benefits of alcohol, but in the years preceding the Civil War, they increasingly opposed its indiscriminate dissemination, substituting their preference for medical consultation before dispensation (Varner, V. 1951, 123–129).

Drawing on his experiences during the Civil War, Navy Surgeon Joseph Wilson authored a book to acquaint readers with "the leading principles of hygienic management" onboard American ships. Wood acknowledged the medicinal benefits of whiskey, brandy, and rum, but he commended the decision to ban the grog ration and replace the strong drink with tea and coffee in the morning and evening (Wilson 1870, 75–81).

High-profile courts-martial alleging alcohol-related misconduct also presumably hardened the military's official response to misuse. Shortly after the Civil War began, a Navy general court-martial convened at the New York Navy Yard on September 23, 1861, to consider the case of Commander Edward R. Thompson, Commanding, USS *Seminole* (Thompson 1861).

Seven Navy officers, including five captains, constituted the tribunal and listened as Judge Advocate Peter Woodbury accused Thompson: "that on or about the twelfth and thirteenth days of September, in the year eighteen hundred and sixty-one ... [he] did drink intoxicating liquors to such an excess as to become incapable of performing his duties as Commander of the said Steamer Sloop Seminole." Thompson pleaded not guilty and relied on the assistance of two lawyers, Theodore Hinsdale and Edward Patterson, for his defense (Thompson 1861).

Lieutenant Henry S. Newcomb, attached to the USS *Seminole*, was Woodbury's first witness. The USS *Seminole* was part of the Potomac Flotilla under the command of Captain Thomas T. Craven and around September 10, 1861, arrived offshore near Indian Head, Maryland. According to Newcomb's testimony, Thompson reported the ship's arrival to Craven, and upon returning to the USS *Seminole* "I then noticed something unusual in his manner. I attributed it to nervousness from smoking ... On the eleventh the next morning ... the officer of the deck informed me that the Captain's Steward had reported to him that the Captain [Thompson] had been drinking very hard" (Thompson 1861).

After receiving the report, Newcomb went to Thompson's cabin and discovered the officer lying in bed, partially clad, with labored breathing, and unresponsive. Newcomb added, "on the 12th and 13th I saw him twice during those days ... his condition was that of a man under the effects of drink or some stimulant." Thompson's condition continued to deteriorate and on September 14, 1861, Newcomb ordered Surgeon George Peck to examine the insensate officer (Thompson 1861).

The surgeon judged Thompson unfit for duty from the "free use of intoxicating drink." Upon receiving Peck's report, Captain Craven relieved Thompson of command and ordered Newcomb to assume those duties. After consulting with the surgeon, Newcomb entered Thompson's cabin and "found there several empty ale bottles, several empty bottles which contained either brandy or whiskey, a demijohn partially full of liquor." Thompson's defense attorneys vigorously cross-examined Newcomb, questioning whether nervous exhaustion or poisoned alcohol accounted for the accused's behavior. Newcomb demurred on both questions but did admit never seeing Thompson drink alcohol (Thompson 1861).

Surgeon George Peck, attached to the USS *Seminole*, testified next and provided extensive details regarding his medical care of Thompson. Peck's first visit to the commander's stateroom on September 14, 1861, showed Thompson "lying upon his bed in a stupid condition from which I aroused him with difficulty." For the next three days, the surgeon meticulously attended to the officer, diligently documenting each intervention in his medical log. He was concerned that Thomson's tremors, nervousness, excessive thirst, and "wild appearance" suggested the early signs of delirium tremens. Peck's timely administration of brandy and opiates successfully averted the potential crisis (Thompson 1861).

The court-martial members reviewed Peck's medical records and learned that the first intervention was "emetic of Ipecac and a cathartic of Magnesia," which emptied the officer's stomach. To help quiet the man's nerves and induce sleep, Peck prescribed chloral hydrate, opiates, and brandy. Thompson responded to the treatment and Peck pronounced him cured on September 17, 1861 (Thompson 1861).

The two defense attorneys interrogated Peck and focused on "Captain Thompson's habit as to smoking." Peck acknowledged the commander's habitual use of tobacco and testified, "I should suppose it would produce more or less nervous excitability." In a further attempt to establish a different narrative, Thompson's attorneys proposed nervous exhaustion as the root cause of his behavior. Judge advocate Peter Woodbury closed his case with the testimony of the surgeon's steward, whose comments closely paralleled those of Dr. Peck (Thompson 1861).

Thompson's defense opened with a brief biography, reminding the court that his Navy career spanned thirty-four years. He then called Commander Thomas Crabbe as a character witness. Crabbe was in command of the Africa

Squadron from 1855 to 1857, and during that time, Thompson was in command of the USS *Dolphin*. Crabbe's testimony was indifferent, remembering the accused as a good officer, but without direct knowledge of his temperance. The remaining defense witnesses were Captain Joshua R. Sands, Lieutenant John C. Horrell, and Commander Augustus S. Baldwin, each testifying that through many years of close social contact they had never witnessed Thompson intoxicated (Thompson 1861).

The defense statement was a lengthy oratory, beginning with a complementary profile of the accused's Navy career, but it then attacked the surgeon's diagnosis and insinuated Newcomb's dark motivation to seize command of the USS *Seminole*. The alleged incapacitation was a thorny issue and required an alternate explanation. Thompson's defense statement claimed that "the truth is that the unusual manner of the accused on that occasion was the result of fatigue occasioned by over exertion, and nervousness super adduced by habits of smoking and chewing tobacco." The court-martial members did not accept the defense's arguments and found Thompson guilty, and sentenced him dismissed from the Navy (Thompson 1861).

Thompson's sentence was subsequently mitigated, sparing his dismissal, but the USS *Seminole* was his last seafaring duty. His succeeding assignments at the Philadelphia Navy Yard and later at the New York Naval Rendezvous culminated in a promotion to commodore in 1866 (Thompson 1879).

Recruiting for the Navy in New York at a Naval Rendezvous (*Frank Leslie's Illustrated Newspaper*, 1861. NH 73735 49522, courtesy Naval History & Heritage Command).

With the stroke of a pen, on July 14, 1862, President Lincoln terminated the official debate and abolished the Navy's cherished grog tradition. The provision stated "that from and after this first day of September, eighteen hundred and sixty-two the spirit ration in the Navy of the United States shall forever cease, and thereafter no distilled spiritous liquors shall be admitted on board vessels-of-war, except as medical stores ... each person in the Navy now entitled to the spirit ration, five cents per day in commutation" (Langley 2015, 266).

In a scene replicated throughout the Navy, Commander James Alden, Commanding, USS *Richmond*, West Gulf Blockading Squadron, stated that on August 31, 1862, "all hands were called to muster, when the order was read to stop the grog in the Navy forever ... we had heard the drum roll for the last grog in the Navy" (Stewart 1905, 754).

An unknown author aboard the USS *Wabash* celebrated the decision that "for the first time in the history of the American navy, the sailors and marines ... went to breakfast without their grog ... the men, [it] seemed, so far from grumbling at the change, welcome[d] it ... The whiskey ration ... was at the bottom of all quarrels and insubordination among those who drew it" ("News from Port Royal" 1862).

A more critical and more representative assessment came from "a meeting of sailors ... in New York ... to consider the stoppage of grog in the navy." The men voiced their resolve never to serve in the Navy until authorities revoked the loathsome provision, in a pledge that declared "that the abolition of grog in the navy was uncalled for ... that the two gills of whiskey per day which we got was not enough to intoxicate anybody" ("A Meeting of Sailors" 1863).

Despite the Navy's ban, the lure of alcohol continued to snare servicemen. Rear Admiral John A. Dahlgren, Commanding, South Atlantic Blockading Squadron, preferred charges against Acting Third Assistant Engineer William Gaul, attached to the flagship USS *Philadelphia*, for violating the Navy's strict prohibition of alcohol onboard ships. Marine Corps First Lieutenant H.J. Bishop, assigned as the judge advocate, read the specification on August 15, 1864, to the five assembled Navy officers, accusing Gaul of bringing "five gallons of whiskey more or less for his own use" onboard the USS *Philadelphia* on or about June 30, 1864. Gaul pleaded guilty and offered no defense. The court-martial reduced Gaul to a first class fireman and exacted three months' pay (Gaul 1864).

The Marine Corps followed the Navy's directives and consequently lost their grog allotment at the same time, but in the months preceding that intervention an unknown, teetotalling sailor sarcastically observed that "the marines all take their grog" ("Letter from the Navy" 1861).

A central figure in the Marine Corps' march to abstinence was Colonel

Franklin Wharton. the third Commandant of the United States Marine Corps, whose directives in 1805 sought to stem the use of alcohol. His first effort at abolition failed when official orders increased the rum ration, forcing Wharton to mitigate the damage by declaring that "as the late Increase of Rum to the Rations, has greatly tended to the Increase of Intoxication, among the Troops of the Garrison, it is Ordered, That in future one half of the Rum allowance per day be issued in the Morning, the other half reserved for Dinner" (Evans 1916, 52).

Official regulations from the Army and the Navy during the Civil War acknowledged the harmful military effects of alcohol but scant evidence suggested their effectiveness at curtailing rampant consumption. Although limited, modern historical research on the subject suggests that excessive alcohol use at all levels in the military contributed to disciplinary problems and battlefield losses.

In *Drinking in America: Our Secret History*, author Susan Cheever explores the use of alcohol during the Civil War and broadly concludes that "the history of the American military is a drunken one, but there is no correlation between generals who drank and generals who lost battles" (Cheever 2015, 105). At the same time, Cheever chronicles drunken routs on the battlefield, officers under the influence of alcohol, and the staggering number of alcohol-related courts-martial. A questionable conclusion stated that surgeons substantially contributed to the Civil War's morbidity "because of the high incidence of drunken incompetence and drug-addled lack of judgment" (Cheever 2015, 107).

Mark Will-Weber regales the reader with entertaining narratives from diaries and newspapers, brimming with anecdotes in *Muskets and Applejack Spirits, Soldiers, and the Civil War* (Will-Weber 2017). The author unequivocally asserts alcohol's behavioral dominance, pointing to the vast numbers of soldiers and sailors who upended the federal efforts to control the beverage with the "ingenuity of the Civil War soldier to obtain liquor ... woven through the diaries, memoirs, and letters of that era" (Will-Weber 2017, 27–28). Even draconian punishments such as "hanging a soldier by his thumbs, or forcing the captive to 'wear the barrel suit'... and made to lug it around camp" failed to dent the demand for alcohol (Will-Weber 2017, 35).

Many factors accounted for alcohol's resilience during the Civil War. Access restrictions weighed heavily on enlisted service members. Military leaders spared officers that inconvenience, based on a conviction that officers would provide an exemplary example of self-restraint, but countless inebriated officers vitiated that belief (Martin 2011, 69). Enlisted service members spared no effort bypassing regulations, securing their liquor through theft, foraging, packages mailed from friends and family,

Drunken soldiers tied up for fighting and other unruly conduct (LC-DIG-ppmsca-21215, Library of Congress Prints and Photographs Division, Washington, D.C.).

surgeons, and, as a last resort, improvised recipes that sometimes contained adulterants such as turpentine and strychnine (Martin 2011, 70).

A United States Sanitary Commission report submitted to the Secretary of War on December 9, 1861, examined the sutler's role in supplying soldiers with alcohol. The Sanitary Commission's survey identified 31 regiments that allowed sutlers to sell liquor, 169 regiments prohibiting it, and in another 177 regiments, the soldiers freely obtained alcohol. Even with ready access, the Sanitary Commission struck an optimistic note in the early months of the Civil War, asserting that "it must not be understood, however, that in all the regiments which had access to liquor there was any serious habitual excess in its use. Intoxication was acknowledged to be common in only six (6) regiments. In thirty-one (31) it was said to occasionally occur, though not deemed a serious evil; and in one hundred and sixty-three (163) the Inspectors were assured, and had no reason to doubt, that it was very rare. In the majority of regiments there is very little dram drinking, except shortly after payday. The volunteers are believed to be more temperate than any European army" (US Sanitary Commission 1866, 24–25).

James M. McPherson in *For Cause and Comrades: Why Men Fought in the Civil War* offered a scholarly analysis of the factors that motivated men to fight and die based on a representative sample of 1,076 soldiers that included 647 Union and 429 Confederate service members (McPherson 1997, 183). McPherson insisted that "references to a liquor ration before combat are extremely rare. More common—but highly suspect—are references to enemy soldiers drunk on whisky." At the same time, the author does not dismiss "liquid courage" as an anxiety-assuaging tonic, a practice more common among officers on the eve of combat (McPherson 1997, 52–53).

The twin concepts of masculinity and honor take center stage in a study by Lorien Foote in *The Gentlemen and the Roughs: Violence, Honor, and Manhood in the Union Army* (Foote 2013). Foote's social analysis relies on three broad sources: general courts-martial records, regimental order books, and the personal reminiscences of the combatants. A novel contribution is the author's inclusion of regimental courts-martial, a two-edged sword that broadens the understanding of disciplinary actions at a level below the general court-martial, but the records are perfunctory and "provide very little information about the offense of the soldier or the proceedings of the trial" (Foote 2013, 11). The paucity of information leaves the author concluding that regimental courts-martial found most soldiers guilty, regardless of their pleadings, in a finding not unlike general courts-martial.

During the Civil War, Foote contended that a soldier's consumption of alcohol characterized their masculinity and honor. How much a man could drink and still act rationally conferred masculinity, but drunken, riotous behavior degraded the man. Conduct unbecoming an officer and a gentleman was a formal military charge levied against drunken, boisterous officers. According to Foote, alcohol was a factor in 18 percent of Army general courts-martial, and he estimated that "thousands more were punished" for drunkenness at regimental courts-martial (Foote 2013, 30).

A study of 75,964 Army general courts-martial framed the factual foundation for Thomas P. Lowry in *Irish and German Whiskey & Beer— Drinking Patterns in the Civil War*. Using the search terms whiskey, beer, wine, brandy, drunkenness, inebriation, and intoxicated, Lowry discovered that alcohol was a factor in 18.5 percent of general courts-martial (Lowry 2011, 2). After classifying the predominant ethnic composition of Army regiments, Lowry determined that 22.4 percent of Irish soldiers' general courts-martial involved alcohol, versus 18 percent for German soldiers and 15 percent for American soldiers (Lowry 2011, 82).

This volume broadened the scope of research by analyzing a representative database that included service members from the Union Army, Navy, and Marine Corps. Included in this sample are 833 individuals (n = 5,000, 16.7%) charged with an alcohol-related offense by a military tribunal.

The representative database included 681 soldiers (n = 4,078, 16.7%), 123 service members from the Navy (n = 786, 15.7%), and 29 men from the Marine Corps (n = 136, 21.3%). In a further description of those charged with an alcohol-related offense, 357 were officers (n = 833, 42.9%): 315 officers from the Army (n = 357, 88.2%), 37 officers from the Navy (n = 357, 10.4%), and five officers from the Marine Corps (n = 357, 1.4%). Enlisted and noncommissioned officers accounted for the remaining 476 alcohol-related trials. Among this group, there were 366 Army service members (n = 476, 76.9%), 86 Navy personnel (n = 476, 18.1%), and 24 Marine Corps service members (n = 476, 5.0%).

In terms of the distribution by year in this representative database, there were 117 alcohol-related trials in 1861, 283 trials in 1862, 197 trials in 1863, 192 trials in 1864, and 44 trials from the truncated year of 1865.

Judge advocates collectively charged the 833 service members with 1,730 crimes, with 204 (n = 833, 24.5%) service members charged with a solitary alcohol-related offense. In the remaining trials, military officials charged 629 service members (n = 833, 75.5%) with an average of 2.4 (n = 1,526/629) military crimes.

In 76 cases, the trials found the service members not guilty (n = 833, 9.1%). Among those found not guilty, there were 31 officers; the Army contributed 28 officers (n = 31, 90.3%), the Navy two (n = 31, 6.5%), and the Marine Corps one (n = 31, 3.2%). The representative database identified 45 enlisted and noncommissioned officers found not guilty: 40 from the Army (n = 45, 88.9%), four from the Navy (n = 45, 8.9%), and one from the Marine Corps (n = 45, 2.2%).

A closer inspection of the not guilty verdicts revealed a precipitous decline beginning in 1863. Of the seventy-six not guilty verdicts in the representative database, courts returned 25 in 1861 (32.9%), 35 in 1862 (46.1%), seven in 1863 (9.2%), eight in 1864 (10.5%), and only one in 1865 (1.3%). The representative database identified that pattern among both officers and enlisted. Courts found nine officers not guilty of an alcohol-related offense in 1861 (n = 31, 29.0%), 14 in 1862 (n = 31, 45.2%), three in 1863 (n = 31, 9.7%), five in 1864 (n = 31, 16.1%), and none in 1865. Among the enlisted, courts found 16 not guilty in 1861 (n = 45, 35.6%), 21 in 1862 (n = 45, 46.6%), four in 1863 (n = 45, 8.9%), three in 1864 (n = 45, 6.7%), and only one in 1865 (n = 45, 2.2%).

General courts-martial returned 757 guilty verdicts (n = 833, 90.9%). The 757 guilty verdicts included 332 officers (43.9%). Junior officers led the list, as exemplified by the Army, which contributed 289 officers (n = 332, 87.0%) of all ranks with 181 lieutenants (n = 289, 62.6%) and 74 captains (n = 289, 25.6%). Navy general courts-martial charged 39 officers (n = 332, 11.8%) with an alcohol-related offense, with the largest contingent being 16 engineers consisting of 10 acting assistant engineers and six acting chief engineers (16/39, 41.0%). This sample also included four Marine Corps officers charged with an alcohol-related crime (n = 332, 1.2%), comprised of three lieutenants and one captain.

This representative database included 425 enlisted and noncommissioned officers found guilty of an alcohol-related crime. The Army accounted for 326 (n = 425, 76.7%), with the rank of private leading the list with 284 soldiers (n = 326, 87.1%). Navy general courts-martial added 82 cases (n = 425, 19.3%) which primarily consisted of 27 landsmen (n = 82, 32.9%), 23 seamen (n = 82, 28.0%), and 20 acting master's mates (n = 82, 24.4%). The Marine Corps sample added 17 cases (n = 425, 4.0%) in a number dominated by 13 privates (n = 17, 76.5%).

Courts-martial charged 629 (n = 833, 75.5%) service members with at least one other crime in addition to the alcohol-related charge. Military authorities commonly charged officers with wrongdoing such as conduct unbecoming an officer and a gentleman, conduct prejudicial to good order and military discipline, disobedience, abusive language, and drinking with enlisted service members. Unauthorized absences, disobedience, and disrespect represented many of the additional charges levied against enlisted service members.

The guilty verdicts resulted in a variety of punishments. Courts-martial dismissed 163 officers (n = 332, 49.1%), cashiered another 145 (n = 332, 43.7%), recommended incarceration for eight officers with sentences from six months to fifteen years, and for the remainder, the courts-martial sentenced the officers to suspensions, reprimands, and loss of pay.

Enlisted and noncommissioned officers suffered a wide variety of punishments. Penalties imposed by courts-martial included forfeiture of pay, reduction in ranks, dishonorable discharge, hard labor, bound by a ball and chain, incarceration, and various public humiliations. In this representative database, forfeiture of pay was the most common punishment, followed by the imposition of hard labor of varying durations, usually coupled with some degree of incarceration.

Courts-martial sentenced 45 enlisted and noncommissioned officers to prison (n = 425, 10.6%) with terms ranging from one month to life, reserving the longest periods for alcohol misconduct and violence. Less commonly, general courts-martial resorted to public humiliation to deter alcohol-related misconduct. In the representative database, general courts-martial sentenced eight soldiers to wear a placard emblazoned with some version of "drunkard," forced two soldiers to wear a barrel with similar labels, branded three soldiers on their hips with the letter D, shaved five soldiers' heads, required 13 soldiers to carry a heavy knapsack or log around the camp, and sentenced ten soldiers drummed out of their regiments.

General courts-martial remitted or mitigated 53 cases (n = 757, 7.0%) and reversed the trial proceedings in 23 cases (n = 757, 3%). Convening authorities even-handedly dispensed this merc,y with enlisted and non-commissioned officers receiving 32 (n = 425, 7.5%) remitted or mitigated sentences and 11 reversals (n = 425, 2.6%). Among the officers, convening authorities remitted or mitigated 21 sentences (n = 332, 6.3%) and ordered 12 reversals (n = 332, 3.6%).

The proceedings in the Navy general court-martial of First Assistant Engineer George S. Bright at the Philadelphia Navy Yard on June 25, 1863, opened an intriguing window into the defense of alcohol-related misconduct. Seven Navy officers assembled to hear Judge Advocate H.H. Goodman accuse Bright of "scandalous conduct tending to the destruction of good morals" (Bright 1863).

Goodman alleged "that on or about the fifth day of May in the year eighteen hundred and sixty-three, the said first Assistant Engineer George S. Bright was drunk at the Astor House in New York." With the assistance of his legal counsel Robert Eden Brown, Bright pleaded not guilty. Goodman approved Bright's request to call five Navy officers for his defense (Bright 1863).

Goodman's prosecution opened with a letter written by the accused to Secretary of the Navy Gideon Welles, around May 21, 1863. In the letter, Bright admitted his inebriation but explained, "I attribute it to my being very weak from the severe spell of sickness I had whilst I was in Beaufort, N.C. It is the first offense that I can remember ... and I most respectfully ask and beg that it may be overlooked" (Bright 1863).

The Secretary of the Navy rebuffed Bright's entreaty and referred the matter to a general court-martial. After reading Bright's futile letter to the court, Goodman called Lieutenant Commander Edward Barrett as the first prosecution witness. Barrett testified that on May 5, 1863, in the early evening, "I visited the Astor House New York City, and while in the Bar Room saw several officers, one of whom was considerably under the influence of liquor" (Bright 1863).

Barrett's testimony lacked conviction because he could not positively identify the accused, but that did not deter Goodman's probing inquiry, which only documented Bright's tottering gait. Bright pointedly cross-examined the witness, scoring points when Barrett agreed that he never observed him drink, that his demeanor at the time was nonviolent, and "I believe he did say something about it being an accident ... that he had just returned from the South" (Bright 1863).

Barrett estimated that the accused had been drinking for ten minutes. Bright challenged that statement and asked Barret how anyone could become intoxicated in such a brief time. The witness reasonably responded, "That depends on the quantity he can stand. Some men can stand a great deal, and some cannot ... but I should judge it would have taken considerable liquor to get him in that state." A member of the court-martial pointedly asked Barrett if Bright's mere presence in the bar influenced his impression of the accused's condition. Once again, the witness hesitated but he admitted the possibility (Bright 1863).

The prosecution's case ended with Barrett's testimony, after which Bright took his turn by presenting Chief Engineer John P. Whipple as the first defense witness. Whipple admitted serving with the accused in the Navy for six years and he denied any knowledge of the man's intemperate habits (Bright 1863).

The second day of Bright's trial began with the accused submitting written testimonials proclaiming his good character as a Navy officer. Bright then presented Chief Engineer Robert W. McCleery as the next defense witness. McCleery offered robust testimony based on his close personal observations when the pair sailed together. Goodman could not undermine McCleery's confident assertions that Bright was a temperate man and earnest officer (Bright 1863).

Assistant Paymaster Jesse P. Woodbury introduced the first evidence supporting Bright's illness by recalling "he was sent out of the vessel at Beaufort North Carolina on account of his health ... He went to the Army Hospital. He joined the vessel again ... some three or four weeks after leaving." Woodbury also testified that on or about May 5, 1863, he left the USS *Passaic* with Bright and together they visited several sites in New York City before they arrived at the Astor House. During their travels, Woodbury recalled Bright drinking a glass of wine at one location, an ale at another, and one other unspecified drink, after which "he said that he felt ill and wanted to go to his room." Woodbury accompanied Bright to his room and testified that he appeared sober but physically exhausted, and in a most compelling statement declared, "he did not drink at the Astor House" (Bright 1863).

Bright's next witness was Third Assistant Engineer William A. Dripps, who endorsed the accused's general sobriety and ill health. Recalling a layover at Beaufort, North Carolina, Dripps stated, "He was taken very ill with typhoid fever. He was taken off the ship and taken to the Hospital." According to the witness, Bright's month-long convalescence did not cure the man and he remained physically feeble after rejoining the ship. Dripps echoed Woodbury's testimony about the events at the Astor House, adding that Bright seemed ill (Bright 1863).

Under cross-examination, Goodman forced the witness to concede that Bright "in my opinion ... was under the influence of liquor. I don't think he was drunk." A puzzled Goodman questioned the difference

Crewmen on the USS *Passaic* (NH 42803, courtesy Naval History & Heritage Command).

between being under the influence and drunk, with Dripps responding that "a man intoxicated I should suppose would be hallooing and laughing, and cutting around, or something of that kind" (Bright 1863).

Bright's trial began on the third day with Chief Engineer William W. Duncan testifying on behalf of the accused. Duncan had the highest praise for the accused, unequivocally asserting that "I know of no young man in the service that stands higher." Duncan was the final defense witness, and with the court's permission, Bright spent the next day preparing his closing defense statement (Bright 1863).

Up to this point, military trial procedures barred Bright's legal counsel from directly addressing the general court-martial, but that changed when attorney Robert Eden Brown received permission to read the defense statement. Brown took advantage of the opportunity and presented a lengthy argument beginning with respectful deference to the court members' integrity and open-mindedness. He then pivoted and vigorously attacked Goodman's accusation of drunkenness based on one observer and refuted by five defense witnesses (Bright 1863).

Brown derided the prosecution's testimony from Lieutenant Commander Barrett as nothing more than "an overzealous and over hasty performance of what he [Barrett] considers a duty, [that] has cast a stain upon the character of this young man, which no act of atonement ... can ever wipe out." Bright's counsel reminded the court that the prosecution's witness was also drinking liquor at the Astor House (Bright 1863).

Brown turned his argument to the core issue of intemperance, beginning with an acknowledgment that "drunkenness is undoubtedly a moral crime, as well as a monstrous social evil." He also admitted that drunkenness aggravated criminal culpability, but then started drawing distinctions that favored his client. Referring to the 45th Article of War, Brown emphasized that Bright was off duty and the law required that an officer be "found drunk on his guard, party, or other duty under arms." Brown dismissed the allegation of scandalous conduct, equating habitual drunkenness and public rowdiness as justifying that charge, a definition that excluded Bright (Bright 1863).

Brown reviewed the events on May 5, 1863, beginning with an emotional ploy: "On that day, feeling unwell, the consequences of that pestilent and tenacious disease, Typhoid fever, he goes on shore for a few hours relaxation." Swinging back to the prosecution's only witness, Brown rhetorically wonders who "could be physically prostrated, as the accused was—under the influence on one glass of Ale, one glass of sherry and one other glass" (Bright 1863).

Bright's letter to the Secretary of the Navy was damaging, but Brown countered by claiming that had the judge advocate "deemed that letter conclusive ... there would have been no need of this trial." Brown's lengthy oratory concluded with an appeal for justice and mercy.

Brown's eloquent and enthusiastic defense failed to win an acquittal. The court-martial returned a guilty verdict, but in response to Bright's otherwise unblemished service and the evidence adduced, they punished Bright with a six-month suspension and a reprimand by the Secretary of the Navy (Bright 1863).

A court-martial convened at Otterville, Missouri, on December 31, 1861, and charged First Lieutenant David L. Baker, 15th Regiment, Illinois Infantry, with conduct unbecoming an officer and a gentleman and violation of the 45th Article of War. Seven specifications detailed instances of alleged alcohol-related misconduct. On August 15, 1861, Baker "was so drunk that he was unfit for duty, and did, while in that condition, draw a pistol on two enlisted men." In mid–October 1861, he "pretended to be sick, and did falsely report himself sick, when, in fact, he was drunk." Two specifications involved Baker's drunken behavior over three days while in Tipton, Missouri, and a fifth alleged that he was "continually drinking with, and procuring liquor through enlisted men, thereby, destroying all discipline by his example." The sixth specification charged Baker with loaning his uniform to a civilian to buy whiskey, and the final allegation stated that Baker was drunk and unfit for guard duty (Baker, D. 1862).

Without elaboration the court-martial acquitted Baker, ignoring the patterns of alcohol misuse and military misconduct. Major General Henry Halleck interpreted the legal proceedings differently, convinced that the "testimony positively establishes specifications five, six ... and the accused should have been found guilty and dismissed the service." Halleck disapproved the court-martial's findings but let the verdict stand. Baker escaped an ignominious outcome and returned to active duty, exonerated by sympathetic court-martial members (Baker, D. 1862).

Second Lieutenant William H. De Freest, Company B, 1st Regiment, Iowa Cavalry, was less fortunate. De Freest appeared before a general court-martial at Camp Lake Springs, Missouri, around August 1863, charged with "being found drunk on duty." Three specifications described the military charge. Around April 7, 1863, De Freest "met Sutler's wagon, and [did] get there from liquors and drink to such an extent as to become beastly intoxicated, so that he had to be helped from that place to camp and to his quarters." A more embarrassing incident occurred on April 24, 1863, when De Freest was "intoxicated and fell off his horse" near Springfield, Missouri. The man was drunk again on duty just a few weeks later, around May 12, 1863. The court-martial rejected the accused's not guilty pleading and declared the man guilty of the military charge, sentencing De Freest "to be cashiered" (De Freest 1863).

Captain James Eutwistle, 176th Regiment, New York Infantry, pleaded not guilty to conduct unbecoming an officer and a gentleman at a general court-martial convened at Savannah, Georgia, on January 25, 1865. The judge advocate accused Eutwistle of being "beastly intoxicated, and in that condition was found by the Provost Guard, in a public square or park, in the city of Savannah, Georgia, wholly unable to take care of himself." The court-martial accepted the judge advocate's argument and sentenced Eutwistle to be dismissed from the army. In reviewing the case, Major General Quincy Adams Gillmore accepted a petition for mercy from "the Brigadier General Commanding the second Division Nineteenth Army Corps" and remitted Eutwistle's sentence, restoring the freed man to active duty (Eutwistle 1865).

Drunkenness afflicted men regardless of rank or status. Colonel Henry W. Hudson, 82nd Regiment, New York Infantry, and a frequent general court-martial president, faced the embarrassment of appearing before such a tribunal, accused of drunkenness. Brigadier General John C. Caldwell presided at Hudson's court-martial that convened at Falmouth, Virginia, on May 8, 1863. Without any details, the court found Hudson guilty and sentenced the man to be cashiered (Hudson 1863a).

A letter from the Adjutant General's Office in Washington, D.C., dated May 28, 1863, informed the Governor of New York of the trial's outcome. Hudson subsequently implored President Lincoln to remit the sentence. The appeal was successful, as evidenced by another letter from the Adjutant General's Office in Washington, D.C., dated August 13, 1863, that informed the Governor of New York that "you are authorized to re-appoint him to his former position" (Hudson 1863b).

Inappropriate actions while intoxicated regularly uncovered drinking issues. Such was the case with First Lieutenant Jackson McFadden, 8th Regiment, Pennsylvania Cavalry, who created a public spectacle when he "did appear on the streets of Washington, D.C., mounted, and in a gross state of drunkenness, and did ride his horse on the side-walk of Pennsylvania avenue, thereby disgracing himself and the service to which he belongs." McFadden's frolic earned him a general court-martial, charged with conduct unbecoming an officer and a gentleman. Inexplicably, the man pleaded not guilty, but the court-martial members were not amused and sentenced the man dismissed from the Army (McFadden 1862).

An even more ignominious tale unfolded when Lieutenant William L. Bath, 45th Regiment, New York Infantry, inadvertently lived up to his name. A general court-martial convened at "the camp of Blenker's Division" on November 19, 1861, and prosecuted Bath for drunkenness on duty and conduct unbecoming an officer and a gentleman. The unbecoming conduct flowed from the man's drunkenness when Bath showered his "vomit, soiling his clothes, floor, and seats around him" in the presence of the unfortunate occupants of an officer's car. Bath pleaded not guilty, but the court reasoned otherwise, found the odious officer guilty, and sentenced the man to be cashiered (Bath 1862).

In a harbinger of a hardening attitude toward wanton drunkenness, Major General George B. McClellan complained that "another court martial considered that an officer picked from the gutters in front of the principal hotels of this city, drunk to insensibility, was adequately punished by a reprimand." McClellan lamented the lenient treatment but endorsed McFadden's punishment and approved the sentence (McFadden 1862).

Lieutenant Colonel Edward A.L. Roberts, 28th Regiment, New Jersey Infantry, almost escaped punishment for two discrete episodes of intoxication. The general court-martial convened at Fort Ethan Allen, Virginia, on November 2, 1862, and charged Roberts with drunkenness on duty. Roberts pleaded not guilty to the two specifications. After hearing the evidence and reviewing the case, the court-martial tossed the first instance of intoxication because the military charge did not identify the location where the offense occurred. Roberts was not so fortunate with the second specification and was found guilty and cashiered from the service (Roberts 1863).

Lieutenant Commander S. Livingston Breese, in command of the gunboat USS *Sagamore*, appeared before a Navy general court-martial at the Philadelphia Navy Yard on Saturday, September 26, 1863. Judge Advocate H.H. Goodman read the military charge of drunkenness to the five assembled Navy officers along with the solitary specification "that on or about the twenty ninth day of August, in the year eighteen hundred and sixty-three, the said Lieutenant Commander S. Livingston Breese ... was drunk on board said vessel" (Breese 1863).

In an interesting sidebar, Breese was unable to promptly enlist the services of legal counsel and, in an effort not to delay the trial, asked the court's permission to cross-examine the prosecution witnesses that testified in the attorney's absence. The court agreed and then listened as Goodman presented Navy Lieutenant John Weidman as the first witness for the prosecution (Breese 1863).

Weidman was the executive officer on the USS *Sagamore* and was greeting Breese as his new commander on August 29, 1863, when a senior officer interrupted the meeting with an order to immediately leave Newport News, Virginia. Weidman ordered the ship's crew to "heave up the anchor," and with a casual glance he observed Breese staggering on deck. A brief time later, Breese directed Weidman "to slip the anchor," an order Weidman protested as dangerous. Breese withdrew the order while unsteadily propping himself against the ship's turret plates, a posture that Weidman associated with intoxication (Breese 1863).

Attorney R.E. Brown joined the court-martial on the trial's second day as Breese's legal counsel. Weidman continued his testimony from the prior day and acknowledged relieving Breese of command. Breese interrogated Weidman during a lengthy cross-examination, eventually asking the witness, "Were you not yourself excited and irritated in being suddenly superseded in command and did you not show this irritation in your manner to the accused?" Weidman denied the imputation but was forced later to concede that it was getting dark when Breese supposedly staggered and swayed on board the ship (Breese 1863).

Acting Paymaster George A. Emerson was sitting on a bench when Breese "came to sit down, I smelled his breath, and smelled some liquor, and I judged that he was not in a sober state." The court listened incredulously as Emerson was uncertain if Breese was actually in command of the ship, even after he attended the official change of command ceremony (Breese 1863).

The third day began with the prosecution's next witness, First Assistant Engineer Edmund Duplaino. Duplaino considered Breese intoxicated because he "staggered somewhat" and seemed unfamiliar with steamships, but he offered no other specific examples to support his opinion. In a telling exchange, Duplaino admitted that the officers were unhappy with Breese's appointment as commander of the ship (Breese 1863).

After Duplaino's shaky testimony, Goodman called Assistant Surgeon William S. Fort, attached to the USS *Sagamore*. The witness's first meeting with the accused was on August 29, 1863, at which time "I smelt his breath very plainly and saw him staggering. I saw him moving about on deck in a manner that convinced me that he was under the influence of liquor" (Breese 1863).

Goodman concluded the prosecution's case with Fort's testimony. Even before presenting his defense witnesses, Breese's cross-examination poked holes in Goodman's case, exposing the witnesses' contradictory statements and vague descriptions of the accused's supposedly drunken behavior (Breese 1863).

Acting Master Peter J. Hargous was the first defense witness, and he crisply denied any unusual behavior in the accused and reiterated the position when queried by the court. Goodman declined the opportunity to cross-examine Hargous (Breese 1863).

Breese's next witness, Lieutenant Clark Merchant, attended the change of command on board the USS *Sagamore* and provided detailed descriptions of the accused's behavior before, during, and after the ceremony, none of which appeared irregular. Once again Breese focused on his reception as the new commander, an inquiry opposed by Goodman as "irrelevant." Breese argued that his question was an effort to examine the witnesses' prejudice and disaffection with his appointment as their commander. The court reviewed Goodman's objection and sustained it (Breese 1863).

Breese took a different approach when the court-martial resumed the next day, and he asked Merchant, "What was the conduct of Lieutenant Weidman upon learning that he was superseded?" Merchant replied, "He appeared to be quite angry from his actions." In what appeared to be further evidence of the crew's sabotage, Merchant criticized their dawdling, as "they were not acting with that promptness which the emergency of the case required" (Breese 1863).

Goodman vigorously attacked Merchant's testimony, provoking three objections from Breese, all of which the court dismissed. Despite the withering cross-examination, Merchant steadfastly denied that the accused was drunk and even managed to impugn the testimony of Assistant Surgeon William S. Fort, who "was very sorry that" Breese replaced Weidman (Breese 1863).

Robert E. Brown, Breese's counsel, read the defense statement to the court on October 1, 1863, and immediately attacked the prosecution witness's bitter resentment of Breese's arrival onboard the USS *Sagamore*. Brown accused the witnesses of fomenting a "conspiracy nurtured in misrepresentation, if not falsehood" (Breese 1863).

Brown castigated "these mere fledglings, these beardless boys ... cruelly intent upon the ruin of one ... a brother officer." Shaking his head in consternation, the attorney alternately expressed his sadness, pitied Breese's immature accusers, and passionately assailed their behavior as a blight on the Navy. After hurling those broadsides, Brown blamed Lieutenant Weidman as the malevolent architect "who in consequence of charges which he very greatly preferred is now in command" of the USS *Sagamore* (Breese 1863).

By accusing Breese of drunkenness, Weidman shrewdly chose the perfect allegation, where every slip of the tongue or footing defines that condition. Not content with smearing Breese, Weidman enlisted the fawning assistance of other officers. When ordered to leave port, the crew dallied, and Breese grew irritable and anxious—further evidence of his drunkenness according to the prosecution witnesses (Breese 1863).

Brown delivered a withering rebuke when "in this galaxy of wonders, comes the never to be forgotten 1st Assistant Engineer Mr. E.A.E. Duplaine, who cannot speak to the condition of the accused as he did not speak with him." Similarly, Brown savaged the assistant surgeon who claimed Breese smelled of alcohol but then testified "there was nothing in the language of the accused to convince me that he did not understand what he was doing" (Breese 1863).

With a quick recitation of the defense witnesses' testimony, Brown humbly asked the court to remember Breese's seventeen years of faithful service, dismiss the weak evidence, and restore the man's honor. After a brief deliberation, the court-martial acquitted Breese (Breese 1863). Breese continued his Navy career unscathed by the court-martial and retired as a rear admiral (Bateman and Selby 1912, 1065).

Courts-martial commonly charged service members with multiple offenses. First Lieutenant Charles N. Smith, Company G, 90th Regiment, New York Infantry, was among this group when a general court-martial convened at the United States Barracks, Key West, Florida, on March 9, 1863, to consider neglect of duty and conduct unbecoming an officer and a gentleman. The crux of both charges centered on an allegation that Smith "did permit and encourage an enlisted man who was drunk to occupy and sleep in his (the said Lieutenant Charles N. Smith's) quarters, and to create an uproar, to the disturbance and annoyance of the officers in the same building." Smith allegedly supported the enlisted man's raucous language, littered with profanity, that loudly insulted the barrack's officers. The court-martial found Smith guilty of both charges but excluded the words "encouraging" and conduct "unbecoming an officer and a gentleman." With those revisions, the court punished Smith with a reprimand from his commanding officer (Smith, C. 1863).

The case of Captain Isaac S. Catlin, 3rd Regiment, New York Infantry, highlighted an inherent conflict between military law and combat operations. A court-martial convened on November 29, 1861, in Baltimore, Maryland, to consider the military charge of conduct to the prejudice of good order and military discipline. Catlin "was drunk and disorderly and conducted himself at the Officers' Mess in a very rude and unbecoming manner, and did use disrespectful and insulting language" (Catlin 1862).

Catlin's drunken, indecorous expostulations resulted in a guilty verdict. The court-martial suspended his rank and pay and limited his excursions to the confines of the camp for three months. Major General George B. McClellan approved the trial's proceedings but not the sentence. McClellan could not abide by the suspension, which effectively precluded Catlin's participation "in the active military operations for which this army has been organized." Catlin pledged his future good conduct, an assurance that also encouraged McClellan's decision to return the man to duty (Catlin 1862).

Colonel Alfred W. Taylor, 4th Regiment, New York Infantry, probably sighed with relief when the court-martial members announced their decision, an exultation that faded with subsequent events. Taylor's trial convened in Baltimore, Maryland, on November 29, 1861, to hear the judge advocate read three military charges. The first was drunkenness on duty, involving an incident that occurred around August 3, 1861, when Taylor "was so drunk while in command of his said Regiment as to be unable to communicate." Taylor's second military charge seemingly left little doubt about his conduct unbecoming an officer and a gentleman, when the officer "was grossly intoxicated while absent on leave, and did publicly expose himself while so intoxicated." Taylor was the butt of jokes following the public performance, and fellow officers mercilessly mocked the man. The judge advocate construed the accused's subsequent silence when ridiculed by his fellow officers as conduct prejudicial to good order and military discipline because Taylor "did publicly receive and submit to gross indignities and personal chastisement in the presence of officers and soldiers ... without resenting the same in a proper manner or taking any measures to punish the offence" (Taylor, A. 1862).

The court-martial decided that Taylor was not guilty of all three military charges but tagged the man for "being under the influence of intoxicating liquors while on duty" and recommended that Division Commander Major General John A. Dix officially reprimand his behavior. Dix was not pleased with the trial's outcome and expressed his dissatisfaction to the court-martial members. In response to the criticism, the court-martial reconvened on February 27, 1862, and revised its findings.

The chastised court-martial altered Taylor's sentence and recommended that the man be cashiered (Taylor, A. 1862).

Offshore near New Orleans, Louisiana, a Navy general court-martial convened on October 21, 1863, for the trial of Marine Corps Second Lieutenant E.B. Sturgeon. The judge advocate read the two military charges, "absence from his station or duty without permission" and "drunkenness." According to the first charge, another officer on board the USS *Pensacola* arrested Sturgeon after he failed to return from a shore assignment, a delay caused by his inebriation that supported the second military charge. Sturgeon pleaded not guilty to the first charge and guilty to the second (Sturgeon 1863).

First Assistant Engineer John Purdy, attached to the USS *Pensacola*, accompanied Acting Master Frederick T. King, the principal arresting officer, to the St. Charles Hotel in New Orleans. Purdy observed Sturgeon lying in bed and testified that the man was drunk because his "face was flushed, his eyes very red, his clothes dirty," but he admitted when cross-examined that he did not witness the accused drink any alcohol. King found the man at the hotel "in a condition not fit to be taken on board the ship," a euphemism for Sturgeon's supposed drunkenness (Sturgeon 1863).

Sturgeon submitted a one-sentence defense statement requesting resignation in place of punishment. After "carefully considering the evidence adduced," the court-martial found Sturgeon guilty of both charges, rejected his resignation, and sentenced him to be dismissed (Sturgeon 1863).

Pettiness and patriotism dominated a Navy general court-martial on November 2, 1864, aboard the USS *James Adger*, lying off the South Carolina coast, in the case of Acting Second Assistant Engineer Gilbert W. Scoby. Judge Advocate Acting Paymaster Charles S. Perley read the single charge of "scandalous conduct leading to the destruction of good morals" to the seven-member tribunal. Perley accused Scoby of taking "distilled spiritous liquor" from Acting Second Assistant Engineer John Lardner's room on the Fourth of July 1864 (Scoby 1864).

Scoby pleaded guilty, but to mitigate punishment he offered the testimony of two character witnesses. Acting Chief Engineer Edward A. Whipple described the accused as "attentive to duty, well behaved, and he has been an excellent character for sobriety and orderly conduct." Commander Thomas H. Patterson, Commanding, USS *James Adger*, recalled an early incident of disrespect toward the executive officer but aside from that, Scoby "attended to all his duties with great cheerfulness and ability. I have never heard his honesty questioned except by Mr. Lardner" (Scoby 1864).

Scoby's witnesses offered credible evidence of his good character, but his defense statement was even more compelling. The accused began his argument by recalling Lardner's stern warning against bringing liquor onboard the USS *James Adger*, but ignoring his own advice "Lardner brought concealed two galls whiskey which he kept in his state room" (Scoby 1864).

On the Fourth of July 1864, Scoby and another officer, Acting Second Assistant Engineer James Mitchell, spied the whiskey in Lardner's room and in a celebratory mood "drank to the Army and the Navy and Mr. Lardner's health." Lardner was not amused and promptly preferred the military charge that Scoby believed arose from the man "being jealous of me ... to ruin my character ... He did not bring charges against his friend Mr. Mitchell who was equally guilty" (Scoby 1864).

The court-martial confirmed Scoby's guilty pleading and recommended his admonishment by Rear Admiral John A. Dahlgren, Commanding, South Atlantic Blockading Squadron. The court-martial members justified the lenient sentence based on the accused's good character, Lardner's duplicity, and that the "offense is alleged to have been committed [on] the Anniversary of our Glorious Independence" (Scoby 1864).

The same tribunal met again on November 4, 1864, and considered the identical military charge and specification lodged at this second trial against Acting Second Assistant Engineer James Mitchell. Like Scoby, Mitchell pleaded guilty but contrasted his case by offering no witnesses. In his two-paragraph defense statement, the officer admitted taking the liquor but "not intending it to be kept a secret but more as fun at a Mess Mates expense with whom I was on good terms." The brief trial culminated with Mitchell's defense, after which the court-martial endorsed his guilty plea and sentenced the man "to be reprimanded and cautioned as to future conduct by the Rear Admiral" (Mitchell 1864).

The day of reckoning for Acting Second Assistant Engineer John Lardner followed Mitchell's conviction. Perley accused Lardner of bringing "on board the said Steamer one or more gallons of distilled spiritous liquor which he kept in his possession." Lardner pleaded guilty, provided no witnesses, and waived the option to read a defense statement. The court-martial extended no mercy and sentenced Lardner to be dismissed. According to Navy law, Rear Admiral John A. Dahlgren could not influence the officer's dismissal and he referred the case to the Navy Department (Lardner, John 1864). The Navy Department ultimately commuted Lardner's sentence to three months suspension without pay (Lardner, J. 1864).

Rear Admiral David G. Farragut convened a court of inquiry on board the flagship USS *Hartford* on October 1, 1862, to ascertain the facts regarding the behavior of Lieutenant Commander James S. Thornton, Commanding, USS *Winona*. Farragut detailed three senior Navy officers and appointed Edward Gabaudan as the court's recorder. The court granted Thornton's request to have Paymaster George Plunkett as his defense counsel (Thornton 1862).

The essence of the court's inquiry focused on allegations that Thornton was suffering from delirium tremens and was unfit for duty over the inclusive dates from September 19, 1862, to September 25, 1862. Winfield Scott Schley, the USS *Winona*'s Executive Officer, lodged the complaint that became the basis for the investigation (Thornton 1862).

According to Schley, Thornton's erratic behavior typified delirium tremens, an accusation amplified by his testimony. The first hint that something was amiss occurred shortly after the USS *Winona* left Pensacola, Florida, en route to Mobile, Alabama. Thornton complained of seasickness, and the heavy seas created by gale-force winds gave credence to the man's professed ailment. The USS *Winona* joined other ships anchored near Mobile on Sunday, September 21, 1862, and Thornton, prostrate in his stateroom, asked Schley to report their arrival to the fleet commander (Thornton 1862).

Just before midnight that Sunday, Schley testified that "Cap't Thornton sent for me and told me that he wished me to investigate the conduct of his boy Robert whom he suspected of having poisoned him." For unknown reasons, Schley did not follow through, and several hours later Thornton summoned the officer for an explanation. Schley assured Thornton that he would investigate Robert in the morning (Thornton 1862).

Schley dutifully reported to Thornton Monday morning, but "I found him so much deranged and his conversation so incoherent that I concluded his sickness to be more than seasickness." Over the succeeding days, Thornton's behavior deteriorated, alarming the crew with his rambling speech and irritable outbursts. On several occasions, Thornton attempted to jump overboard but alert crewmembers foiled his efforts. To protect the enfeebled man and the crew, Schley confined Thornton to his cabin and posted a watch as an additional security measure (Thornton 1862).

Thornton's suicidal tendencies did not abate with confinement, and the next morning's breakfast ended abruptly when the officer of the deck reported "that the Captain had his razors and was about to cut his (meaning Cap't Thornton's) throat." Fortunately, Thornton surrendered the lethal weapons without a struggle, but the man's desperation forced Schley to thoroughly search his stateroom and remove all potentially harmful objects, during which "I found a demijohn, nearly full of spirituous liquor of some sort" (Thornton 1862).

With the quiet assistance of Paymaster George Plunkett as his defense counsel, Thornton cross-examined Schley, concentrating on the rough weather and his subsequent seasickness as the more likely explanation for his behavior. Schley disagreed, claiming that the transition from innocuous symptoms to an unsound mind was inconsistent with seasickness (Thornton 1862).

Schley relied on the medical support provided by Assistant Surgeon Arthur Matthewson as the ordeal on board the ship progressed. Thornton initiated the first encounter with the surgeon on Sunday, complaining of seasickness. Matthewson was probably sympathetic, suffering himself with the same ailment, and "I administered an opiate. At the same time I noticed some muscular tremors; he appeared quite rational except in the belief that his boy had poisoned him" (Thornton 1862).

Assistant Surgeon Matthewson returned the next morning and found Thornton still vomiting but now agitated and hallucinating. "He imagined at times that he was surrounded by rattlesnakes which were attempting to bite him, he imagined himself the object of conspiracies against his life and thought that he was a prisoner." In response, Matthewson increased the opiates, and "stimulants in the form of ale were given to him during the day." Despite the surgeon's ministrations, Thornton's mental faculties worsened, aggravated

Assistant Surgeon Arthur Matthewson, USN (NH 48079, courtesy Naval History & Heritage Command).

by a merciless agitation that prevented a restful night's sleep (Thornton 1862).

Three days of medical treatment failed to turn the tide and Thornton's physical and emotional descent worried Matthewson. On Wednesday, September 24, 1862, Matthewson left the USS *Winona* and made the short traverse to the nearby USS *Richmond*, seeking consultation with Surgeon Andrew A. Henderson. Henderson suggested increasing "the dose of opium and the stimulant to two ounces of whiskey and fifty drops of laudanum every two hours." Thornton's condition improved with the revised treatment plan (Thornton 1862).

Matthewson testified that Thornton suffered from delirium tremens, the result of "the too free use of spiritous liquor." The surgeon dismissed Thornton's contention that tobacco could cause delirium tremens and insisted that the most probable cause was alcohol (Thornton 1862).

Court Recorder Edward Gabaudan presented Jonathan M. Foltz, the Fleet Surgeon of the West Gulf Blockading Squadron, as the next witness, clearly in an attempt to use the man's position to the prosecution's advantage. Thornton immediately objected to Foltz's testimony, arguing that the surgeon never observed the accused onboard the USS *Winona*. The court agreed, but Gabaudan sidestepped the decision and reintroduced Foltz as an expert witness, provoking another objection from Thornton. After taking a moment to consider the objection, the court overruled Thornton. Foltz restated the symptoms of delirium tremens, insisted that only liquor, and not tobacco, caused the disorder, and testified that hallucinations of "snakes are one of very common occurrence" (Thornton 1862).

Acting Master's Mate Henty D. Burdett, attached to the USS *Winona*, recalled Thornton's efforts to jump off the ship: "He seemed incoherent ... I was walking the deck ... When I looked next, I saw him evidently trying to get out of the Starboard after port. The Quartermaster ... stopped him by taking hold of him. He then tried a few minutes after to get over the taffrail aft" (Thornton 1862).

Anticipating fireworks, Gabaudan asked the court "to consider whether the testimony of the negro servant of Lieut. Comdr Thornton, cited to appear by the Recorder, would be admitted." The court approved Gabaudan's request, but Thornton stridently objected to the testimony of Robert Jones "on the ground that the witness is a negro and a fugitive slave. That such persons have no rights that white men are bound to respect." Thornton further claimed that the United States Supreme Court decision in *Dred Scott v. Sandford* precluded Robert Jones's citizenship (Thornton 1862).

The court of inquiry dismissed Thornton's objections and allowed Robert Jones to testify. Before doing so, the court evaluated the 15-year-old's competence to testify, making sure he understood the need for honesty and the consequence of false statements. Jones's simple answers satisfied the court and Gabaudan proceeded to take his testimony (Thornton 1862).

Jones's testimony was ambiguous. Three times he stated, "I saw nothing wrong with him." Gabaudan wondered why he reported Thornton's suicide attempt with a razor, considering those comments, but Jones simply referenced an order from Schley "not to give him [Thornton] anything any ways sharp." Pushed by Gabaudan again, Jones testified that Thornton "imagined he saw snakes and wild geese" (Thornton 1862).

Only one prosecution witness observed Thornton surreptitiously imbibing from the demijohn. Assistant Paymaster Samuel F. Train testified that the demijohn was nearly empty as a result. The court of inquiry retired to consider the body of evidence after Train's testimony and determined that "the testimony elicits the facts that Lieut Cmdr Jas. S. Thornton ... was incapacitated from duty by a fit of Delirium Tremens, and attempted self-destruction" (Thornton 1862). The court's findings seemingly had no adverse effect on Thornton's distinguished Naval career, as he progressively assumed future commands rising to the rank of captain (Thornton 1862).

From the Philadelphia Navy Yard, H.H. Goodman prepared the prosecution of Acting Third Assistant Engineer David M. Howell, on August 14, 1863, for two military charges, disobeying a lawful order of his superior officer and drunkenness. Both offenses occurred on July 5, 1863. According to the judge advocate, the first charge occurred when Howell left the USS *Kensington* without permission, and the second military charge accused Howell of drunkenness on board the ship. Howell pleaded guilty to disobedience but not guilty to drunkenness, and with the court's permission he read a statement defending his unauthorized absence (Howell 1863).

Howell claimed that the day before the ship arrived in New York, "I had been sick with dysentery. Doctor James having no medicine to do me any good, I got permission from the Chief Engineer to go on shore." Not content with a few hours on shore, Howell petitioned Captain Higgins for permission to stay overnight and in return received an expletive-laden response ending with "I will have time to attend to you bye and bye." Unfazed by Higgins's reply, Howell dismissed the friction-laden encounter and joined a shore party headed to New York City. When Howell returned the next day, Higgins summoned the errant officer to his stateroom and notified him of the charges preferred. Howell countered by submitting his resignation, prompting Higgins to propose withdrawing the charges in exchange for the officer remaining. They both agreed to the pact, but Admiral Hiram Paulding refused the brokered deal (Howell 1863).

Acting Assistant Surgeon Hiram H. James, attached to the USS *Kensington*, was the prosecution's first witness. James considered the accused a temperate man and confirmed Howell's illness because "he was suffering from diarrhea, and afterwards from constipation ... I gave him some brandy three or four times during the passage, but I think it was not on that day." Acting Master's Mate James McGlathery was the officer of the deck, and from that pivotal position he observed Howell's behavior and confirmed the surgeon's testimony (Howell 1863).

Goodman completed the prosecution with McGlathery's testimony, and the accused had no witnesses. The court recessed, reviewed the evidence, and found Howell not guilty of drunkenness, but guilty of disobedience, and sentenced him to be dismissed from the Navy (Howell 1863).

Acting Assistant Surgeon Peter P. Gilmartin brought his bedside manner to court when he agreed to serve as the defense counsel for Acting Ensign Felix McCann, attached to the USS *Champion*. The general court-martial members convened on November 24, 1863, aboard the USS *Choctaw*, and listened as Judge Advocate Acting Paymaster Edward N. Whitehouse read the military charges, all three of which occurred on October 24, 1863. Whitehouse accused McCann of disobedience of orders, insubordination, and drunkenness. The judge advocate emphasized the accused's belligerent conduct toward Acting Master Alfred Phelps, Jr., Commanding, USS *Champion*. McCann pleaded not guilty to all three charges (McCann 1863).

Acting Master Alfred Phelps, Jr., was the prosecution's first witness. Phelps testified that McCann ignored a maneuver order and when the senior officer asked why, the accused replied that "he had no reason to give." A few hours later McCann approached Phelps and apologized for his behavior which he attributed to a "misunderstanding." Phelps gave the junior officer a lifeline by not punishing the disobedience. He cautioned McCann against future defiance, but "when I made that remark, he in an excited manner raised his fist and said if I am to hang, I may as well hang now as ever, and brought his hand down on the railing." Phelps considered McCann intoxicated, based on the man's aggressive behavior and alcoholic breath (McCann 1863).

Acting Assistant Surgeon Abram L. Vail proved to be a weak witness, lacking knowledge of the first two charges. However, he confidently claimed that McCann was drunk and unfit for duty based solely on his "excited manner." Acting Master's Mate Herman Alms unequivocally declared that McCann was drunk because "he told me he was drunk himself and I saw him dancing in the Ward Room after he was ordered to his room. The only thing I could tell, he seemed a little happier than I have even seen him" (McCann 1863).

For reasons not stated in the court-martial transcript, Gilmartin was absent when the trial entered its second day. In his place, McCann requested the assistance of Acting Assistant Surgeon W.F. McNutt. Gilmartin rejoined the trial as senior counsel the next day and in a remarkable interrogation challenged William Wenthorn, the pilot of the USS *Champion*. Wenthorn observed McCann after his arrest, convinced he was intoxicated because "he appeared to be very excited when he came into the room. He took off his hat and coat and threw it into the room ... He also said he was under arrest and acted as men do when under the influence of liquor." Gilmartin asked the witness if being arrested could account for McCann's behavior, but Wenthorn steadfastly replied, "I should attribute his actions to liquor alone" (McCann 1863).

McCann's defense extended the trial for a third day, along with two accommodating defense witnesses who established the accused's sobriety. At this point, McCann requested a delay in the proceedings to prepare his defense statement. A day later, Gilmartin read the 12-page handwritten statement to the court (McCann 1863).

Gilmartin began by conceding "there might possibly be a dearth of establishing, by direct testimony, the innocence of the accused," but he then pivoted to "the conviction that the charges, from very evidence, are utterly without foundation, in fact, and rather the creation of a highly wrought fancy in nature over-sensitive [rather] than the conclusions of cool, collected thought" (McCann 1863).

McCann's counsel dissected the prosecution witnesses, shredding their credibility by exposing contradictions, half-truths, and factually worthless assertions. Gilmartin mockingly dismissed the testimony of prosecution witnesses who claimed that McCann was simultaneously intoxicated and capable of performing his duties. Dr. Viel diagnosed intoxication based on the accused's excited behavior, a claim Gilmartin acidly noted "is far from deserving the name of drunkenness" (McCann 1863)

Gilmartin ended his long oratory on a positive note, "look[ing] forward with renewed confidence to the impartial decision of the court, which cannot be otherwise than favorable to the cause of a worthy careful officer." After a short deliberation, the four-day trial ended with Gilmartin's faith no doubt crushed, as the court found McCann guilty of all three charges and sentenced him to be dismissed from the Navy (McCann 1863).

Fort Jefferson, Florida, contained a formidable prison on Dry Tortugas Island roughly seventy miles west of Key West. President Lincoln replaced the death sentences of a sizeable number of service members with imprisonment on the lonely outpost (General Orders Number 206, 1864).

Ships delivered supplies regularly to Fort Jefferson that barely dented the austere, windswept landscape. Prison life was miserable and recreation nearly nonexistent, with boredom compounded by the sweltering climate.

Second Lieutenant Morgan Everts, Company E, 110th Regiment, New York Infantry, turned the adversity into opportunity, but he only succeeded at getting court-martialed while at Fort Jefferson (Everts 1865).

Throughout March and April 1865, the judge advocate accused Everts of multiple instances of disobedience of orders, conduct prejudicial to good order and military discipline, and conduct unbecoming an officer and a gentleman. The gist of the charges focused on Evert's alcohol bootlegging, as described in one specification when "2d Lieutenant Morgan Everts, Company 'E,' 110th New York Infantry Volunteers, did sell to one John Dorsey, a prisoner at Fort Jefferson, Florida, two canteens of whisky, and two bottles of whisky, in all about one gallon." Dorsey was the principle conduit peddling liquor between the accused officer and the other prisoners, a rewarding but risky retail enterprise that Everts managed by cautioning Dorsey "to look out and not let the boys get tight, as it would come back on me and raise the devil with me." Everts kept the liquor flowing with fraudulent requisitions (Everts 1865).

Everts pleaded not guilty to all three military charges. The court-martial rendered mixed verdicts, finding Everts not guilty of conduct unbecoming an officer and a gentleman but guilty of disobedience of orders and conduct prejudicial to good order and military discipline: an outcome that did not mitigate the court's sentence ordering the man dismissed from the Army (Everts 1865).

Being under the influence of alcohol had the potential to indirectly harm soldiers, as revealed by the general court-martial of Second Lieutenant William P. Christie, 99th Regiment, Pennsylvania Infantry. The judge advocate charged Christie with neglect of duty after the officer ordered the ambulance's horses unharnessed, an act that deprived wounded soldiers of care and transport on December 13, 1862, near Fredericksburg, Virginia. Christie faced a second charge of drunkenness on duty because of his "use of spiritous liquors." The court-martial found Christie guilty and sentenced the officer to be cashiered (Christie 1862).

Fraternization between officers and enlisted soldiers undermined discipline and respect for authority, but alcohol could dissolve that inviolate boundary, as Captain Fleming Holliday, Company A, 110th Regiment, Pennsylvania Infantry, learned to his chagrin. A general court-martial convened near Falmouth, Virginia, on October 11, 1862, and charged Holliday with three specifications of conduct unbecoming an officer and a gentleman (Holliday 1863).

Holliday was in command of Company A, located in the vicinity of Fort Cass, Virginia, and was drunk on September 21, 1862. Deceptively, the officer ordered the sutler to sell Private William Spitler a bottle of brandy, and once procured, Holliday hosted a party "in his own tent drink[ing] liquor with privates of his Company, to the total subversion of discipline and good order." The court acquitted the officer of being drunk on duty but guilty of cavorting with his enlisted soldiers. Major General Ambrose E. Burnside reviewed the trial proceedings and identified multiple technical errors, but despite the sloppy record, he approved the court-martial's sentence dismissing Holliday from the Army (Holliday 1863).

The same court-martial that heard Captain Fleming Holliday's case turned its attention next to a fellow officer, First Lieutenant John Cottrell, Company G, 110th Regiment, Pennsylvania Infantry, also charged with conduct unbecoming an officer and a gentleman. Cottrell's fetid offenses were twofold, drunk on duty on October 10, 1862, and again two days later "during divine service, and there made a loud and unbecoming noise, and upon being told by the Officer of the Day to keep quiet, replied to him Go to Hell." Cottrell's uncouth church commotion led to his dismissal from the Army (Cottrell 1863).

Like Captain Fleming, Lieutenant William Wills, Company D, 24th Regiment, New York Infantry, also suffered the perils of fraternizing with his enlisted soldiers. Wills's court-martial took place "at the camp of McDowell's Division" on November 25, 1861, and prosecuted the officer for drunkenness on duty and conduct unbecoming an officer and a gentleman, both offenses on October 22, 1861. The latter charge stemmed from the officer playing cards with enlisted soldiers. After reviewing the evidence, the court-martial found Wills not guilty of drunkenness on duty but guilty of playing cards with soldiers, and for that, he was dismissed from the Army (Wills 1862).

The judge advocate prosecuted Major Charles W. Anderson, 13th Regiment, Missouri Infantry, with an array of charges and specifications in a determined approach to convict the officer. The court-martial convened at Benton Barracks, Missouri, on December 8, 1861, to hear the prosecutor read seven military charges clarified by fourteen specifications. Anderson listened as the prosecutor accused the officer of multiple incidents of drunkenness, threats, vulgar language, breaking arrest, and accusing Surgeon John B. Ball, 13th Regiment, Missouri Infantry, of having "drugged or poisoned the liquor" (Anderson 1862).

Anderson pleaded not guilty, and the court-martial, without elaboration, agreed and "fully and honorably acquit him, the said Charles W. Anderson." When the trial's transcript reached Major General Henry Halleck for review, "the General commanding has noticed that after the court had been sworn, and the prisoner arraigned, a supernumerary member reported and was sworn, but not allowed to fill a vacant seat ... The court erred in introducing a new member after it had been sworn." Halleck's criticism of the trial proceedings was important in terms of judicial oversight, but it was not construed as a fatal error and did not overturn the legal proceedings (Anderson 1862).

The general court-martial of Marine Corps First Lieutenant William J. Squires was full of twists and turns, pitting the prisoner against his chief antagonist in a fully contested trial. The court-martial convened at the Marine Barracks, Norfolk Naval Station, Virginia, on November 28, 1864, to hear the judge advocate, Marine Corps Second Lieutenant Kent D. Davis, bring three charges against the accused officer. The judge advocate first leveled accusations of drunkenness against Squires, alleging that the officer was unfit for duty as the officer of the day on October 1, 1864. The second charge against Squires involved disobedience of orders, and the judge advocate described it in two specifications accusing Squires of being absent from duty and not delivering a prisoner to the provost marshal. Both incidents occurred on October 1, 1864. The third charge levied by the judge advocate accused Squires of submitting a false inspection report of the prisoners' quarters. Squires pleaded not guilty to all three military charges and retained "Mr. Chandler" as his defense counsel (Squires 1864).

Judge Advocate Davis presented Marine Corps Orderly Sergeant H. Carlisle as the prosecution's first witness. Carlisle testified that Squires was intoxicated, a conclusion based on his observation that "he was not able to write a legible 'Tattoo' report." Marine Corps Colonel William Dulany reviewed the illegible report, and through Carlisle, ordered Squires to provide a corrected copy. Squires casually replied that he would submit a legible version the following day. During that conversation, Carlisle testified that Squires "asked me several times to repeat what I said." Carlisle attributed the repetition to the accused's drunkenness. During the cross-examination, Squires exposed several contradictions in Carlisle's testimony. For instance, Carlisle claimed that the accused did not "reel or stagger" but he also testified that the accused "reeled

First Lieutenant William J. Squires, USMC (NH 44767, courtesy Naval History & Heritage Command).

while talking ... he appeared to mix words up and pronounce all the words as one" (Squires 1864).

Carlisle also testified that Squires was absent from his duty as officer of the day on two occasions, about one hour in the morning and about four hours in the afternoon. As a result of the absences, Squires was supposedly unable to check the prisoners' quarters, an allegation that supported the judge advocate's accusation that the officer prepared a false inspection report (Squires 1864).

Squires cross-examined Carlisle about Colonel Dulany's criticism of the accused's duty performance on October 1, 1864. To demonstrate the senior officer's hostility and prejudice, Squires asked, "Had there been any other interview of an unpleasant character between Col Dulany and the accused, prior to the time you have just spoken of" (Squires 1864).

Before Carlisle could answer, a member of the court-martial objected. After consulting with his legal counsel, Squires responded, "I would respectfully state the reasons ... Liquor is not the only cause producing the like consequences, if within a short time prior ... a difficulty had occurred between Col Dulany and myself ... I respectfully submit that it is competent for me to show the fact in explanation of my manner ... from anger ... I should be permitted to show that other causes than intoxication may have produced the physical condition spoken of by the witness, it is making him, an Orderly Sergeant, an expert in a matter about which Doctors might well disagree" (Squires 1864).

The court-martial members briefly deliberated and permitted Squire's inquiry. Carlisle subsequently described an acrimonious meeting in Dulany's office, during which the senior officer accused Squires of disrespect. Squires adamantly denied Dulany's accusation and argued that "there were witnesses who could testify as to what he had said" (Squires 1864).

On November 30, 1864, Colonel William Dulany testified and recalled Squire's behavior as officer of the day while inspecting the men: "He did it in a very careless and indifferent manner ... dismissed [the men] without being at his proper post ... and he went off as if he was in a great hurry ... he was drunk, he was very unsteady, he could hardly articulate" (Squires 1864).

Squires vigorously cross-examined Dulany and through the process questioned the man's memory, his conflicting testimony, and his demand that the judge advocate secure additional prosecution witnesses "to prove facts stated." Squires also questioned how Dulany could have known, "in the most positive and unequivocal terms that at 'Tattoo' inspection, the accused, while officer of the day, was drunk in presence of the troops, and that a few minutes afterwards you ordered the accused to perform the important act of duty inspecting prisoners? Why did you allow the accused to remain on duty ... if you knew or believed him to be drunk?" Surprisingly, the court members and the judge advocate did not object to the question. Perhaps they too were curious, but Dulany dodged the trap: "I decline answering the question on the ground that I might criminate myself" (Squires 1864).

The judge advocate presented three witnesses after Colonel Dulany's testimony, all of whom supported the prosecution's three charges. The judge advocate first summoned William Dulany, Jr., who testified that Squires "was drunk, his gait was not steady; in the second place his manner and bearing and articulation were that of a drunken man. I am positive he was not in a fit condition to perform his duties as Officer of the Day" (Squires 1864).

Squires no doubt knew the answer but for the record asked William Dulany, Jr., "Are you the son of Col Wm Dulany, and do you reside with him, and if so, how long have you resided with him?" The twenty-year-old Dulany acknowledged the relationship and admitted living with his father and working as an unpaid clerk. Additionally, he confirmed Squires's claim of authoring his father's criminal complaint. Squires grilled the young man's potential prejudice, but the younger Dulany repelled every attack, implausibly asserting a dispassionate interest in the case (Squires 1864).

Squires and his defense counsel huddled overnight, planning the next day's strategy that began with the younger Dulany's continued examination. Impeaching the witness was the obvious goal of the first question, "How many courts-martial have you been a witness before in the action or results of which your father was interested or before which he was a witness?" (Squires 1864).

Squires continued to probe the witness's bias, but a court member objected without providing any reason and interrupted the proceedings. Squires promptly rebutted the objection, arguing that the younger Dulany was not an impartial witness based on his partisan participation in other trials. The court-martial overruled the court member's objection and forced Dulany to concede that he had previously testified in two trials that supported his father's interests (Squires 1864).

Navy Assistant Surgeon James Kinnier was the first defense witness, in what proved to be an aggressive effort by Squires to weaken the prosecution's case. Kinnier described multiple clinical encounters with Squires from August 30 to November 30, 1864. During those times, Kinnier treated Squires for tonsillitis, chronic diarrhea, bronchitis, pulmonary congestion, acute rheumatism, and typhoid fever, collectively leaving the officer "below the standard of health" (Squires 1864).

Around October 1, 1864, Kinnier advised Squires "to keep out of the night air, and to avoid all excess ... he was Officer of the Day ... he was weak and exhausted, and hardly able to go about." Squires pointedly asked the doctor if the diseases' symptoms would be like drunkenness, prompting Kinnier's response that "certainly they would resemble some of them." The surgeon also advised Squires to use liquor as a fatigue-fighting stimulant (Squires 1864).

Kinnier's medical testimony muddled the prosecution's case by introducing alternative, but plausible, explanations for the accused's behavior. Squires then proceeded to call witnesses that attacked Colonel Dulany, an audacious strategy that risked offending the court-martial members. In an unusual move, Squires called a member of his court-martial, Marine Corps Second Lieutenant Edmund P. Banning, of the Norfolk Naval Station, to testify in his defense. Banning testified that Colonel Dulany's "manner has been overbearing, and unofficer like to the other officers of his command with whom he came in contact." Banning believed the senior officer was dishonest, his reputation "bad," and his powers of observation clouded by "the effects of the liquor which he drinks during the day" (Squires 1864).

Squires summoned Marine Corps Captain John H. Higbee, another member of his court-martial, who delivered a second testimony corroborating Banning's opinion that Dulany was "unofficer like and ungentlemanly towards the officers generally." It fell to Marine Corps Major Thomas Y. Field to deliver what the defense hoped would be the knockout blow. Field personally knew both Colonel Dulany and his son. When asked about the younger Dulany's reputation for truthfulness, Field testified that he was truthful but "not in a matter in which his father was interested." Squires then posed the same question to the witness regarding Colonel Dulaney's honesty, but he was no doubt frustrated when Field "respectfully decline[d] answering that question, on the ground that it would form an essential link, in a chain of evidence, that might subject me to punishment" (Squires 1864).

Squires' legal counsel read the defense statement to the court-martial on December 7, 1864. The 26-page document repudiated Squire's drunkenness, and lambasted Colonel Dulany's testimony as "totally unworthy of belief ... he has been impeached in every way known to the law ... his testimony was black-wicked and malicious perjury." Similar words savaged Dulany's son as "totally unworthy." Squires's defense statement summarized his various medical debilities and confessed that "I freely admit that I had ... taken a small amount of stimulant but it was because I was so exhausted." The long monologue tapered to a conclusion with Squires's conviction "that these charges were trumped up against me" (Squires 1864).

The court-martial delivered mixed verdicts, finding the accused not guilty of drunkenness but guilty of disobedience and of making a false report, both modified by the court's favorable rewording of the specifications. Squires's punishment was twofold, an official reprimand by the Secretary of the Navy and a two-year suspension with loss of pay. Immediately after sentencing the accused, the members of the court-martial requested clemency, citing the officer's good conduct and their belief that the false report "may have inadvertently occurred" (Squires 1864).

The court-martial transcript of Squires did not mention an appeal for mercy, but a later pension application indicated that the authorities had mitigated the sentence. His military career peaked with a promotion to Marine Corps Captain around 1867. Two years later, Squires was involved "in the suppression of riots that were caused by the Revenue operation in connection with illicit distilling." The Brooklyn, New York, whiskey riots turned violent and claimed Squires as a victim when an unknown assailant threw a brick that cracked his skull, inflicting a morbid injury that felled the officer's career (Squires 1891).

Before 1863, general courts-martial treated drunkenness with a mixture of monetary fines, short periods of confinement, and various punishments that shamed the perpetrator, exposing him to ridicule, and not so subtly serving as a general deterrent. After 1863, court-martial members hardened their approach, dramatically reduced acquittals, and issued harsher sentences. Even so, courts-martial still punished officers with dismissals and cashiering, both representing humiliating dishonorable discharges, but they rarely imposed imprisonment and they never implemented a death penalty. Conversely, enlisted service members and noncommissioned officers suffered the strictest penalties.

Private Richard Kavenaugh, Company D, 1st Regiment, United States Infantry, was among the fortunate few exonerated for drunkenness. Kavenaugh's general court-martial convened at Otterville, Missouri, on December 31, 1861. The judge advocate charged the man with being "so much intoxicated as to be unfit to perform his duty as a member of the guard. This at Sedalia, Mo., on the 15th day of December 1861." Kavenaugh pleaded not guilty and following the court-martial's agreement, he returned unscathed to duty (Kavenaugh 1862).

Shortly after the Civil War began, Corporal Edward E. Sheridan, Company G, 3rd Regiment, United States Infantry, faced a general court-martial in Washington, D.C., for two interrelated charges of conduct to the prejudice of good order and military discipline and disobedience of orders. Both charges stemmed from his behavior on August 13, 1861. Sheridan was drunk on duty that day and refused to leave the parade ground. He admitted his guilt, and in response, the court-martial reduced the soldier's rank to private and fined him ten dollars (Sheridan 1861).

Recurrent bouts of intoxication subjected the offender to greater consequences, as demonstrated in the trial of Private William Andrie, Company C, 11th Regiment, Missouri Infantry (Union). Andrie's general court-martial convened at Cape Girardeau, Missouri, on December 18, 1861, to consider the military charge of conduct prejudicial to good order and military discipline. The judge advocate accused Andrie of being "drunk on the 3d day of December, 1861, and was drunk almost every day previous, for the last two months." Andrie pleaded not guilty, but the court-martial decided otherwise and sentenced the man "to walk in a twenty foot ring from reveille till retreat, allowing one hour for dinner, with a twenty pound stick of wood strapped on his back, for four consecutive days, and be placarded on the back 'For Drunkenness,' and for each time he takes it off, an additional day be added" (Andrie 1862).

Private Michael English, another soldier from the 11th Regiment, Missouri Infantry (Union), faced the same tribunal as Private Andrie for conduct to the prejudice of good order and military discipline and disobedience of orders. English stole a bottle of liquor from a store owner in Cape Girardeau, Missouri, on January 10, 1862, but before the hapless thief could consume his ill-gotten gain an officer ordered the soldier to return it, which he refused to do. The court-martial determined that the accused was guilty of the specification regarding the theft but somehow reasoned he was not guilty of the military charge. No such ambiguity existed in the court-martial members' decision declaring English guilty of disobedience, after which he was ordered "to walk in a forty foot ring, for two days, from reveille till retreat, except for one hour for dinner, with a placard marked, 'Stealing Whiskey and disobeying orders'; to have one-half of his monthly pay deducted for four months: and to be publicly reprimanded by the Colonel of the Regiment" (English 1862).

Alcohol's sedative effect jeopardized Private Anderson Budy, Battery A, 5th Regiment, United States Artillery, after an officer posted the man as a sentinel guarding prisoners. Anderson was so drunk on September 20, 1861, that he fell asleep on the guard detail. The general court-martial convened on October 18, 1861, at the Headquarters of the Army of the Potomac, Washington, D.C., and after finding the soldier guilty sentenced him "to forfeit ten (10) dollars of his pay for eighteen months; to undergo solitary confinement for fourteen days, fed on bread and water" (Budy 1861).

A general court-martial convened at the Norfolk Virginia Navy Yard on July 17, 1862, to consider the case against Marine Corps Private Samuel Rothrauff. The judge advocate charged the accused with desertion and resisting arrest on July 4, 1862. The prosecutor added a second military charge of drunkenness because Rothrauff was intoxicated and "riotous" at the time. Rothrauff pleaded not guilty and requested permission to summon three defense witnesses (Rothrauff 1862).

The judge advocate's case primarily relied on Sergeant John Hoben, who reported a noisy disturbance and, upon inspection, identified Private Rothrauff outside the Navy Yard's wall. Hoben testified that he "heard a noise outside of the entrance Gate and looked through a loophole in the Gate, and saw that there were some Marines outside." When Hoben went outside and ordered the men to return, they refused, which forced him to momentarily retreat while he gathered reinforcements. Although the show of strength convinced most of the Marines to return peaceably, Rothrauff refused and resisted angrily, prompting Hoben to use force to detain him. Private William Haskins helped corral Rothrauff, and testified that "I took him to be crazy drunk" (Rothrauff 1862).

Private Michael Evers was the first defense witness and he freely admitted being among the Marines standing outside the Navy Yard's gate. The small group never ventured far from the Navy Yard, prompting a court member's puzzlement as to their intentions. Evers denied the obvious and claimed no intention to desert. Up to this point, Evers's testimony was shaky, but with more certainty, he claimed "that he [Rothrauff] was under the influence of liquor." The two remaining defense witnesses conceded that Rothrauff was drunk but they both insisted that he had no intention of deserting (Rothrauff 1862).

Rothrauff's defense statement was an artful, patriotic appeal that denied desertion because "the day '4' July you will all admit is one that every citizen wishes to celebrate, not getting permission to go to town caused me to get such a thought in my head." The "thought" led the intrepid Marine to covertly arrange boat passage from the waterfront just after roll call, and to return the same way after celebrating in town. Rothrauff admitted that he celebrated too much, and "I was so much intoxicated that I do not recollect anything that transpired for a few hours previous to my being taken in by the Guard" (Rothrauff 1862).

Perhaps Rothrauff's patriotic indulgence struck a responsive chord in the court-martial's decision finding the accused not guilty of desertion but inescapably guilty of drunkenness. His celebration ended with more than a hangover after the court-martial sentenced him "to confinement in the Cells, with a Ball and Chain ... and to be employed in the daytime doing Police Work on the Garrison for the term of three calendar months and to forfeit all pay for ... three months" (Rothrauff 1862).

Commander Napoleon B. Harrison, Commanding, USS *Minnesota*, preferred charges of "unfitness for duty from habits of intemperance" against Boatswain Paul Atkinson, a matter investigated by a court of inquiry at the Charleston, Massachusetts, Navy Yard on December 17, 1862. As the testimony unfolded, the witnesses revealed their collective reluctance to candidly address Atkinson's poor duty performance, alcohol misuse, and age: a hesitation based on the man's long and loyal service in the Navy (Atkinson 1862).

As the first witness in the court of inquiry, Commander Harrison recounted the letter he had sent to the Secretary of the Navy Gideon Welles, in which he had questioned Atkinson's fitness for duty. Harrison testified that while the USS *Minnesota* was undergoing repairs in Portsmouth, New Hampshire, "I noticed the boatswain was not attending properly to his duty. Thought it was in consequence of drinking, but no report had been made to me that he had been." On December 4, 1862, after leaving Portsmouth, Harrison testified that Atkinson was not at his place of duty, and upon further investigation he learned that the boatswain was on the sick list. Harrison then "sent for the Boatswain and found him in a wretched condition, very nervous, and shaky, which I believe the consequence of intemperance." Harrison recalled no prior incidents of drunkenness and believed the man faithfully discharged his duties "except such as arose from his being too old for the performance of his duties in that ship ... He did the best he could" (Atkinson 1862).

Lieutenant Commander Edward C. Grafton, the executive officer on board the USS *Minnesota*, testified next and noticed Atkinson's intoxication "on several occasions," which he reported to Commodore Gershom Jacques Van Brunt. Although Grafton acknowledged that he had never seen Atkinson drunk, he held the belief that the man lacked the necessary force or physique to hold the position of boatswain on a vessel of such size. While in Portsmouth, Atkinson was on light duty after suffering a sprained knee, and with little to do, he asked Grafton for permission to go ashore. When Atkinson returned, he "was stupid and unable to do his duty and he left the deck." Suspecting intoxication, Grafton asked Surgeon John S. Kitchen to examine the man. Kitchen dutifully complied and reported that Atkinson was not intoxicated, but "seemed to be suffering from the effects of a debauch" (Atkinson 1862).

Kitchen was the court's last witness, and during his testimony he described the examination of Atkinson. The surgeon recalled that he knocked several times before Atkinson, appearing groggy and disheveled, opened the door. After examining the man, Kitchen had doubts about his illness, declined to include his name on the sick list, and voiced his suspicions of malingering to the executive officer (Atkinson 1862).

Atkinson's defense statement reminded the court of inquiry of his twenty-five years of loyal service in the Navy. Atkinson earned his promotions through arduous work but regrettably noted that his many recommendations "were destroyed with all my private property on board the Minnesota in her action with the rebel steamer Merrimack, a shell exploded ... and destroyed all my effects." Citing his age, Atkinson openly acknowledged, "I have not now the physical strength to perform the duties of Boatswain on such a vessel as the Minnesota." Notably absent from Atkinson's defense statement was any reference to intoxication (Atkinson 1862).

The court of inquiry determined "that Boatswain Atkinson has been addicted to the use of intoxicating drinks—that this use taken in connection with his age has rendered him unfit to perform so arduous duty." After weighing all the evidence, the court "recommended him to the favorable consideration of the Department" in recognition of his previously unblemished Navy service (Atkinson 1862).

Boatswain Atkinson's Navy career continued despite periodic hospitalizations. Doctors discharged Atkinson from the United States Hospital in Chelsea, Massachusetts, around February 1864. In January 1865, Boatswain Atkinson wrote a letter to the Secretary of the Navy Gideon Welles, in which he declared that his health had been fully restored and he was now prepared to resume his duties (Atkinson 1864).

During a court-martial proceeding, Private Martin Fallon, Company E, 17th Regiment, Massachusetts Infantry, was clearly under the influence of alcohol. The court-martial arrested the soldier "for appearing before them as a witness while intoxicated." Fallon's imprudence resulted in thirty days of confinement with the added weight of a twenty-four-pound ball and chain (Fallon 1862).

Three mysteriously intoxicated soldiers never revealed the source of their liquor at a general court-martial convened at St. Augustine, Florida. Private David A. Perry (Company A), Private John Evans (Company K), and Private Michael McGrath (Company F), all from the 24th Regiment, Massachusetts Infantry, faced the same two military charges. The judge advocate accused each soldier of conduct prejudicial to good order and military discipline, alleging that they "did ... take and drink a portion of the contents of a keg containing Lager Beer, the property of Dr. Adolf Majer, Surgeon in charge of the convalescent Hospital. This at St. Augustine, Florida, on or about the 10th day of December 1863." The judge advocate charged each soldier with drunkenness on duty, but in doing so, he overlooked the obvious correlation between their intoxication and the theft of beer. Perhaps it was that omission that persuaded the court-martial to acquit the men of tapping the keg, but not of drunkenness on duty. The court sentenced the three soldiers to hard labor and forfeiture of pay for one month (Perry, Evans, and McGrath 1864).

Private Philip Wells, Company E, 5th Regiment, Connecticut Infantry, exemplified the lenient punishment of drunkenness in the early years of the Civil War. The judge advocate accused Wells of being absent from his company without leave and drunkenness on October 8, 1861. The judge advocate additionally charged Wells with conduct prejudicial to good order and military discipline for assaulting an officer and for the wanton destruction of private property after shooting a citizen's pig. Wells pleaded guilty to all the charges except the assault. The court-martial found Wells guilty of all four military charges and leniently sentenced the soldier to hard labor and forfeiture of pay for three months (Wells 1862).

The trial of Private Winterfield of Company D, 8th Regiment, New York Infantry, for assaulting an officer resulted in a different outcome. Winterfield's court-martial considered three charges involving drunkenness, theft "of a barrel of vinegar, to the value of about $2.50," and threatening his commanding officer to leave him alone or "he will get a ball into his head." The court-martial returned three guilty verdicts and sentenced the soldier "to have the buttons torn from his uniform, and to be dishonorably drummed out of his Regiment, and then to be confined in the penitentiary of the District of Columbia for the term of one year" (Winterfield 1862).

A general court-martial tried Private Mersereau Wood, Company G, 67th Regiment, New York Infantry, for a distinct type of alcohol-related offense. Instead of drunkenness, the judge advocate accused Wood of supplying alcohol to other soldiers, who subsequently became intoxicated while on duty. The court-martial charged Wood with two specifications of conduct to the prejudice of good order and military discipline "while doing duty as a wagoner in said Regiment, secretly and clandestinely procure and bring into camp spiritous liquor," resulting in a drunken sentry and several intoxicated Union prisoners. After a brief trial, the court found Wood not guilty of distributing the liquor to the prisoners, but guilty of bringing the beverage to the sentry. In an interesting outcome, the court reasoned that as "the liquor given to [the sentry] was small in quantity and not sufficient to intoxicate, the Court attaches no criminality to the specification, and recommends the release of the prisoner" (Wood 1862).

Major General George B. McClellan considered two sides of drunkenness in reviewing the court-martial of Private Charles Hoegenauer (Hagenauer), Company B, 27th Regiment, Pennsylvania Infantry. The judge advocate charged the soldier with sleeping on post while detailed as a sentinel at Baily's Crossroads, Virginia, on October 14, 1861. At the same time, the judge advocate accused Hoegenauer of drunkenness on duty and disrespect to his superior officer when the man proclaimed, "I'll be damned if I am drunk" (Hoegenauer 1862).

Sleeping when posted as a sentinel was a serious military crime that exposed the regiment to a surprise attack and courts-martial typically imposed harsh punishments, including the imposition of the death penalty. Hoegenauer may not have understood the implications of pleading guilty to sleeping on post and perhaps thought that drunkenness was more serious. In any event, Hoegenauer pleaded not guilty to drunkenness and disrespect (Hoegenauer 1862).

The court-martial found Hoegenauer guilty of all three charges and sentenced the soldier "to be shot by musket fire till dead," an outcome that emphasized the danger of sleeping on post. Major General McClellan reviewed the legal proceedings and stressed "the sacredness of the duty of sentinels" before reasoning that if Hoegenauer "became drunk after being posted as sentinel, it was an aggravation of his offence. If he was drunk before being posted, his offence is lessened in a slight degree by being shared with the negligent officer of the guard who posted a drunken man." Since McClellan was unable to find satisfactory answers to his questions, he ultimately ruled in Hoegenauer's favor, remitted the sentence, and allowed the soldier to return to duty (Hoegenauer 1862). Private Hoegenauer (Hagenauer) was later killed in action at the Battle of Missionary Ridge, Tennessee, on November 23, 1863 (Bates 1869a, 399).

Post-trial reviews of courts-martial proceedings were influential in shaping the practice of military law, particularly in cases where a convening authority challenged the outcome. Colonel George W. Taylor was the president of a general court-martial assembled near Alexandria, Virginia, on October 9, 1861, to discipline 36 soldiers accused of various crimes, including being AWOL, disobedient, and drunk. Private Thomas Spear, Company F, 2nd Regiment, New Jersey Infantry, was typical of this group. The judge advocate charged Spear with drunkenness and "resisting his superior officer and abusing him" with a mixture of threats and violence. In deciding the case, the court-martial dismissed the drunkenness because there was "no offence known to the service being charged therein" but the court found Spear guilty of "resisting his superior officer and abusing him." Spear's punishment was a lenient loss of one month's pay (Spear 1862).

Private Christopher Fleming, also a member of Company F, 2nd Regiment, New Jersey Infantry, faced charges like Spear of being under the influence of liquor and threatening his commanding officer. Despite the court-martial finding the soldier guilty of blatant attacks on discipline and authority, he received only ten days of extra duty as punishment. Remarkably, the same court-martial members continued with their lenient sentencing approach, even after considering the more egregious behavior of Private Aleck Barnett, Company E, 3rd Regiment, New Jersey Infantry. Barnett was already in confinement for drunkenness when he voiced "gross disrespect to his superior officer" and threatened to kill his company commander. The court-martial cited Private Aleck Barnett's previous good behavior as a prisoner and sentenced him to twenty days of confinement, with any time already spent in detention being credited toward the sentence (Fleming and Barnett 1862).

Major General George B. McClellan reviewed and approved the courts-martial's collective findings with a stern caveat "that in many instances the punishment and the offence are all out of measure with each other; the error in every such instance being on the side of undue lenity. This is not the mode of infusing a soldierlike spirit into an army, nor is it even a means of securing the good will of the men. They soon learn the value of a rigid observance of discipline" (General Orders Number 6, 1862).

Bringing liquor on board a ship was a hazardous undertaking, but Master-at-Arms Charles Eldridge found a way to dodge the risk. A Navy general court-martial met on board the USS *Alleghany* at the Port of Baltimore, Maryland, on June 4, 1862, with Judge Advocate George M. Weston reading the charges to the five Navy officers. Weston accused Eldridge, attached to the USS *Fernandina*, of scandalous conduct tending to the destruction of good morals and embezzlement. The incriminating incident occurred on April 4, 1862, when Eldridge allegedly "purloined from the spirit room a quantity of the ship's whiskey and gave it ... to the crew, thus inciting them to misconduct." Eldridge entered a plea of not guilty, and the trial proceeded without any assistance from a defense counsel (Eldridge 1862).

The prosecution's main witness was Captain of the Top William Hillman, who testified, alongside his brother John Hillman and Michael Henry, that they had received a bottle of whiskey from Eldridge. After establishing Eldridge's involvement, the judge advocate summoned Acting Master John R. Dickinson to the stand. Despite being questioned about the official Navy regulations regarding liquor, Dickinson claimed ignorance, stating that "we were all volunteers and did not fully understand the rules of the Navy." Despite this admission, Dickinson insisted that he restricted the crew's access to the spirit room. When questioned by the accused, Dickinson spoke highly of Eldridge's performance of duty, except for a previous incident of intoxication (Eldridge 1862).

Eldridge conducted a spirited defense. He cross-examined witnesses and presented the testimony of two defense witnesses. His defense statement pitifully opened with, "as master of arms, which is a very unthankful situation, I had very few friends." Eldridge probably had enemies and John Hillman was among them. Hillman was an inveterate card player and resented Eldridge's constant interference. According to Eldridge, it was Hillman's hostility "which induced him to say that I furnished the liquor." Eldridge's defense convinced the court-martial, which then acquitted him, demonstrating a lack of certainty in the prosecution's case (Eldridge 1862).

According to charges filed in a trial conducted on December 14, 1863, on the USS *Portsmouth* near New Orleans, Louisiana, Acting Master's Mate Henry Heliker devised a devious scheme to bring liquor on board the USS *Arizona*. Seven officers listened as Judge Advocate Paymaster C.W. Hassler accused Heliker of drunkenness and "encouraging spiritous liquors to be brought on board ship ... and did order or request Henry Jackson, Landsman ... to bring spiritous liquors on board the US Steamer Arizona at New Orleans" (Heliker 1863).

Acting Ensign William Harcourt testified that on December 8, 1863, Heliker was drunk, staggering on deck, swearing, and giving unintelligible orders, forcing Harcourt to order the drunken man to his room. Landsman Henry Jackson testified that "Mr. Heliker told me to bring the whiskey on board and keep it for him." Hassler concluded the prosecution's case with just two witnesses, apparently convinced it was sufficient for a conviction (Heliker 1863).

Acting Master's Mate John H. Mallow testified on behalf of Heliker and contradicted Jackson's damning testimony. He insisted that Heliker told the Landsman "Not to take a drop of liquor aboard the ship." In his defense statement, Heliker restated his innocence and attributed his "drunken" behavior to being "unwell and unable to attend to my duties as officer of the deck having a heavy fever on me at the time," and he adamantly denied ordering Jackson to bring liquor on board the ship. In weighing the evidence, the court-martial members sided with the prosecution's case, found Heliker guilty of both charges, and ordered his dishonorable discharge from the Navy (Heliker 1863).

It was common for service members to admit to drunkenness, believing that the befuddling effects of intoxication excused or at least lessened their misbehavior. From the perspective of a young illiterate service member contending with a board of officers at a court-martial, usually without defense counsel, drunkenness might have been the only explanatory argument. Sometimes the strategy worked, but more typically courts-martial considered excessive alcohol use as an aggravating factor, as illustrated in the case of Marine Corps Fifer James Carrigan.

Carrigan's Navy general court-martial took place on board the USS *Clara Dolsen*, on December 4, 1863, at Cairo, Illinois, to consider military charges of drunkenness and theft. Carrigan pleaded guilty to being drunk at the Cairo Marine Barracks on November 6, 1863, but contested "steal[ing] from Private Augustus Formhoff eleven birds, the property of Corporal George W. Cline" (Carrigan 1863).

In what seemed to be much ado about nothing, the judge advocate summoned five witnesses to testify before the court-martial members. Corporal Cline, the prosecution's main witness, explained that "I was out gunning and brought into the barracks, the birds mentioned in the charge," Second Lieutenant C.H. Humphrey testified that both Cline and Formhoff accused Carrigan of stealing the birds. Marine Corps Captain M.R. Kintzing saw Carrigan leaving the barracks with the birds, but "thought nothing of it." After learning of the alleged theft, Kintzing questioned Carrigan, who insisted that the birds were given to him by Private Formhoff (Carrigan 1863).

Carrigan had two defense witnesses, both of whom testified that Formhoff gave the birds away. In his defense statement, Carrigan provided details about a casual conversation that led to Formhoff giving the birds away. Carrigan probably torpedoed his defense by waffling on the effects of the alcohol and admitting that "a lady friend made a stew with the birds." As it turned out, both the birds and Carrigan ended up in hot water. The court-martial found him guilty of drunkenness and theft and sentenced the man to three years in prison, the loss of all pay, and a dishonorable discharge (Carrigan 1863).

Throughout the Civil War, Navy courts-martial repeatedly assembled to prosecute violations of the rule prohibiting alcohol on board ships. Marine Corps Private Daniel Jordan was among those willing to take the risk, based on a calculation no doubt shared by others who believed that apprehension was an unlikely outcome. Jordan's general court-martial convened at the Marine Barracks in Brooklyn, New York, on May 14, 1863, to consider his "unlawfully introducing spirituous liquor on board a vessel of war" (Jordan 1863).

The judge advocate charged Jordan with bringing liquor on board the USS *Sabine*, alleging that he had violated the Secretary of the Navy's order of July 17, 1862. Commodore Cadwalader Ringgold, the prosecution's main witness, had long harbored suspicions that crewmembers smuggled alcohol aboard the USS *Sabine*. As evidence of the unlawful behavior, Ringgold cited an outbreak of rowdy, intoxicated Marines and a chance encounter that uncovered the scheme. It was late at night on April 7, 1863, when a loud noise awakened Ringgold. An investigation discovered that Jordan was drunk and "interfering with the muskets at the rack," after which a ship's officer arrested and confined the Marine. The next morning Ringgold offered to release Jordan in exchange for information about the smuggling of alcohol on board the ship (Jordan 1863).

Jordan accepted Ringgold's offer and confessed that "he smuggled a quantity of liquor from a boat under the bow, hauling it up by a line sent on by a boy in the boat." Ringgold kept his end of the bargain and released the prisoner from confinement, but then set the wheels in motion for the court-martial. In an interesting twist, the prosecution's remaining witness was Marine Corps Captain Charles Heywood, a member of the court-martial, whose testimony paralleled Ringgold's comments (Jordan 1863).

For his defense, Jordan presented Marine Corps Private John Moore, a wobbly witness who did more damage than good. During the trial, Moore claimed that he had not witnessed the accused bringing any liquor on board the ship. However, a court member pressed him on the vague nature of his testimony, compelling the witness to concede that "the accused [could] have smuggled liquor and you not notice it." Jordan summarily concluded his defense following Moore's testimony. The court-martial subsequently found Jordan guilty and leniently punished the man with solitary confinement and loss of pay for one month (Jordan 1863).

Rear Admiral Samuel Phillips Lee, Commanding, Mississippi River Squadron, preferred the charge of "drunkenness while on post as a sentinel" against Marine Corps Private Charles H. Moore, resulting in a Navy general court-martial that convened on November 28, 1864, at the United States Naval Station, Mound City, Illinois. Moore pleaded guilty to the July 31, 1864, incident, obviating prosecution witnesses, but he presented Marine Corps Orderly Sergeant Carl Wagner as a witness for the defense. Wagner described the accused as "always clean, and orderly, and prompt to obey," and in response to a court member's inquiry, he added that the accused was placed on sentry duty only a few hours after returning from liberty (Moore 1864).

The court-martial endorsed the guilty plea and in recognition of the serious crime sentenced Moore "to be confined six months at hard labor ... with loss of half his pay during that time." Rear Admiral Lee approved the trial's proceedings "but in consideration of his long confinement before trial, his previous good character, and the fact that there is no evidence to show that he got drunk while on post, I hereby remit the execution of the sentence" (Moore 1864).

Drunkenness possibly spared Seaman Robert Hyman from being charged with mutiny when Commodore Henry H. Ball preferred a less serious charge of riotous conduct. A Navy general court-martial convened on board the USS *Portsmouth*, near New Orleans, Louisiana, on January 7, 1864. The judge advocate accused Hyman of being disobedient and "drunk, noisy, and abusive" while onboard the USS *Hollyhock* a week earlier (Hyman 1864).

Acting Master Meletiah Jordan was the prosecution's first witness. Jordan testified that Acting Master's Mate Lewis Milk informed him on January 1, 1864, "that the men had rum in the forecastle and were very noisy." Jordan went to the forecastle and demanded the men's silence, prompting an unknown voice to angrily scream, "come down and take the rum away from us." Ignoring the threat, Jordan and his fellow officers moved to the Hurricane Deck with the motley crew following close behind. Hyman's boisterous belligerence continued unabated, and with the situation descending into anarchy, Jordan ordered the ringleader put in irons. At the same time, Jordan quietly sent an officer to a nearby ship for reinforcements (Hyman 1864).

Perhaps sensing the consequences, the rebellious crew retreated, and Jordan subdued and shackled Hyman. The drunk and defiant seaman slipped out of his restraints the next morning, and his unceasing raucous, threatening behavior resulted in one of the ship's officers gagging "him with a piece of iron and lashed his irons behind him around a post." Proving himself once again an escape artist, Hyman removed the gag, but an officer wisely suggested he replace it or suffer even greater punishment. A semblance of calm surfaced in the man and he compliantly replaced the iron gag (Hyman 1864).

Hyman defended his misconduct, claiming that "the liquor was brought on board and some of it given to me. I had no intention of getting drunk but only intended to take one glass as much to allay suspicion on the part of the others as any love of liquor. This one glass, however so far deprived me of judgment that I took more and became intoxicated. Then while deprived of reason I was guilty of the excesses found against me" (Hyman 1864).

The court-martial members most likely reasoned that Hyman had consumed alcohol of his own volition, which was strictly prohibited on board the ship and constituted a breach of military regulations. Regardless of his defense, Hyman was ultimately convicted and handed a harsh sentence of four years in prison without pay, as well as a dishonorable discharge (Hyman 1864).

A high-powered group of officers consisting of Rear Admiral Samuel L. Breese, Commodore William C. Nicholson, Commodore Henry Eagle, Captain James Glynn, Commander George A. Prentiss, Lieutenant James A. Doyle, and Lieutenant Bayse N. Westcott gathered together in the Navy general court-martial of Acting Master's Mate David Fader at the Brooklyn, New York, Navy Yard on December 7, 1864 (Fader 1864).

Judge Advocate Philip Hamilton charged Acting Master's Mate David Fader with drunkenness, using insulting and abusive language toward his superior officer, and assaulting his superior officer. All three incidents occurred on November 5, 1864. On that date, the prosecutor alleged that Fader was drunk and when ordered to board a receiving ship saltily replied, "Who in Hell are you." Lieutenant Commander Leonard Paulding ordered Fader's arrest, further infuriating the accused, who responded by assaulting the senior officer (Fader 1864).

Fader pleaded not guilty and declined the assistance of defense counsel, after which Hamilton called Marine Corps Drummer John Ross as the prosecution's first witness. Ross described the events he witnessed on

November 5, 1864, at the Navy Yard's Lyceum when a scuffle took place between Lieutenant Commander Leonard Paulding and the accused. Fader, in a forceful manner, yanked on the officer's coat. Paulding scanned the surroundings, noticed Ross, and ordered him to escort the accused to the receiving ship. Fader was a large man and, with a volley of obscenities and his determined resistance, he thwarted Ross's mission. A nearby group of Marine guards responded to the fracas and subdued the stubborn man with hand irons and a rope about his legs. Ross was adamant that Fader was "very much intoxicated," deliberately attacked Paulding, and in response to a question from the accused again stated "he [Fader] was drunk. He was carried on board" the receiving ship (Fader 1864).

The victim of Fader's attack, Lieutenant Commander Paulding, first observed the accused "slightly staggering and as I supposed under the influence of liquor." Paulding approached the man, inquired of his name, and in return "he became very violent ... kept up his vituperative language." From that point, Paulding's account mirrored Ross's testimony, while adding that Fader "struck me on the right shoulder with his fist ... and having no other means of defence I returned the accused's blow." Fader cross-examined Paulding and asked, "Do you think I knew what I was doing?" Paulding conceded that the accused was "partially conscious of what he was doing ... I do not think the accused was in a state to take care of himself" (Fader 1864).

After the prosecution's case, Fader called Acting Third Assistant Engineer Gilbert Webb as a defense witness. Webb recalled the incidents preceding the Navy Yard imbroglio when the accused was drinking alcohol with several officers at a Brooklyn, New York, hotel, and "he was in a crazy state so much so that he did not know me." Webb offered a different account of the alleged assault and did not recall Fader using opprobrious language. He further testified that Fader accidentally fell on Paulding during the struggle, which led Paulding to strike Fader. Aside from the incident in question, Webb stated that Fader was normally a sober man (Fader 1864).

Fader called three other defense witnesses, all of whom testified to the accused's sobriety, good character, and long, devoted Navy career, comments supported by Lieutenant Commander Samuel Magaw, Commanding, USS *Florida*. Acting Ensign Cornelius Washburne offered high praise for the accused, citing his courageous behavior when "he was attacked by the rebels with two field pieces." In another gallant act, Fader was in command of a small boat "with Admiral Lee on board for the purpose of reconnoitering some rebel works." After beaching the little craft, Admiral Lee and eight men advanced on foot, arousing the attention of concealed Confederates who opened fire on the intrepid group. Fader immediately recognized the danger and "carried the Admiral five or six rods and put him in the boat" (Fader 1864).

Fader presented a lengthy, nine-page defense statement that detailed his extensive seafaring career, which commenced in 1850. The statement included a meticulous account of his service in various Navy vessels, descriptions of battles he had participated in, and a forceful rebuttal of allegations of drunkenness. In an interesting twist, Fader speculated that "on the morning of the day specified in the charges I was in New York City ... took a glass of hot whiskey and then went to the Brooklyn Navy Yard and on board of the 'Newbern' ... after being on board awhile I felt a pain in my head and stomach, which I now sincerely affirm and believe was the consequence of a drug which must have been mixed with the whiskey." After drinking the supposedly poisoned beverage, Fader's memory faded and he "remember[ed] nothing of what happened until I found myself in irons on board the North Carolina" (Fader 1864).

After Fader concluded his defense statement, the court-martial retired to deliberate over the evidence. Upon their return, they found the accused guilty of all charges, sentencing him to one year in prison, forfeiture of all pay, and a dishonorable discharge. The ink was barely dry before the court-martial members recommended clemency, swayed by Fader's heroism and unswerving fealty to the Navy (Fader 1864). It was a compelling petition joined by the highest ranking members of the court-martial and was successful, as suggested by Fader's April 11, 1866, appointment as a mate in the United States Navy (Fader 1866).

Contributory negligence was a dominant theme in a Naval general court-martial convened on board the USS *Choctaw* on December 31, 1863, for the trial of First Class Fireman Edward McClain, attached to the USS *Osage*. Acting Assistant Paymaster Edward N. Whitehouse read the five military charges preferred by Rear Admiral David Porter that included disobedience of orders, mutinous conduct, treating with contempt his superior officer, attempting to assault his superior officer, and drunkenness. McClain pleaded not guilty to all the charges except for the drunkenness and then requested that Paymaster's Clerk Albert Praxton serve as his defense counsel. All five charges stemmed from an incident on October 7, 1863, when the accused was a member of an expedition probing Confederate forces between the Red River and the Mississippi River (McClain 1864).

The prosecution called six witnesses to testify, three of whom, including Acting Chief Engineer Thomas Doughty, provided unhelpful responses of "I know nothing" to the five contested charges. Doughty's professed ignorance would later boomerang as the legal proceedings unraveled. The prosecution's most loquacious witness was Acting First Assistant Engineer George H. Hobbs, with a verbosity that tangled the man in a web of alleged deceit (McClain 1864).

Hobbs began his narration by testifying that "Edward McClain kept

Crewmen on deck amidships, USS *Choctaw* (NH 55577, courtesy Naval History & Heritage Command).

hollering and shouting and I ordered him to stop. He did not stop until we got to the river." Hobbs repeated the order and McClain angrily cursed the man, and then sat down and refused to budge. Despite the earlier altercation, McClain continued with his march toward the river, but along the way, he struck yet another man with his rifle. Once again, Hobbs wheeled into action and demanded McClain surrender the rifle, leading to a scuffle during which, the officer claimed, "he struck at me with the rifle" (McClain 1864).

It took a question from Albert Praxton, McClain's counsel, for Hobbs to admit that the accused was drunk on the march back to the ship, but it was Praxton's next question that upended the trial. "Who furnished him with liquor?" Praxton inquired, followed by Hobbs's damning declaration, "Some was dealt out by Mr. Doughty's orders ... some he helped himself to" (McClain 1864).

Perhaps sensing a trap, Hobbs clumsily and unbelievably replied "I do not know" when Praxton asked if it was customary to give enlisted men a whiskey ration and whether the practice violated "an act of Congress." In an apparent effort to mitigate his peril, Hobbs insisted that he ordered the men not to drink any liquor other than that supplied by the officers and "not to drink too much." In defiance of his orders, Hobbs blamed the accused for sneaking more liquor from the unguarded jug (McClain 1864).

In his defense statement, McClain relied on the legal expertise of Praxton, who invoked the paymaster clerk's initial accusation against Acting Chief Engineer Thomas Doughty for distributing illegal whiskey rations, as well as First Assistant Engineer Hobbs's alleged involvement in the process. Praxton then made a dramatic plea, arguing that his client had been temporarily rendered insane due to consuming whiskey provided by the ship's officers, and was thus incapable of being held accountable for his actions at the time (McClain 1864).

The court-martial retired after Praxton's arguments and upon returning pronounced McClain guilty of the five military charges and then summarily ordered him "to be hung by the neck until dead." The severe penalty probably stunned Praxton and the accused, but the court-martial softened the blow by mentioning extenuating factors, chief among them, "had the officers in charge of the expedition exercised proper diligence the condemned would not have conducted himself in the manner in which it is proved that he did." With that addendum, the court-martial members forwarded the trial's transcript to the convening authority with a recommendation for mercy (McClain 1864).

In a setback to McClain, Rear Admiral David D. Porter denied the court-martial's recommendation for mercy, reasoning that the evidence proved the man's guilt and "in my opinion, getting drunk on such an occasion is but an aggravation of the offences committed by McClain. If drunkenness was admitted as justification of mutinous conduct, there would be an end of discipline and of safety for an officer who could at any time be assaulted under pretence of drunkenness." Porter acknowledged the officers' complicity in the illegal distribution of the whiskey and insisted that both should be dismissed from the Navy. He then singled out "the loose and contradictory evidence given by Acting First Assistant Engineer G.H. Hobbs ... He is scarcely exonerated from the charge of perjury" (McClain 1864).

In a letter to the Secretary of the Navy Gideon Welles, dated January 20, 1864, Porter addressed the duplicity of Doughty and Hobbs and accused them of being the "cause of all the trouble" with a further swipe at Hobbs, who "in giving his evidence, prevaricated so much" (Porter D. 1864). On October 30, 1864, Captain Alexander Mosely Pennock, the Fleet Commander of the Mississippi River Squadron, wrote a letter to Gideon Welles informing him that McClain had been held in confinement on board the USS *Osage* following his trial until September 19, 1864. On that day he was transported to the Naval Hospital in Memphis, Tennessee, where he remained under observation (Pennock 1864). A veteran pension form later listed Edward McClain as an invalid applicant, a testament to his avoiding the hangman's noose (Pension Number 28669).

Without any explanation, an unknown hand-scrawled "illegal proceedings" on the court-martial transcript of Gunner's Mate William B. Taylor, attached to the USS *Arkansas*, in a trial held on board the USS *Portsmouth* near New Orleans, Louisiana, on December 21, 1864. To be sure, the case was anomalous, a fact not apparent when Judge Advocate Acting Ensign Dennis W. Mullan accused Taylor of drunkenness, scandalous conduct tending to the destruction of good morals, disobedience, and assault (Taylor, W. 1864).

The four military charges all stemmed from Taylor's misconduct on December 1, 1864, when an officer refused the intoxicated man's shore leave, prompting his angry retreat to the ship's armory. From there, Taylor fired a barrage of bullets and when ordered to stop, threatened to shoot the officer (Taylor, W. 1864).

To prove his case, Mullan first called Acting Ensign Richard C. Dawes, who recalled the accused's behavior after the officer denied his request for shore leave. "I was afterwards sent down to order him to stop discharging firearms ... He then went into the armory, and I returned to the deck." While in the armory Taylor seized two pistols and began firing randomly, forcing Dawes to once again order him to stop. Taylor again refused and threatened to shoot Dawes, although adding, "I do not wish to injure you." To prevent any further escape attempts, an officer barricaded the armory door and held Taylor there for approximately twenty hours until he had sobered up (Taylor, W. 1864).

Witnesses testified that Taylor was intoxicated when he came on board the USS *Arkansas* and he no doubt hoped to continue his revelry when he requested another shore leave. Without regard to the charged offenses, the prosecution witnesses and Taylor's two defense witnesses collectively lauded the man's good character (Taylor, W. 1864).

The court-martial found Taylor guilty on all counts and recommended he "be confined on the dry Tortugas for the period of fifteen (15) years at hard labor," forfeit all pay, and receive a dishonorable discharge. While admitting the prisoner's abject guilt, the court-martial members discreetly criticized the ship's officers and recommended mercy for Taylor because "the accused had been on liberty and returned to the vessel in a state of intoxication, and had the proper and usual precautions been taken, the court is satisfied that no disturbance would have arisen." Commodore James S. Palmer, Commanding, West Gulf Blockading Squadron, reviewed the trial and condemned the "want of discipline so manifest on board of the USS Arkansas," and mitigated Taylor's confinement to one year (Taylor, W. 1864).

Under Navy regulations, any Navy or Marine Corps officer could be appointed as a judge advocate in a court-martial, which resulted in Surgeon Thomas J. Turner being assigned to the trial of Seaman Daniel Green, attached to the USS *Kanawha*. Green's court-martial convened on board the USS *Lackawanna*, near Mobile Bay, Alabama, on July 9, 1863, to consider three military charges of being AWOL from the USS *Kanawha*, disobedience, and drunkenness. Green pleaded not guilty to the unauthorized absence but otherwise admitted his guilt (Green 1863).

Surgeon Thomas J. Turner, USN (NH 119298, courtesy Naval History & Heritage Command).

Surgeon Turner prosecuted Green with three witnesses, each of whom described events that transpired when the USS *Kanawha* was at the Pensacola, Florida, Navy Yard for coaling. While there, Green went ashore without permission and became severely intoxicated and rowdy. During the brief trial, Green cross-examined the prosecution witnesses and established his previous good conduct, a character trait bolstered by the testimony of two defense witnesses (Green 1863).

In Green's defense statement, he openly conceded, "I was drunk, and I lost my senses ... it was the first time I'd been on shore for 18 months." Green predicated his innocence of being AWOL on the factual admission that "I left the coal barque and not the Kanawha," but the court-martial still found the man guilty except for the words referencing the USS *Kanawha*. After considering the evidence, the court-martial members punished the man with the loss of six months' pay and confinement in double irons for one month (Green 1863).

Serendipity spoiled a salacious celebration on board the prize ship *Gypsy* when Seaman Owen Riley, attached to the USS *Ethan Allen*, stabbed Seaman Redmond Dalton on March 20, 1863. In a Navy general court-martial convened near Key West, Florida, on board the USS *Santiago de Cuba*, on April 29, 1863, Rear Admiral Theodorus Bailey, Commanding, East Gulf Blockading Squadron, preferred the three military charges of attempt to kill, drunkenness, and insubordination (Riley 1863).

Walter C. Maloney, a distinguished citizen of Key West, served as the judge advocate (Rerick and Fleming 1902, 616).

Riley pleaded guilty to drunkenness and then requested the counsel of Acting Assistant Paymaster Nathaniel C. Freeman to support his defense of the two remaining charges, but Freeman refused. Without the benefit of defense counsel, Riley listened as Maloney then presented the prosecution's case. Acting Master Isaac A. Pennell, Commanding, USS *Ethan Allen*, testified that the accused was among a group of sailors from the prize ship *Gypsy*, and "some returned sober, some half drunk, some dead drunk." Two-thirds of the returning crew were intoxicated and among them was a man wounded in the shoulder from a "sharp pointed knife." Pennell probed further and learned that Redmond Dalton was the man stabbed (Riley 1863).

Unsurprisingly, Maloney faced difficulties in dealing with the prosecution witnesses from the *Gypsy* as most of them were intoxicated, which led to a blurring of their recollections. Even the victim of the attack admitted being drunk, unaware of the culprit, and insisted Riley was his best friend. Pennell seemingly rescued the prosecution's case when Riley confessed to the attack two weeks after the incident, when he admitted, "I must have been drunk when I did it" (Riley 1863).

Without Riley's aggressive behavior, it would be reasonable to conclude that military authorities would not have prosecuted the use of alcohol on board the *Gypsy*. Pennell testified about the widespread misuse of alcohol, but the court-martial members were indifferent and demonstrated no curiosity regarding the lack of discipline or the source of the liquor. Interestingly, the court-martial found Riley "guilty of stabbing, but not guilty of an intention to kill" and acquitted the man on the first charge. For disobedience and drunkenness, the court-martial sentenced Riley to 18 months of confinement at hard labor and forfeiture of his pay (Riley 1863).

Seaman Albert D. Parker, attached to the USS *Cherokee*, overcame multiple adversities at a general court-martial held on board the USS *Dale* near Key West, Florida, on March 17, 1865. Judge Advocate Acting Assistant Paymaster Henry Lunt accused the sailor of drunkenness, for becoming intoxicated on the prize ship *Emma Henry*, and for mutinous conduct when the man "did attempt to draw his revolver upon his superior officer," Acting Ensign Theodore F. De Luce, on December 8, 1864. After pleading not guilty, Parker asked Commander Reed Werden to be his defense counsel, but the officer declined the invitation (Parker 1865).

Werden's refusal surely disappointed the sailor when the judge advocate launched a parade of prosecution witnesses. The judge advocate's first witness was Acting Lieutenant William E. Dennison, Commanding, USS

USS *Cherokee* (NH 55211, courtesy Naval History & Heritage Command).

Cherokee, who captured the *Emma Henry* and sent Acting Ensign Theodore F. De Luce to take charge of the prize ship. Dennison later boarded the *Emma Henry* and witnessed "the accused ... in a state of intoxication." Dennison watched as De Luce ordered the accused to drop a bottle and threatened Parker that "if you attempt to put rum in that boat, I will shoot you." From a distance, Dennison noted Parker's hand as it gravitated toward his sidearm, and fearing the worst he "sprang toward him ... and placed him under arrest" (Parker 1865).

Members of the court-martial interrogated Dennison and elicited testimony favorable to the accused. Parker was on the USS *Cherokee* and participated in the Second Battle of Fort Fisher, North Carolina, and Dennison recalled that "on or about the 13th of December [1864] during the action at Fort Fisher he was released from confinement and volunteered to serve in working his gun ... and made the best shooting of any man on board the ship." The court-martial requested the logbook of the USS *Cherokee* at the close of Dennison's testimony (Parker 1865).

Parker deftly cross-examined the prosecution witnesses and then presented three defense witnesses. Seaman John Sheerin claimed that the accused raised his sidearm and cutlass to clear the railing when boarding the boat back to the USS *Cherokee* and not to threaten De Luce. Sheerin also testified that De Luce pointed his revolver at the accused and angrily stated, "I'll blow your bloody brains out," evoking Parker's meek response,

"I hope not, Mr. De Luce." The remaining two defense witnesses denied Parker's alleged drunkenness and supported Sheerin's pugilistic description of De Luce's behavior (Parker 1865).

In a surprising turn of events the court-martial acquitted Parker, a verdict reached because "the evidence in this case plainly shows ... that Mr. De Luce himself was in a high state of excitement and by reference to the Log Book of the Cherokee it is observed that a few days after this transaction, this officer was arrested for disobedience and drunkenness." After savaging De Luce's misconduct, the court-martial dismissed Parker's drunkenness, citing a lack of evidence, and praised the sailor's courageous action at Fort Fisher. In a final scathing criticism, the court-martial "feels bound to express its surprise that after an offence so venial and services so good, the accused ... should have been brought before a Court Martial" (Parker 1865).

Seaman William Morgan, attached to the USS *Kineo*, suffered one of the more severe punishments handed down by a Navy general court-martial. Five Navy officers, including one who testified for the prosecution, convened on board the USS *Portsmouth* on January 30, 1865. The judge advocate accused Morgan of drunkenness, scandalous conduct tending toward the destruction of good morals, and desertion. Morgan pleaded guilty to the first two charges, but not guilty to desertion (Morgan, William 1865).

Morgan did not contest the drunkenness and scandalous conduct, both charges stemming from his misconduct on May 22, 1864, while on board the USS *Kineo* patrolling the Gulf of Mexico. In the area near Velasco, Texas, the USS *Kineo* captured a schooner and Morgan was "serving at that time in the capacity of coxswain, being in charge of a boat's crew on board a prize schooner." Morgan and his crew got drunk and lost the prize ship, a careless act that resulted in the capture of one officer and four sailors (Morgan, William 1865).

Desertion was the third charge, an allegation based on Morgan's absence of "24–26 hours" on December 20, 1864, when the USS *Kineo* was near New Orleans, Louisiana. From the evidence, Morgan overstayed an authorized leave of absence and was then arrested without incident. Morgan chose not to call any witnesses or make a defense statement, opting instead to rely on the testimony that had already been presented during the trial. After examining the prosecution's evidence, the court-martial returned three guilty verdicts and sentenced Morgan to fifteen years in prison, the forfeiture of all pay, and a dishonorable discharge (Morgan, William 1865).

Sailmaker's Mate Joseph Bowden, attached to the USS *Marblehead*, faced a Navy general court-martial on November 3, 1863, on board the

USS *Pawnee*, near Morris Island, South Carolina. Judge Advocate Paymaster George Lawrence read the two charges of scandalous conduct tending to the destruction of good morals and mutinous conduct. Both offenses occurred on October 21, 1863, when Bowden was "sent in the Launch to haul the seine, got drunk and suffer[ed] the boat to get aground." The intoxicated man, seemingly aware of his predicament, defied an order to return to the USS *Marblehead* and proceeded to hurl profanities at the executive officer. He also tried, without success, to enlist the support of the launch's crew (Bowden 1863).

Bowden pleaded guilty to drunkenness and, with the assistance of Third Assistant Engineer Mosher A. Sutherland, contested the mutiny charge. The prosecution's witnesses described a crew full of drunken sailors on the grounded launch, but only Bowden offered resistance when ordered off the craft. After several objections by a court member, Sutherland succeeded in revealing that the rebuked officer pointed a revolver at the accused, needlessly escalating the encounter. Bowden failed to rally the intoxicated crew to his cause but finally returned to the USS *Marblehead*, swearing at the officers once on board and later while in confinement (Bowden 1863).

Sutherland actively cross-examined the prosecution witnesses and repeatedly documented that Bowden was not disobedient but was willing to leave the launch "as soon as he helped" another sailor get out of the boat. Defense witnesses corroborated the officer's threat to shoot Bowden, and after surmounting another objection, Sutherland forced the admission that the officer was also drunk. In the closing defense statement, Sutherland admitted that he initially balked at accepting Bowden's request "to act as his counsel, feeling as I did my inexperience and incompetency ... but a desire to see justice ... has caused me to appear on his behalf." With that admission, Sutherland emphasized the conflicting testimony regarding Bowden's intoxication and the officer's inappropriate intimidation (Bowden 1863).

Bowden's defense partially succeeded. The court-martial found the accused guilty of both military charges but removed the mutinous language. The man's punishment was less severe due to the court's decision to remove mutinous language from his charges. As a result, he was sentenced to one year of imprisonment involving hard labor, loss of pay, and a dishonorable discharge (Bowden 1863).

Rear Admiral John A. Dahlgren, Commanding, South Atlantic Blockading Squadron, received the legal proceedings, and "in order to enable me to judge fully as to my action in the sentence it is necessary to be informed of the previous character and conduct of the accused." In compliance with the request, the court-martial reconvened, and Sutherland presented defense witnesses who spoke favorably of the accused, with one exception. In a damaging recollection, one of the witnesses described an earlier insubordinate altercation between Bowden and an officer. The testimony presented at the subsequent court-martial was probably sufficient justification for Dahlgren to approve the sentence that was originally handed down (Bowden 1863).

Four

Violent Misconduct

Violence and desertion were the two military crimes most often associated with courts-martial during the Civil War. This chapter explores violent misconduct and in doing so provides a comprehensive analysis that frames both a complex and nuanced understanding of the subject. For purposes of this study, the author defined violence as intentional behavior undertaken to harm persons or property. Military charges in the representative database for this volume consistent with that definition included assault, murder, mutinous conduct, rape and other sexual crimes, threats of violence, marauding, manslaughter, maltreatment, pillage, plunder, and torture.

The representative database of 5,000 trials included 1,353 Army officers, 290 Navy officers, and 12 Marine Corps officers, most of whom were indicted for more than one offense. With that in mind, military courts indicted 761 (n = 5,000, 15.2%) Civil War service members in this database for an act of violence, 134 (n = 761, 17.6%) of whom were officers. Military courts charged 98 Army officers (n = 1,353, 7.2%), 35 Navy officers (n = 290, 12.1%), and one Marine Corps officer (n = 12, 8.3%) with a violent offense. In the Army most were junior officers, with 24 second lieutenants (n = 98, 24.5%), 24 first lieutenants (n = 98, 24.5%), and 37 captains (n = 98, 37.8%). A different pattern unfolded in the Navy, with 16 engineers (n = 35, 45.7%), followed by six acting ensigns (n = 35, 17.1%) and six acting masters (n = 35, 17.1%). The Marine Corps contributed one lieutenant and one captain to the tally.

Military courts indicted 627 (n = 5,000, 12.5%) enlisted Civil War service members in this representative database for an act of violence. The entire database included 2,725 Army, 496 Navy, and 124 Marine Corps enlisted members. For purposes of comparison, military courts indicted 491 Army (n = 2,725, 18.0%), 115 Navy (n = 496, 23.2%), and 21 Marine Corps (n = 124, 16.9%) enlisted men with a violent crime. Like the officers, junior enlisted men with Army privates (452/491, 92.1%), Navy seamen (50/115, 43.4%), Navy landsmen (18/115, 15.7%), Navy coal heavers (10/115,

8.7%) and Marine Corps privates (19/21, 90.5%) led the lists of their respective services.

Based on the representative database, military trials from the Army, Navy, and Marine Corps indicted 108 service members in 1861 (n = 761, 14.2%), 221 in 1862 (n = 761, 29.0%), 191 in 1863 (n = 761, 25.2%), 202 in 1864 (n = 761, 26.5%), and 39 (n = 761, 5.1%) in the Civil War's final year in 1865. Calculating the indictments by the number of months per year reveals a different picture. Allowing nine months for 1861 reveals an average of 12.0 indictments per month, 18.4 per month for 1862, 15.9 per month for 1863, 16.8 per month for 1864, and for the three full months of 1865 an average of 13.0 per month. These data show a relatively consistent number of indictments for violent misconduct throughout the three full years of the Civil War.

Seasonality is another way to examine indictments for violent misconduct. Military courts indicted 311 service members (n = 761, 40.9%) in the winter months of December, January, and February, 136 (n = 761, 17.8%) in the spring months of March, April, and May, 127 (n = 761, 16.7%) in the summer months of June, July, and August, and 187 in the autumn months (n = 761, 24.6%) of September, October, and November. These data clearly show that trials peaked in the winter, a finding that tracked the decline in battlefield operations during the colder months. Only a small number of major battles took place in the winter, such as the Battle of Stones River in 1863, the Battle of Nashville in 1864, Sherman's 1864 March from Atlanta to the Sea, and the First Battle at Fort Fisher in 1864 (Kennedy, F. 1998, 150, 396, 405, 401). Several factors could explain the spike in indictments during the winter season, such as reduced outdoor activity and more idleness among service members due to inclement weather, greater availability of alcoholic beverages, and more officers available to conduct trials.

The representative database included the first five military crimes courts-martial charged against each service member. The 761 service members in aggregate faced 1,526 military charges, an average of two allegations at each trial (1526/761, mean = 2.01). In some cases, the service member faced multiple charges of violent misconduct. In those cases, the author added the most violent crime to the following groups.

An assault was the most frequent violent misconduct lodged against service members (348/761, 45.7%), with declining incidents of mutinous conduct (154/761, 20.2%), murder (91/761, 11.9%), and rape (24/761, 3.2%). The remaining military charges involved threats of violence, marauding, manslaughter, maltreatment, pillage, plunder, torture, and other sexual misconduct. Drunkenness was the most common extra charge, with 144 (n = 761, 18.9%) of the service members receiving that additional military charge in addition to their violent misconduct. Courts-martial convicted the majority (675/761, 88.7%) of violent offenders, at a rate that spared neither enlisted (560/627, 89.3%) nor officer (115/134, 85.9%).

Sentencing closely tracked a crime's seriousness. For less serious offenses mitigated by extenuating circumstances, courts-martial commonly imposed penalties that included forfeitures of pay, reductions in rank, hard labor, and short periods of confinement. In some cases, the punishment included rations reduced to bread and water, wearing a ball and chain, branding, head shaving, drumming out, and the use of an iron neck yoke.

Punishments meant to mortify a service member sometimes resembled torture. In the early winter of 1863, a court-martial convicted an unidentified soldier with the 75th Regiment, Indiana Infantry, for desertion and assault. The hapless man appeared before the assembled regiment and sat near a blazing fire. "A barber lathered his head ... and then proceeded to shave it until it was bare ... a red-hot iron from the fire [was] pressed ... against the right cheek—a siz and jet of steam—the iron is withdrawn, and there is a large D upon the cheek." After branding the man, musicians played the Rogue's March, paraded the prisoner around the encampment, and he was then forcibly "taken beyond the Union lines ... and set adrift" (McGee 1882, 104).

Modern historians study violence by examining the social, economic, and political forces in a broad context, with the Civil War being one of the key events along a continuum that began with America's revolution. However, those four years were particularly significant in shaping society. Before the battlefield carnage, deeply divisive issues such as slavery, religious fissures, and friction between states and regions frothed and boiled for years before exploding into violent conflict (Oliver and Hilgenberg 2018, 210–214).

As men were drafted for military service, the rate of violent crime in cities decreased, though this decline was somewhat illusory, a result of the concerted efforts of provost marshals and military leaders to curb aggressive behaviors among recruits and service members in urban settings. However, this general trend was punctuated by events like the draft riots, which underscored the volatile nature of urban environments during times of conscription (Oliver and Hilgenberg 2018, 215–219).

The *Enrollment Act of 1863* set the stage for the draft riots that enveloped New York City beginning on July 13, 1863. At its core, the rioters protested the Enrollment Act's language that exempted Black men and allowed the affluent to evade the draft for three hundred dollars. The poor and aggrieved men keenly felt the inequity, an injustice further inflamed by the belief that Black men would take their jobs. The rioters took to the city streets as a large group and for three days exacted unmitigated violence against innocent Blacks and their property. Impotent police could not quell their lust for vengeance, leaving the restoration of order to 10,000 beleaguered troops returning from the Battle of Gettysburg. Casualties from the riot included hundreds injured and 105 individuals killed, including the vicious murder of Colonel Henry F. O'Brien, 11th Regiment, New York Infantry (Oliver and Hilgenberg 2018, 215–219).

A riot erupted in Boston, Massachusetts, on July 14, 1863, fueled by similar grievances. The incident began with a confrontation between an officer serving conscription notices and an Irish woman, which quickly escalated when the woman slapped the man. Incensed by the assault, the officer threatened to arrest her, with the woman responding with ear-piercing screams that brought a multitude to her rescue. In the ensuing melee, hundreds of rioters gathered, throwing taunts and brinks. Boston authorities quickly responded with a riot-quelling show of force, but not before a large crowd surrounded an armory. While securing the armory, members of the 1st Regiment, Massachusetts Heavy Artillery, fired their rifles to disperse the crowd, an action that stirred the angry crowd's efforts to breach the building. The commanding officer, fearing that the rioters would succeed, ordered the firing of a cannon. An unknown number of rioters were subsequently injured or killed, but the prompt intervention by responsible authorities limited the damage throughout the city (Hanna 1990, 262–273).

Except for the draft riots in 1863, murders in New York City declined during the Civil War in a trend repeated in other northern cities. An axiomatic explanation concludes "that the poor, young, and underemployed males responsible for most urban homicides were drawn off into the army, where killings won medals and applause" (Lane 1997, 143). While it may be true in some cases, that broad assessment oversimplifies any relationship between murder and combat and conflates legally sanctioned acts of violence in a wartime setting with criminal acts of homicide. That conclusion also implies that acts of violence are celebrated in the military. In reality, military awards for combat actions are typically given for acts of bravery, sacrifice, and service that are considered to have protected lives, which stands in stark contrast to the selfishness of criminal violence.

Author Aaron Sheehan-Dean in *The Calculus of Violence—How Americans Fought the Civil War* devoted a chapter to Army "Discipline, Order, and Justice." The author acknowledged "the violence committed by soldiers against each other, most of it inspired by alcohol," but also concluded that military units experiencing idleness had a significant increase in the number of assaults and murders (Sheehan-Dean 2018, 240). The representative database examined for this volume supported Sheehan-Dean's contention based on the seasonal fluctuations in military trials that consistently reached a peak during the winter months, along with courts-martial charging nearly one-fifth of violent offenders with drunkenness as well.

When brought to trial, author Sheehan-Dean noted, Army courts-martial convicted 85 percent of the offenders, a statistic nearly identical to the representative database for this volume (Sheehan-Dean 2018, 241), In a sobering comment, the author speculated that punishment failed as a general deterrent and paradoxically boomeranged when enlisted soldiers vented their anger against officers, who reciprocated by using force when subordinates challenged their authority (Sheehan-Dean 2018, 241). The representative database analyzed for this volume provided evidence for this tit-for-tat escalation, as nearly one-fifth of all enlisted service members' assaults were aimed at officers.

Sheehan-Dean reflected on the increase in military prosecutions as the war progressed, and when combining courts-martial and courts of inquiry, speculated that "enhanced enforcement not increased criminality is to blame" (Sheehan-Dean 2018, 246). While that may be true, the findings in the representative database for this volume did not identify a significant year-over-year increase in general courts-martial among the Army, Navy, or Marine Corps. A greater emphasis on strictly enforcing military law through general courts-martial also seemed less likely given the enduring tension between staffing a trial or manning a battlefield. Officers could have straddled this divide by preferring lesser charges in subordinate courts, resorting to extrajudicial punishments, or turning a blind eye, all in favor of preserving battlefield strength.

In *Baring the Iron Hand: Discipline in the Union Army*, author Steven J. Ramold asserted the view that Army officers increasingly tempered discipline to preserve manpower. Ramold's thesis relies on the presumed clash between the Regular Army martinets and the laissez-faire citizen-soldiers who chafed at the regimentation and reprimands. Officers increasingly relaxed enforcement or mitigated punishment, even for serious crimes such as desertion and violence, to placate soldiers and conserve fighting strength (Ramold 2010, 44).

Ramold's analysis comports with the representative database for this volume, which found a flat year-over-year trend in general courts-martial, lending plausibility to the argument that officers resorted to more efficient summary punishments to enforce their authority.

Mutinous Conduct

Mutiny was the ultimate act of defiance, and the representative database for this volume identified 147 examples (n = 5,000, 2.9%), a tally that included courts-martial charges for both mutiny and mutinous conduct. By service, the Army contributed 30 officers (n = 1353, 2.2%), the Navy six officers (n = 290, 2.1%), and none for the Marine Corps. In terms of enlisted service members, the Army indicted 78 (n = 2,725, 2.9%), the Navy charged 32 (n = 496, 6.5%), and the Marine Corps added one (n = 124, 0.8%).

Mutiny or mutinous conduct was a serious infraction of military discipline and courts-martial responded accordingly. Mutiny often arose from defiant disobedience, which could escalate to assault and murder in some cases. As a result, the punishments for mutiny ranged from forfeiture of pay to execution. Courts-martial sentenced 21 enlisted service members to death (n = 111, 18.9%), but on further review, 12 (n = 21, 57.1%) were either mitigated to prison or reversed. The most serious punishments imposed by courts-martial against officers included 18 dismissed and five cashiered.

The line between mutiny and mutinous conduct was an exercise in prosecutorial discretion, with the former more likely when linked with physical violence. Far more common but less severe military charges, such as disobedience, contempt, and insolence, spared many service members the ignominious allegations of mutiny or mutinous conduct.

Allegations of mutiny and mutinous conduct were common in the Army, Navy, and Marine Corps, but historians have mostly neglected the subject or concentrated on singular examples. An exception is Webb Garrison's *Mutiny in the Civil War*, which chronicles nearly two hundred incidents in the Confederate and Union armies and includes the respective navies. Garrison contended that "it is widely believed that mutiny was rare among fighting forces in both Blue and Gray." This erroneous idea rests in part upon the fact that the huge index volume of the Official Records (OR) includes only six references to "mutiny," plus a single reference to "mutineers" (Garrison 2001, 294).

The representative database studied for this volume confirmed Garrison's finding that mutiny was indeed not rare. Military courts-martial charged both officers and enlisted service members with mutiny and mutinous conduct and found the preponderance guilty.

General courts-martial charged mutiny mostly against enlisted service members. In the representative database studied for this volume, 78 soldiers faced allegations of mutiny, 32 Navy enlisted, and one Marine Corps private. Enlisted service members also faced severe consequences, with 19 convicted Army soldiers being executed (*Proceedings of U.S. Army Courts-Martial and Military Commissions of Union Soldiers Executed by U.S. Military Authorities, 1861–1866*). In a further observation, 14 of the 19 Army soldiers executed for mutiny were Black, a disparity that "seems strange that so disproportionate a number mutinously defied the authority that had become engaged in ending slavery" (Westwood 1985, 222).

Historians examining racial disparity rotate along two competing axes. One group contends that race prejudiced courts-martial sentencing, while a counterargument insists that Army court-martial procedures applied evenly to both Blacks and Whites and "afforded blacks substantially more rights than slaves ever claimed" (Samito 2007, 173). In support of the latter, even a cursory review of courts-martial transcripts reveals Black soldiers challenging White witnesses, and "despite the gravity of the mutineers' crime, many officers seem to have realized that they grounded their protests in legitimate grievances" (Samito 2007, 201). Courts-martial reserved the death sentence for leaders of a mutiny or instances involving an aggravated assault (Samito 2007, 188).

Racial prejudice was an undeniable factor that contributed to a Black soldier's mutiny. With their newfound freedom and army service, Black soldiers chafed at their unequal treatment and lack of respect. Racial tensions were often inflamed by high-handed White officers who abused Black soldiers. Additionally, the War Department refused to commission Black soldiers, and a persistent pay gap that favored White soldiers were core complaints leading to some mutinies (Kynoch 1997, 109; Reid 1990, 147; Reis 2009, 61).

Research focused exclusively on soldiers executed for mutiny distorts the subject. The representative database analyzed for this volume provided a comprehensive analysis of cases that confirmed the blurred boundaries between mutiny, mutinous conduct, and the far more common allegations of disobedience, contempt, and insolence. Commanders justified the more serious charges based on the severity of the disobedience, or possibly, as a general deterrent to quash nascent insubordinate sentiments.

Unknown standing Black soldier with rifle and fixed bayonet (LC-DIG-ppm-sca-11520, Library of Congress Prints and Photographs Division, Washington, D.C.).

In the representative database analyzed for this volume,

courts-martial considered mutiny or mutinous conduct against 147 service members, most of whom were found guilty (n = 131/147, 89.1%). Courts-martial found all six Navy officers guilty, and 24 Army officers guilty (n = 30, 80%). Among enlisted service members, Army courts-martial convicted 71 soldiers (n = 78, 91.0%), the Navy 29 (n = 32, 90.6%), and the Marine Corps convicted one enlisted service member.

The cases presented in the following sections mostly avoid trials of soldiers executed for their crimes, a topic that historians have explored in detail. Therefore, this volume has examined the less dramatic but more common proceedings, which broadened the understanding of courts-martial in the Union Army, Navy, and Marine Corps.

Defiance was the basis for a spectrum of preferred military charges, ranging in severity from several types of disobedience such as conduct to the prejudice of good order and military discipline, to mutinous conduct, and finally to mutiny. Military law lacked precise legal definitions of these crimes, and without substantive differentiation, ambiguity reigned. As the following courts-martial demonstrate, military leaders often charged mutiny and mutinous conduct for trivial insubordination. During the early years of the Civil War, courts-martial often dealt with cases of disobedience leniently. However, as widespread disobedience began to undermine combat operations, punishments for such behavior became more severe, ostensibly serving as a general deterrent.

One of the earliest cases in the representative database analyzed for this volume documented the trial of Private George Leighton, Company H, 37th Regiment, New York Infantry, held at Fort Washington, Maryland, on September 16, 1861. The judge advocate charged Leighton with the overlapping crimes of mutinous conduct and disobedience of orders when the man refused to "fall into ranks for drill" and salted his disobedience by saying, "you need not be in such a damn hurry about it ... I will go to the Guardhouse before I drill." After a brief trial, the court-martial members found Leighton guilty and, perhaps with a touch of irony, confined the soldier to the guardhouse for 60 days along with the loss of one month's pay (Leighton 1861).

The trials of Private Daniel M. Stillwell, Private Walter Allen, and Private Edward Adams, all with Company F, 18th Regiment, New York Infantry, provided insights into how general courts-martial juggled sentencing. All three faced general courts-martial convened on August 10, 1861, near Alexandria, Virginia, for violations of the 6th and 9th Articles of War for disobedience and mutiny. The charges grew out of the three soldiers' steadfast refusal to obey an order for guard duty from Captain H.M. Donovan on August 9, 1861, and by "words and actions, to prevent others from obeying said order, thus inciting to mutiny" (Stillwell, Allen, and Adams 1861).

The abbreviated proceedings resulted in Private Stillwell's acquittal. Private Allen was found guilty of both charges and was sentenced to a three-year prison term. Private Adams was found guilty of mutiny and was sentenced to a ten-year prison term. In a twist, the Headquarters of the Army of the Potomac ordered the court-martial reassembled "to complete the business before it" on September 5, 1861. The "business" involved the court-martial members convening to review the original sentences, and after careful consideration, they decided to execute each man (Stillwell, Allen, and Adams 1861).

Major General George B. McClellan applauded the court members' support of military discipline "but the sentences awarded are considered too severe for the offences ... and where the orders are not important ones it is deemed inexpedient to select such cases for the impressive lesson which a death sentence will involve." McClellan restored all three soldiers to duty and hoped they had learned a valuable lesson about the consequences of future disobedience (Stillwell, Allen, and Adams 1861).

At a general court-martial convened on September 23, 1861, near Alexandria, Virginia, Private Daniel Callaghan, Company K, 2nd Regiment, United States Infantry, listened as the judge advocate charged the soldier with mutinous conduct and habitual drunkenness. The first military charge stemmed from Callaghan's defiant assault on the sergeant of the guard, and the habitual drunkenness arose from six weeks of incessant alcohol use leaving him "totally unfit." The court-martial members perfunctorily sentenced Callaghan "to be indelibly marked on the right hip with the letter W... and be drummed out of the service" (Callaghan 1861).

A Navy general court-martial convened on October 14, 1861, at the New York Navy Yard, to hear evidence in the case of Seaman Frank Leslie, charged with mutinous conduct and AWOL. Leslie's alleged mutinous conduct occurred after returning from an unauthorized absence and consisted of striking a master-at-arms and two ship's corporals and threatening an officer, on October 7, 1861, at Fort Ellsworth, near Alexandria, Virginia (Leslie 1861).

Lieutenant James M. Prickett, the executive officer at Fort Ellsworth, was the prosecution's chief witness. According to Prickett, Leslie secretly left a work detachment without permission and did not return until later in the evening. Upon his return, in what appeared to be an unprovoked attack, Prickett witnessed the accused viciously hit the master-at-arms, and when reinforcements arrived, he continued fighting. Nearly two hundred men gathered to watch the melee before Prickett arrived with a revolver and faced the angrily posturing Leslie. Master-at-Arms John M. Banks, the principal victim, recalled Leslie striking him twice and rendering him nearly unconscious. The two ship's corporals, while suspecting the accused of having some liquor, endorsed Leslie's normally superior performance and sobriety during duty. In passing judgment, the court-martial members cited Leslie's character and sobriety to justify the mild punishment of "solitary confinement for thirty days and forfeit one half his pay for three months" (Leslie 1861).

The judge advocate accused Sergeant John A. Boyles, Company F, 76th Regiment, Pennsylvania Infantry, of violating the 7th Article of War by inciting a mutiny after Boyles believed he was making a justifiable intervention. Boyles's court-martial convened at Hilton Head, South Carolina, on August 12, 1862. The specification described an incident that took place on August 7, 1862, when Boyles witnessed Lieutenant Buttinger punishing Private Jackson Williams. Boyles dashed across a street after observing the officer attempting to forcibly restrain Williams. The intrepid sergeant curtly confronted the officer, saying, "Jack, they shan't buck and gag you while I am about and can help it." Boyles begged other service members to join his crusade, but no one heeded his pleadings. The members of the court-martial also ignored the man's pleadings, and after considering the evidence, reduced the sergeant in the ranks and required him to stand "in the center of a hollow square formed by the regiment, to receive a reprimand from the commander of the regiment" (Boyles 1862).

Perhaps if Boyles knew what preceded his rash dash, he could have avoided a court-martial. Private Jackson Williams, Company D, 76th Regiment, Pennsylvania Infantry, was not victimized by a brutish officer but instead he instigated a series of events that required a forceful response (Williams, J. 1862).

Like Boyles, Private Williams faced a court-martial for mutinous conduct. The military specifications alleged that Williams was absent from duty and upon his return, Lieutenant Buttinger punished the man by ordering him to carry a heavy log and then stand on a barrel, presumably for drunkenness. Williams defiantly refused, after which, Buttinger ordered the soldier tied and gagged. Williams broke the bonds and ran to his tent. Lieutenant Buttinger and several other soldiers attempted to arrest Williams, who responded by lunging at them with a bayonet. Williams threatened further violence after "being overpowered and tied and gagged, [and] he used insulting language toward the Lieutenant." Williams's raucous behavior earned the man "one year at hard labor at Tortugas, with six pound ball and four feet of chain attached to the left leg, also half of pay to be stopped during the time" (Williams, J. 1862).

Three soldiers stationed in hot, humid Fernandina, Florida, refused to join a dress parade on August 4, 1862, and resolutely declared their intentions to "do no more duty." To emphasize their determination, the three soldiers stacked their weapons outside the officer's quarters. In a way,

Private John Wallace, Private Charles E. Lee, and Private James Ward, Company C, 1st Regiment, New York Engineers, achieved their stated goals when military authorities relieved them from duty and placed them in confinement pending a court-martial for mutinous conduct. Their blatant insubordination ended with a journey south to the prison at Fort Jefferson, Florida, for 12 months of hard labor (Lee, C., Ward, and Wallace 1862).

Except for his rank, the facts in the case of Sergeant William Postwiller, Company K, 5th Regiment, Missouri Cavalry (Union), resembled other trials that alleged mutinous conduct when disobedience was the only misbehavior. The events unfolded on July 9, 1862, when Postwiller refused to strike his tent and join the company's march. After hearing the evidence, the court-martial members who assembled in St. Louis, Missouri, brushed aside the accused's not guilty pleading and sentenced Sergeant Postwiller to be shot to death. General Samuel Curtis disapproved of the findings "for the reason that the specifications do not support the charge under which they are brought." General Curtis also disapproved of the sentence because the court-martial transcript did not document that two-thirds of the members approved the death penalty. The fatal errors made by the court-martial spared Postwiller's life, and Curtis returned him to duty not out of mercy but due to these errors (Postwiller 1863).

USS *Susquehanna* (NH 57515, courtesy Naval History & Heritage Command).

Seaman Thomas Roscommons undoubtedly had an anger problem, manifested by frequent conflicts with officers on board the USS *Hartford* that culminated in his Navy general court-martial. Rear Admiral David G. Farragut convened the trial on board the USS *Susquehanna* on October 20, 1862. Farragut preferred two military charges, the first for using mutinous and treasonable language and the second charge for treating his superior officers with contempt (Roscommons 1862).

In September 1862, a summary court-martial convicted Roscommons of unspecified misbehavior. This conviction led to his confinement on board the ship for 30 days, being placed in double irons, fed only bread and water, and deprived of pay for five months. Restrained and infuriated by the punishments, Roscommons lashed out on September 16, 1862, heatedly exclaiming, "I will never fire another gun under the American flag. Next time I fight it will be on the other side. Hurrah for Jeff Davis ... he is a better man than Farragut." Several other officers also endured most of the man's invective, with Roscommons taking special aim at Midshipman John H. Read, declaring, "you ought to be hung." Roscommons's intemperate behavior lasted mere moments, but it was a costly outburst that justified his subsequent general court-martial (Roscommons 1862).

On the trial's first day, the judge advocate perfunctorily asked the accused if he objected to any member of the court-martial. Perhaps Roscommons surprised the judge advocate with his request to remove Captain James S. Palmer, Commanding, USS *Hartford*. After a brief recess to consider the objection, the members of the general court-martial agreed, and Palmer left the courtroom. Roscommons then pleaded guilty to both military charges, despite the judge advocate's ardent warning to reconsider the pleading given the gravity of the allegations (Roscommons 1862).

Roscommons presented two witnesses for his defense, an officer and a seaman. During the naval engagements at Vicksburg, Mississippi, both witnesses testified to Roscommons's steadfast performance while firing a ship's gun. Furthermore, they could not recall any prior incidents of him using treasonous language. Assisted by the judge advocate, Roscommons drafted a one-page defense statement that highlighted his loyalty to the Union. He cited examples of valorous conduct and attributed his incendiary outburst to the five-month pay forfeiture "and the knowledge of the suffering that would necessarily be caused to a widowed mother by the loss of her main support." Roscommons's guilty plea guaranteed a conviction, and the court-martial subsequently penalized the man with a two-year prison sentence followed by a bad conduct discharge (Roscommons 1862).

Federal authorities relied on the military to suppress the 1863 draft riots in New York City. Admiral Hiram Paulding contributed to that effort by directing a Navy battalion under the command of Lieutenant Commander Richard W. Meade, Jr., to help quash the uprising. Meade's attention was naturally focused on the rebellion occurring in the streets, leaving him unprepared for the possibility of a similar uprising among his men (Conway 1863).

Meade's moment came on July 15, 1863, around noon, when "I ordered the different gun's crews to be marched into the buildings to get their rations." A brief time later a loud commotion startled the officer. Meade suspected trouble, a hunch confirmed when he entered the raucous room and several angry men confronted the officer, with one "pointing to some bread and cheese. Is this stuff fit for a man to eat? Or a proper ration for a man?" (Conway 1863).

Meade could have been a bit more sympathetic to the complaint, but perhaps feeling defensive, he carefully examined the bread and cheese and then openly concluded, "I don't see that you have any just cause of complaint." As might be expected, Meade's summary dismissal of the crews' complaints exacerbated their resentment. At this point, Seaman John Conway, whom Meade considered slightly intoxicated and the malcontents' ringleader, rudely roared "that he had been damned near starved since he had been in New York, and that he thought it a hard case that men should be treated like dogs, to have to sleep on a hard plank and get nothing to eat" (Conway 1863).

Murmurs of agreement from the other men threatened an escalation. Meade tried to reason with the men; he acknowledged their rapid deployment, unusual duty in New York City, and the fact that they were surviving on Army rations that fell short of their shipboard provisions. In an attempt to calm the crisis, Meade reminded Conley that he, as an officer, had to live and sleep under the same conditions as his men (Conway 1863).

Meade's half-hearted efforts to sympathize with his men's plight took a turn for the worse when Conway continued to press his complaints, backed by a group of surly men. The officer tried to shame the rebellious crew: "The marines had been marched all over the city through the rain for nearly twenty-four hours and yet had not complained." Meade then demanded the restive crew be quiet, but Conway persisted with "mutinous language." After exhausting his patience, Meade struck Conway's face fiercely, ordered his confinement, and instructed the guard "to bayonet him if he made any disturbance" (Conway 1863).

Seaman John Conway's court-martial convened at the Philadelphia Navy Yard, on August 21, 1863, and H.H. Goodman charged Conway with mutinous conduct for the affray on July 15, 1863. Lieutenant Commander Richard W. Meade, Jr., was the prosecution's sole witness. Meade narrated the events and justified his striking Conway as a means to quell the three other men involved in the incident, admitting that "I had no side arms, otherwise I should have cut him down, his language was so insolent" (Conway 1863).

Conway cross-examined Meade on two points, first by suggesting that other men complained of the food, an allegation the officer denied. Conway next asked, "Are not complaints frequently made directly [to] the commanding officer?" Meade bristled at the question and curtly replied, "Not to my knowledge in a well disciplined ship" (Conway 1863).

Goodman closed the prosecution following Meade's testimony. Conway's first defense witness was Acting Master's Mate Robert T. Topping, who witnessed the events. Topping's version of the events differed drastically from Meade's, portraying Conway as a sleep-deprived man who respectfully approached the officer on behalf of some of the men about the meager food. Topping testified that Meade then angrily "doubled up his left hand and hit Conway on the cheek." More importantly, Topping described the pitiful rations as "a small piece of bread and a small piece of cheese. The bread was soft ... about a quarter pound and the cheese about the same size at each meal ... They had coffee once the first day and once in the second." Making matters worse, Topping claimed that the officers patronized local restaurants for their meals (Conway 1863).

Acting Ensign Hubert Oberley was Conway's next defense witness and testified, "I was giving out the bread and cheese to the men. Most all the men found fault with it not being enough. I directed them to report it to Lieutenant Commander Meade." Oberley confirmed Topping's observations, and perhaps most damning was his claim that the officers had a separate table for some of their meals, with "ham, sandwiches, bread and butter and cheese, some lobsters" (Conway 1863).

Surgeon James McClelland was the final defense witness. McClelland served with Conway for 15 months, and based on his observations, he testified that Conway "always conducted himself with the greatest propriety." The court-martial adjourned for deliberations following the surgeon's testimony and on returning found Conway not guilty (Conway 1863).

Perhaps Surgeon Thomas J. Turner believed that the Hippocratic Oath's nonmaleficence principle applied only to doctor–patient relationships when he accepted Rear Admiral David G. Farragut's appointment to serve as a judge advocate (Polhill 1863). Without seemingly considering medical ethics and dual agency, the Navy allowed any officer, while at sea, to potentially serve as a judge advocate. This created a potentially nettlesome issue when the surgeon then resumed his medical duties on board the ship.

Turner charged Seaman Charles Polhill with mutinous conduct at a court-martial that convened on board the USS *Lackawanna*, off Mobile

Bay, Alabama, on July 2, 1863. The events took place on a cutter returning to the USS *Vincennes* on May 25, 1863. During the 15-minute voyage, a kerfuffle erupted between Seaman Thomas Shannon and the officer onboard, with Polhill spurring Shannon on. Acting Master William H. Churchill ordered Polhill to cease his interference, provoking an insolent reply: "I won't stop my noise for you ... I don't care a damn for anything you can do." Polhill kept unleashing a stream of profanity-filled attacks at the officer until Churchill finally stepped in and ordered him confined on board the USS *Vincennes* (Polhill 1863).

Polhill pleaded not guilty and Acting Master Oliver B. Warren agreed to serve as his defense counsel. After those preliminaries, Judge Advocate Turner called Acting Master William H. Churchill as the prosecution's first witness. According to this witness, four seamen in a cutter left the USS *Vincennes* on May 25, 1863, bound for nearby Ship Island. While returning from their shore duty, Shannon suddenly attacked the officer, spurred on by Polhill's aggressive encouragement (Polhill 1863).

Acting Master Warren, Polhill's defense counsel, may have surprised the general court-martial members when he objected to Churchill's testimony "upon the ground that the witness has been guilty of perjury before a Summary Court-martial." The court-martial took a brief recess to consider the matter and upon returning denied the objection because the summary court-martial did not convict Churchill of lying under oath. In an interesting admission, the court-martial chastised Polhill's defense counsel because "the objection should have been made to the witness at the time the oath was administered." With the objection dismissed, Turner's prosecution continued with additional witnesses, none close enough to the cutter to positively identify the participants. In a damaging disclosure for the prosecution, the cutter's coxswain testified, "I could not remember a word Polhill said, not one word" (Polhill 1863).

Polhill's first defense witness, Seaman Thomas Ford, of the USS *Vincennes*, disputed the prosecution's allegations and testified that Polhill "asked Shannon to sit down and said can't you behave yourself as I am." Two additional defense witnesses agreed with Ford and testified that Polhill was quiet on the return trip even though he was "tipsy" but not drunk (Polhill 1863).

After reviewing the evidence, the court-martial members rejected Turner's mutinous conduct allegations. The credibility of Churchill's testimony may have been a factor in the court-martial's reasoning when weighed against Polhill's witnesses. Polhill was not acquitted, however, but convicted of the lesser charge of insubordination and sentenced "to be confined during his watch below in single irons for three months and to forfeit six months' pay" (Polhill 1863).

About eight months after the end of the Civil War, on December 1, 1865, the United States Government carried out the execution of six Black soldiers for mutiny at Fernandina, Florida. In an article titled "The Jacksonville Mutiny," Captain B. Kevin Bennett, Judge Advocate General's Corps, thoroughly examined the legal proceedings and extensively documented the racial prejudices at play (Bennett 1991, 157–172). Twenty years later, John F. Fannin returned to the subject and exposed once again the harsh racial injustices that impacted the Black soldiers who were executed on that day (Fannin 2010, 368–396).

The 1865 Jacksonville Mutiny belatedly attracted the attention of Civil War scholars, but another less well-known mutiny occurred two years earlier in Fernandina, Florida. In this case, a general court-martial convened on March 21, 1863, to consider charges of mutiny against Privates Henry Cole, Owen Dinneny, George Adams, and other unnamed soldiers, all from Company D, 7th Regiment, Connecticut Infantry (Cole and Adams 1863).

The allegations stemmed from an incident on February 21, 1863, when Captain B.F. Skinner ordered Sergeant Eli D. Seely to arrest a drunk and disorderly Private George Webb. Private Henry Cole violently assaulted Seely, making every effort to free Webb while also issuing threats and using profane language. Private Dinneny, Private Adams, and others joined the brawl as the anarchy spread, and "it became necessary to turn out the greater part of the Company under arms to put down the mutiny" (Cole and Adams 1863).

Skinner's show of force quelled all the agitators except for Cole, who "continue[d] to threat, challenge; curse and strike, and did also endeavor to induce others to assist, in overpowering the guard, and did not desist until finally overpowered by the non-commissioned officers and men." After a few minutes, Cole managed to break free and continued with his verbal attacks, while also futilely urging the onlookers to join in a rebellion. Overpowered at last, Cole threatened Skinner: "I don't care a damn, Capt. Skinner, if you ever live to strike New Haven dock, you will never breathe in Danbury" (Cole and Adams 1863).

The judge advocate considered Private Henry Cole and Private George Adams as the two instigators and charged the pair with mutiny. Citing unspecified extenuating circumstances, the court-martial sentenced both soldiers to "six months hard labor, with ball and chain, on left ankle, 24 pound ball, six feet chain, iron not more than one-half inch or less than one-fourth inch in diameter," followed by 28 days solitary confinement, and forfeiture of half pay for seven months (Cole and Adams 1863).

The Fort Jackson mutiny of 1863 in Louisiana was another tragic event that is not as widely recognized as the 1865 Jacksonville Mutiny but is nonetheless significant. On Christmas Day in 1863, a correspondent from the *New York Times* journeyed to Fort Jackson and offered readers of the newspaper a firsthand report of the mutiny. As the reporter noted, events unfolded rapidly after a group of ten Black soldiers crossed the guard line without permission, provoking the ire of Lieutenant Colonel Benedict, who "in a fit of anger" seized a teamster's whip, and gave each of them "a half dozen well laid on." Long-simmering tensions finally boiled over, leading to a group of around one hundred armed Black soldiers burning Benedict's tent, firing their weapons wildly, and searching the USS *Suffolk* for Benedict, who was suspected to be aboard. Benedict was not found, despite the search lasting for four hours. Authorities restored order the following day, an outcome the reporter praised because "I know of few instances of moral courage greater than that displayed by the officers in arresting thirteen of the insurgents and confining them to the custody of their companions—a confidence which was not misplaced" ("Department of the Gulf, The Mutiny in Fort Jackson" 1864).

Aside from the *New York Times* article, the mutiny received scant contemporary coverage. In a two-paragraph description, the *Utica Daily Observer* dismissed rumors "that every white man in the fort had been massacred" and insisted that during the half-hour disturbance the Black soldiers "never intended to create a mutiny or shed blood" ("Interesting From New Orleans" 1863).

Fred Harvey Harrington's critical analysis shed light on the fateful events that occurred on December 9, 1863, ultimately leading to mutiny in the 76th Regiment of the United States Colored Infantry. Harrington laid the blame for the mutiny squarely on 24-year-old Lieutenant Colonel Augustus W. Benedict, a merciless man who used intimidation and cruelty to govern. Benedict abused his authority by whipping men, suspending men by their thumbs for minor infractions, "and if a man's dress did not please him, he would knock him about and hit him ... strike men on parade without any cause whatever" (Harrington, F. 1942, 420–431).

The spark that ignited the mutiny occurred on December 9, 1863, when Benedict flogged regimental band members Harry Williams and Munroe Miller. Furious soldiers released prisoners in the guard house, ran amok, and repeatedly sought but failed to punish Benedict. Officers implored the rioters to cease their actions, offering the assurance of an investigation. After an hour's intervention, they were finally able to bring about a degree of calm (Harrington, F. 1942, 422–423).

The serious breach of discipline at Fort Jackson mandated a general court-martial, and military officials charged twelve soldiers with mutiny and one soldier with insubordinate conduct. With the trial's conclusion, the court-martial sentenced Private Frank Williams (Company I) and

Private Abraham Victoria (Company D) to be shot to death, and ordered incarceration for Musician Edward B. Smith (Company B) for one year, Corporal Lewis Cady (Company K) for two years, Private Willis Curtis (Company D) for three years, Private Charles Taylor (Company K) and Private Abram Singleton (Company F) for ten years, and Private Julius Boudro (Company D) for 20 years. The court-martial acquitted Corporal Henry Green (Company G), Private Jacob Kennedy (Company D), Private Volser Verett (Company D), and Private James Hagan (Company B). The court-martial convicted Private James H. Moore, Company F, of being insubordinate and sentenced the soldier to hard labor for one month, a punishment the convening authority reversed for "the evidence being conflicting and unsatisfactory" (General Orders Number 90, 1863). The death sentences of privates Williams and Victoria were subsequently mitigated to imprisonment at Fort Jefferson, Florida (Harrington, F. 1942, 425).

The same court-martial that sentenced the mutineers also considered allegations preferred against Lieutenant Colonel Augustus W. Benedict. Authorities arrested Benedict on December 22, 1863, in advance of his trial. In what appeared to be an effort to forestall the court-martial, Colonel Charles W. Drew, Benedict's commander, penned a letter acknowledging that the accused officer "has been guilty of very indiscreet action which he bitterly repents, and for which he would be willing to do anything to atone. In view of the feeling against him in the regiment ... I respectfully recommend ... an honorable discharge from the service." Drew's intervention failed, forcing his protégé into court (Benedict 1863).

In a letter written to Brigadier General Charles Pomeroy Stone, fellow officer Brigadier General William Dwight outlined Benedict's offenses while sharing his concerns: "I have very little confidence in these 'Courts Martial' where there are so many lawyers ... The legal mind is full of doubts and whims." Dwight was further frustrated that Benedict was exploiting the legal process "to delay matters as much as possible" (Benedict 1863).

The judge advocate charged Lieutenant Colonel Augustus W. Benedict with inflicting cruel and unusual punishment to the prejudice of good order and military discipline. The first specification accused Benedict of ordering two soldiers tied "down to stakes ... with their arms and legs spread out and to smear their faces, hands and feet with molasses" at Baton Rouge, Louisiana, on August 7, 1863. A second specification described a similar act at St. Phillips, Louisiana, on August 25, 1863. The judge advocate's third specification accused Benedict of multiple instances of assaulting soldiers around Baton Rouge between September and November 1863. The fourth and final specification accused Benedict of whipping Harry Williams and Munroe Miller, the incident that precipitated the mutiny (Benedict 1863).

Benedict's campaign of terror at Fort Jackson was a condemnation of the military leadership, as other officers either condoned, downplayed, or ignored his brutal mistreatment of Black soldiers. His rampant racial hostility fused with unchecked brutality ended with a court-martial conviction. Even though Benedict was the catalyst that triggered the firestorm, his only punishment was to be dismissed from the Army (Benedict 1863).

Compared to the Union Army, nearly twice as many Black men, comprising around 20 percent of enlisted personnel, joined the Union Navy. Estimates suggest that 18,000 Black men joined the Union Navy, with most coming from Maryland and Virginia. Many of the Black men who joined the Union Navy were contrabands, which referred to slaves who had escaped their bondage, and the Union Navy's blockade of southern ports served as floating recruitment centers (Tomblin 2009, 189–191).

The Union Navy, as revealed by the database analysis, rarely initiated court-martial proceedings against Black service members for mutinous conduct. An exception was the trial of Coal Heaver Richard Cornelius. His general court-martial convened on board the USS *Clara Dolsen*, near Cairo, Illinois, on September 5, 1863. The judge advocate accused Cornelius of mutinous conduct and striking an officer. The events occurred on August 2, 1863, when Cornelius used "abusive and profane language" toward an acting master's mate. When subsequently "confined by wrist irons, did strike Acting Master's Mate ... by uplifting the irons ... and bring them with force against" the acting master's mate (Cornelius 1863).

Cornelius pleaded guilty to both charges and with the assistance of the judge advocate submitted a written defense statement proclaiming that while on shore duty, "I fell in with some friends, drank, and returned on board ... The acts alleged against me were committed while under the influence of liquor." Three defense witnesses attested to the man's good character. Lieutenant Commander Thomas Pattison, the president of the court-martial, testified, "I looked upon him as very respectful, trustworthy man." After considering the evidence, two-thirds of the court-martial members sentenced the accused "to suffer death by hanging," but then recommended mercy based on the man's reputation as a solid sailor "and his apparent ignorance" (Cornelius 1863).

The representative database analyzed for this volume identified only one member of the Marine Corps charged with mutinous conduct, giving Private Francis Connell a dubious distinction. A Marine general court-martial convened at the Washington, D.C., Marine Barracks, on June 15, 1864. The judge advocate charged Connell with disobeying a lawful order and mutinous conduct. Connell's predicament stemmed from his adamant refusal to do guard duty "and [he] was disrespectful and mutinous in language and deportment" (Connell 1864).

Black crewmembers sewing and relaxing on the forecastle, starboard side, USS *Miami* (NH 55510, courtesy Naval History & Heritage Command).

Connell pleaded not guilty to the more serious charge of mutinous conduct but conceded his guilt in disobeying an order. During the trial, the prosecution called upon two Marine Corps officers as witnesses, both of whom had ordered the accused to guard duty. Connell refused in both instances, resisted arrest, and was then forcibly detained and placed in confinement (Connell 1864).

Connell presented two defense witnesses, Navy Assistant Surgeons Dandridge Kennedy and J.W. Newcomer. Connell asked the witnesses to comment on his health before the altercation: "Did I complain to you of lightness of the head and loss of sleep ... pains through my breast, sides and arms?" Although Kennedy was skeptical of the accused's complaints and considered him fit for duty, both witnesses confirmed his complaints. On cross-examination, the judge advocate received assurances from the assistant surgeons that Connell was sane and mentally competent. The court-martial subsequently found Connell guilty of both military charges and exacted a steep penalty of four years in prison, loss of all pay, and a dishonorable discharge (Connell 1864).

Officers were not immune to charges of mutiny, as Captain Wallace W. Barrett, Captain Edwin L. Hayes, and Lieutenant John B. Stoner, all with the 44th Regiment, Illinois Infantry, learned when a general court-martial convened near Rolla, Missouri, on December 16, 1861. The judge advocate charged the three officers with mutiny and disobedience of orders. Colonel Charles Knobelsdorff, Commanding, 44th Regiment, Illinois Infantry, testified that in late September 1861, the three officers held secret meetings "tending as he is informed and verily believes it to be true, to break up the organization of said regiment." According to Knobelsdorff's testimony, during the incident, Barrett, Hayes, and Stoner actively resisted boarding their men onto the troop transport USS *McDowell* and even refused to provide them with muskets, a clear act of mutinous behavior. The court-martial members rejected Knobelsdorff's accusations and acquitted the three officers (Barrett, Hayes, and Stoner 1862).

Colonel Knobelsdorff subsequently found himself in a difficult position when he was charged by a judge advocate with several offenses, including fraud, insubordination, oppression, disobedience, and drunkenness, effectively turning the tables on him. Knobelsdorff's alleged offenses culminated in his general court-martial on April 24, 1862, at Camp Cross Timbers, Arkansas. Thirteen senior officers listened to the testimony during the two-week trial and decided that the accused was only guilty of disobedience and rebuked the officer with a reprimand. Just four months later, Knobelsdorff faced another court-martial for unspecified military charges that resulted in his dismissal from the Army. The Governor of Illinois removed the stain on Knobelsdorff's record in December 1863 and promoted the man to Brigadier General (Lowry 2003, 34–39).

First Lieutenant Andrew J. Whittier, 4th Regiment, United States Colored Cavalry, did not tolerate his soldiers' maltreatment, a stance that landed the officer in a general court-martial. His trial took place at Port Hudson, Louisiana, on November 9, 1864, and charged the 24-year-old officer with conduct unbecoming an officer and a gentleman and with mutinous conduct. The court-martial subsequently convicted Whittier for loudly protesting that "I will not see my company kicked and cuffed and run over

… I am mustered into this company and I am going to stand by it and see that the men have their rights … at the same time brandishing his clenched Fists." Whittier's outburst resulted in the court-martial sentencing the man to be dismissed from the Army. Major General Nathaniel P. Banks mitigated the harsh sentence to the forfeiture of one month's pay (Whittier 1864).

Mutiny was not always the sole offense that led to a court-martial, as illustrated by the case of Captain Henry Jansen, who served in the 12th Regiment, Illinois Cavalry. The judge advocate seemed determined to convict the officer, alleging four military crimes involving insubordinate conduct, mutiny, conduct unbecoming an officer, and tyrannical conduct. Jansen's angry tirade took place near Greenville, Louisiana, on May 7, 1864, when the officer refused an order to assemble his men for an inspection. The officer's behavior prompted Major H.B. Dox, the commanding officer, to order Jansen's arrest. In response, Jansen "violently dash[ed] his arms down in the Major's tent and proceeded to his quarters, shouting and swearing … and when directed … to stop his disorderly proceedings and confine himself to his quarters, did utterly refuse" (Jansen 1864).

The judge advocate charged Jansen with mutiny because he implored a group of enlisted Germans soldiers to remember "that the Germans could not be run over by any damned Yankee … that he was sorry any Germans ever took arms to serve this country" (Jansen 1864).

The judge advocate described instances of Jansen's tyrannical conduct. In one case, Jansen assaulted Private F. Gagel, 12th Regiment, Illinois Cavalry, by "throwing him down and dashing his head against the ground, thrusting a stick of rough wood, wholly unfitted for the purpose of a gag, breaking his teeth and cutting his mouth badly." In another incident, Jansen drew his sword on Private William Russel, 12th Regiment, Illinois Cavalry, and threatened to "run him through" (Jansen 1864).

Surprisingly, the court-martial found Jansen not guilty of mutiny but guilty of insubordinate conduct, conduct unbecoming an officer, and tyrannical conduct. Jansen's only punishment was a dismissal, despite two instances of aggravated assault (Jansen 1864).

Obedience, not democracy, was the core issue in a Navy general court-martial that ensnared three officers attached to the USS *Argosy*. The group included Acting First Assistant Engineer John W. Rohrer, Acting Second Assistant Engineer Benjamin Nannah, and Acting Third Assistant Engineer Thomas K. Hill. The three officers submitted a petition to Rear Admiral David D. Porter grieving the command of Acting Ensign John C. Morong. In their letter, the officers bemoaned the lack of "a feeling of unity and mutual confidence," citing Morong's "gross blunders and a want of a proper regard for the etiquette of the Navy … and whereas in our judgement the interest of the Navy and US Government imperatively demand that Acting Ensign John C. Morong ... be relieved of his present command." They bolstered their argument with examples of Morong's micromanagement, which often led him to encroach upon the responsibilities of other officers (Rohrer, Nannah, and Hill 1863).

Acting on behalf of Rear Admiral Porter, Lieutenant Commander Thomas O. Selfridge, Commanding, USS *Conestoga*, penned an acid letter on July 7, 1863, to the rebellious officers. Selfridge wrote, "I have read the charges preferred by you against your Captain and inform you they are all extremely ridiculous. You speak of the rules and etiquette of the Navy, your letter too plainly indicates an entire ignorance of both ... you lay yourself open to the charge of mutiny ... The Captain is supreme, in all departments, he is responsible to his superiors and not to you" (Rohrer, Nannah, and Hill 1863).

A Navy general court-martial consequently convened on board the USS *Clara Dolsen* near Cairo, Illinois, on October 3, 1863, and charged the three officers with forming a combination against the commanding officer, disobedience, mutinous conduct, and contempt. In response, Rohrer and Nannah pleaded guilty to all four charges while Hill only disputed the disobedience. All three officers attributed their behavior to ignorance of Navy law. Rohrer insisted, "Had I known that signing the paper in question was an act of mutiny, I should never have had anything to do with it." Nannah asserted the same, adding, "At the time the letter to the Admiral was signed I was sick." Hill conceded that "the errors I have committed in this affair arose from my ignorance of the rules of the Naval Service." Neither character witnesses nor their defense statements spared the officers. The court-martial sentenced all three officers dismissed from the Navy (Rohrer, Nannah, and Hill 1863).

Lieutenant Commander Thomas O. Selfridge's declaration that the "Captain is supreme" proposed an unfettered authority and was probably the prevailing sentiment among officers in the Union Navy (Rohrer, Nannah, and Hill 1863). Even so, Navy laws, customs, and traditions provided an important bulwark protecting service members from abusive practices. In some cases, a Navy general court-martial decided the boundary between reasonable command authority and willful, illegal mistreatment.

An early test came when a Navy court of inquiry convened at the Navy Yard in Washington, D.C., on October 1, 1861, to investigate the conduct of Commander William Chandler, Commanding, USS *Dawn*. Secretary of the Navy Gideon Welles ordered the court of inquiry after receiving complaints that Chandler was "violent and oppressive in his treatment of his officers and crew, has been negligent in the performance of the official duty ... and has expressed ... sentiments of a disloyal tenor." George M. Weston acted as the court of inquiry's recorder and presented the case to three Navy Captains: Elie Augustus Frederick La Vallette, Garrett J. Pendergrast, and Henry W. Morris (Chandler 1861).

Acting Master's Mate Charles W. Pass testified first, recalling an incident on June 28, 1861, when "I was put in double irons and placed in the sweat box and kept there for three days." Pass returned late from shore leave and once onboard the USS *Dawn*, Chandler "shoved me off the poop deck down the ladder, a distance of eight feet ... I was pushed over backwards, head foremost. He had a revolver in his hand and swore he would blow my brains out and walk over my dead body" (Chandler 1861).

According to Pass, the ship's commander was routinely belligerent and profane, and frequently punished crewmembers with double irons and confinement in the sweat box. The sweat box was a stateroom room adjoining the boiler, stripped of births, "five feet by six," and unbearably hot. When cross-examined by Chandler, Pass admitted that the boiler was under repair while he was confined. Ship's Cook John Holland had the unenviable record of four days in the sweat box after striking the boatswain's mate (Chandler 1861).

Chandler's cruelty extended to runaway slaves seeking safety on the USS *Dawn*. The officer repeatedly rebuffed the slaves with the admonishment that they must "shift for themselves." On at least four occasions Chandler refused to board the slaves, insisting they return "to their masters" (Chandler 1861).

Acting Master's Mate Henry Woodstock confirmed part of Pass's testimony, not recalling whether Chandler pushed the man, but he did witness the drawn revolver and the Commander's threat to kill the man "if you attempt to get the upper hand of me." Woodstock acknowledged that Pass "was not sober but he was not much intoxicated" but he was obedient and quiet, contradicting Chandler's assertions. On other occasions, Woodstock recalled that Chandler insulted officers and assaulted a seaman (Chandler 1861).

Acting Assistant Surgeon Louis Michel testified that when Pass returned to the ship "he was in liquor. He did not stagger or tumble down ... Next morning, he was not noisy ... When Mr. Pass went up the forward ladder, [Chandler] seized him, shaking him violently, and threw him down the ladder." The surgeon visited Pass in the sweatbox and testified that "the sufferings I noticed were mental ... not caused by liquor ... but by his fall and confinement. It amounted to temporary derangement and indicated a shock to the nervous system." Michel also described Chandler's incessant abusive language that spared neither officer nor enlisted member and his southern sympathies. It was Chandler's overbearing conduct that motivated the surgeon to resign, a move that triggered the court of inquiry (Chandler 1861).

Chandler vigorously cross-examined witnesses and in his defense produced witnesses that extolled his stewardship, Union loyalty, and calm demeanor. The defense witnesses portrayed Pass as angry, vindicative, disobedient, and threatening, justifying Chandler's behavior in response to the man's mutinous conduct (Chandler 1861).

Chandler's request for a delay to prepare a defense statement was denied by the court, which maintained that the officer had been given enough time to prepare. After begrudgingly complying, Chandler's defense statement failed to sway the court members. The court of inquiry decided "that the said William Chandler ... was violent and oppressive in his treatment of his officers and crew." The court of inquiry also substantiated Chandler's negligence and disloyalty to the Union cause (Chandler 1861). Chandler was subsequently dismissed from the Union Navy (Dudley 1981, 37).

The boundary between obedience and its enforcement was the central issue in the court-martial of Seaman Thomas Hamilton, held on board the USS *New Ironsides*, near Newport News, Virginia, on October 15, 1862. Hamilton was a seasoned sailor serving on the USS *Victoria*. The judge advocate charged Hamilton with mutinous conduct consisting of "assault, and strik[ing], with a broom, several times on the head Acting Ensign William H. Myers" on October 10, 1862. Hamilton pleaded not guilty and then immediately complained that over the preceding four days, the ship's officers had punished him with solitary confinement, double irons, and a diet consisting solely of bread and water (Hamilton, T. 1862).

Acting Ensign William H. Myers was the prosecution's first witness, and he painted a sullen picture of the accused. On the day in question, Myers ordered the accused to lift the Main Deck awning, a task the man "went there to do it, and after trying—or pretending to try to do as I ordered ... he said ... he would see me damned before he would try again." Angered by the seaman's rebuke, Myers responded, "I then said to him you are of no use." Hamilton murmured and sulked, which only served to further annoy the officer. Eventually, the officer ordered Hamilton to sweep water off the Poop Deck, all the while needling and provoking the already upset sailor (Hamilton, T. 1862).

Based on Hamilton's surly behavior, Myers anticipated an attack and reported his suspicions to Quartermaster David Patten. Ten minutes later, Hamilton did indeed hit Myers on the head with a wet broom. In his testimony about the attack, Patten stated that Myers repeatedly and profanely rebuked the sailor, "You are good for nothing damn you" (Hamilton, T. 1862).

Members of the court-martial scrutinized the actions of the next witness, Acting Master Alfred Everson. An incredulous court-martial member asked by what authority the accused was punished before his trial, prompting Everson to reply, "By my order, Sir ... I thought he deserved it." Everson's violation of Navy law troubled the court, but it was a pattern the officer would repeat in the future (Hamilton, T. 1862).

Hamilton's defense statement lamented his harsh treatment on the USS *Victoria*. Citing the endless provocations from the officers, Hamilton complained that "I was punished previous to the preferring of a Charge against me." The court-martial obliquely agreed with Hamilton's argument in a letter sent to the convening authority, observing "that it is more common now than before the War the habit of using reproachful words calculated rather to provoke resistance than to enforce obedience." In the same letter, the court emphasized Everson's illegal punishment. In treading the line between maintaining discipline and mistreatment, the court-martial found Hamilton guilty of mutinous conduct, and sentenced him to six years in prison, but "the sentence of death is not adjudged because the Prisoner was abused ... and already been partly punished" (Hamilton, T. 1862).

Accusations involving an officer's abusive conduct surfaced as the central issue in a Navy general court-martial convened at the New York Navy Yard, on September 14, 1864. Secretary of the Navy Gideon Welles convened six Navy officers, including Rear Admiral Samuel L. Breese, to conduct the trial of Acting Master Alfred Everson. Judge Advocate Samuel Perkins charged Everson with assault with intent to kill and a second crime of maltreatment and cruelty. Both charges stemmed from an incident on March 21, 1863, on board a captured steamer "Nicholas I" near North Carolina. Perkins claimed that Everson "assaulted James O'Neill, fireman ... and without just cause, fired a pistol ... at the said O'Neill with intent to kill him ... O'Neill, one of the crew of the captured vessel," was severely wounded (Everson 1863).

Everson pleaded not guilty, and with the assistance of his attorney, James B. Craig, listened to the judge advocate question James O'Neill, the prosecution's first witness. The 45-year-old native from Dublin, Ireland, recalled coaling the ship, and then taking a break, and was preparing to light a lantern when Everson intervened saying, "I will light it." O'Neill then followed Everson as the officer walked toward the ship's stored gunpowder. According to O'Neill's testimony, Everson then said, "No admittance and before I could stir the ball was through my thigh ... and I felt the blood running down my leg ... Never mind he says, It's all right" (Everson 1863).

O'Neill stumbled away and was on the verge of fainting when another crewmember cut "my trousers and drawers. He took off my boot and stocking. He got a handkerchief and tied it around my leg." A brief time later the ship's surgeon arrived and revived the briefly unconscious man with an unknown "drink." Several other men then placed O'Neill in a canvas sling, hoisted him over the ship's side, and into an awaiting boat for a short journey to the USS *Victoria*. Four days later the wounded man transited Ft. Monroe, Virginia, and then spent 70 days at the Norfolk Hospital (Everson 1863).

As his testimony continued, O'Neill reiterated the inexplicable nature of the shooting, insisting that Everson's attack was utterly unjustified. In response to a question from the judge advocate, O'Neill commented, "To the best of my opinion he was under liquor." A series of probing questions from the court followed the judge advocate's inquiries, none of which changed O'Neill's testimony (Everson 1863).

Everson methodically cross-examined O'Neill, impugning the man with aspersions of drunkenness and disobedience. Before Everson's assault, O'Neill admitted receiving his regular grog ration but claimed he was not drunk because "I only drank a glass what we were allowed ... I was working long enough below to get sober." O'Neill repeatedly rebuffed Everson's efforts to portray him as disobedient. Mistakenly concluding that he had the upper hand, Everson challenged O'Neill's testimony that he was "under liquor." Unfazed by Everson's question, the witness insisted that "a sober man wouldn't shoot a poor man who was working hard" (Everson 1863).

First Class Fireman Thomas Gernon boarded the captured ship and immediately confronted a drunk, quarrelsome crew. With a volley of threats, he quelled the rampage and turned his attention to inspecting the ship's boilers. He discovered the gunpowder and reported the unguarded explosive to Everson, who in turn requested a lantern to inspect the dangerous cargo in the ship's forehold. After hearing a shot, Gernon witnessed O'Neill bleeding profusely and then actively assisted the wounded man. Gernon also corroborated O'Neill's claim that Everson was "under the influence of liquor," explaining that "his face was reddened ... and he staggered slightly" (Everson 1863).

Everson's defense statement was a lengthy point-by-point rebuttal of the prosecution's case and it specifically refuted O'Neill's testimony. Everson argued that O'Neill was drunk and disobedient, although neither circumstance justified the officer's attack. The court-martial found Everson guilty after an 18-day trial and punished him with a one-year prison term followed by his dismissal from the Navy (Everson 1863).

Murder and Assault

An assault was the most frequent violent misconduct charge lodged against service members (348/761, 45.7%), based on the representative database for this volume. Officers confronted violence from the enemy on the battlefield and from service members within their units. Courts-martial charged 147 (n = 761, 19.3%) service members for assaulting an officer, a tally that overwhelmingly accused enlisted personnel (n = 130/147, 88.4%).

The representative database for this volume included 91 allegations of murder, and prosecutors generally charged that crime as the sole offense (n = 67, 73.6%). Only three officers stood trial for murder. Courts-martial convicted 80 service members of murder (n = 91, 87.9%). Courts-martial in this representative database only paired one of the murder charges with drunkenness, in stark contrast to service members facing a military charge of assault. In this representative database, the year 1864 had the highest number of murder trials with 38 (n = 91, 41.8%). In contrast, the preceding year of 1863 had 21 murder trials (n = 91, 23.1%).

Service members convicted of murder and assault tilted the censures toward imprisonment, punitive discharges, and executions. Military authorities typically dismissed (70/115, 60.1%) or cashiered (15/115, 13.0%) officers found guilty of aggravated violence. The remainder received a variety of punishments, including confinement, forfeiture of pay, and reprimands. In this representative database, courts-martial sentenced only one officer charged with murder, Captain Bernard J. McMahon, to be shot to death. On October 29, 1863, a few months after the trial, military authorities discharged McMahon, indicating that he had successfully avoided execution (Bates 1869b, 807).

Courts-martial convicted most service members found guilty of murder (76/91, 83.5%). Enlisted personnel suffered the brunt of severe punishments. Among those specifically convicted of murder, courts-martial sentenced 45 enlisted service members to be hanged (n = 76, 59.2%) and 26 to be executed by a firing squad (n = 76, 34.2%), while the remainder received prison terms.

Secretary of the Navy Gideon Welles directed the formation of a Navy general court-martial at the New York Navy Yard on August 5, 1864, to prosecute an allegation of murder. Commander Daniel Ammen listened as Judge Advocate Samuel C. Perkins accused the senior officer of murder and manslaughter following an incident that occurred on May 15, 1864, on board the USS *Ocean Queen*. According to the specifications, "Commander Daniel Ammen did willfully, feloniously and of his malice aforethought, kill and murder John Kelly, a seaman of the Navy, by firing a pistol loaded with powder and ball ... mortally wounding the said Kelly ... and afterwards ... [Kelly] died." Using identical language, Perkins also accused Ammen of murder and manslaughter in the death of Seaman Alfred Bussell. Ammen pleaded not guilty and requested the assistance of Lieutenant Commander James Parker for his defense (Ammen 1864).

Judge Advocate Perkins called Boatswain Thomas Bell as the first witness. Bell's testimony began with the grumblings of 220 "men in the draft" who were unhappy with their shipboard meals. The steward and regular waiters refused to serve the rambunctious men, forcing Bell "to get the colored sailors we had in the draft" to prepare the Sunday dinner, a meal consisting of roast beef, bread, potatoes, and tea. Bell asked the ringleaders Kelly and Bussell to approve the meal before serving dinner, and both of them gave it their hearty endorsement (Ammen 1864).

Bell hoped that Kelly and Bussell's approval would appease the disgruntled group of men, but when crewmembers served the meal the two instigators surreptitiously left the dining area. Both men then proceeded to the forbidden officers' area and confronted a small group that included the chief engineer and Commander Ammen. Bell followed Kelly and Bussell and vainly begged the men to leave, but neither did. A few minutes later, four pistol shots killed Kelly and Bussell (Ammen 1864).

Before their deaths, Kelly and Bussell channeled the anger of 50–100 men, upset with poor rations and crowded quarters. Acting as a "ship's lawyer," Kelly took charge of the group and pressed the men's complaints, accompanied by his threats, swearing, and "shoving" the ship's captain. In response, the ship's officers promised better food and liquor in a failed effort to quell the mounting anger. Kelly agreed to postpone any further action until he sampled the Sunday dinner, but Bell stated that Kelly's main interest was in obtaining liquor, and he was determined to get it. According to Bell's testimony, Kelly and Bussell, along with about 50 men, had the intention of forcibly seizing the USS *Ocean Queen* (Ammen 1864).

During cross-examination by Commander Ammen, Bell added to his testimony that "Kelly said he had been on board a Man of War and had broken into the Spirit Room and taken liquor from it and that he would have liquor from" the USS *Ocean Queen*. Kelly was no doubt perturbed when Ammen promised the men better food but "liquor was out of the question" (Ammen 1864).

Twenty-three-year-old Navy Steward William Cowen testified next and recounted the ill-fated ship's departure with the newly drafted men. Cowen testified that the drafted men provoked the crew the following morning by throwing their breakfast overboard. Several angry men then threatened and assaulted Cowen. After reporting the attack, Commander Ammen met with the men "and saw the food they were getting—thought it was cooked very well." Ammen's comments did not calm the restive men and the following morning the breakfast again went overboard. The mob then overturned tables and furiously attacked Cowen, who fled the area fearing for his life (Ammen 1864).

Chief Engineer Elisha R. Phelps expected trouble after hearing the men's complaints, and on Sunday "the men made a rush ... I met them at the gate." Phelps pushed one of the agitators away from the gate, but another got through, prompting Commander Ammen's order to fire. During the skirmish, Phelps recalled that "the ball went through my thumb. I had my hand on the left breast of the man at the gate ... and the ball went into his left breast—right through his heart and he fell dead." Phelps justified the killing of the two men by believing that "the safety of the ship ... would be endangered unless the mutineers were forcibly dealt with" (Ammen 1864).

During the trial, Surgeon Edwin H. Gibbs testified that chaos erupted almost immediately after the ship left New York with the 220 draftees, with the men abusing the officers and engaging in fights among themselves. "One of them ... demanded that I should give them liquor. Upon my refusing he said that he or they ... would attend to my case." On another occasion, a sailor was stabbed, and in general "these sailors became so turbulent and used such language and threats that I was unable to attend to my duties forward." Like Phelps, Gibbs unequivocally stated, "I believed then and I still believe that they would have had entire control of the ship within fifteen minutes had not those measures been resorted to" (Ammen 1864).

Despite being responsible for prosecuting the case, Judge Advocate Perkins called witnesses who inadvertently provided testimony in favor of the officer. Even so, the accused officer cross-examined the prosecution witnesses and strengthened his case (Ammen 1864).

Lieutenant Commander James Parker read the lengthy defense statement to members of the general court-martial. According to the defense statement, the USS *Ocean Queen* departed from New York with a large group of civilian passengers, leaving the 220 drafted men to occupy cramped quarters. Ammen and the other officers sympathized with the men's plight and attempted to placate their frustration. As the evolving drama unfolded, Kelly and Bussell quickly assumed the role of chief instigators, bullying both crewmembers and drafted men. Ammen recalled that "Kelly proposed that a little whiskey would make all right—to which I dissented." With tensions mounting, Ammen expected a mutiny, armed his officers with pistols, and when Kelly and Bussell breached the gate, he ordered his men to fire. Interestingly, Ammen's defense statement was "duly sworn" by Stephen Johnson Field, an Associate Justice of the United States Supreme Court, a passenger on the USS *Ocean Queen*. The defense statement concluded with an appeal for acquittal because "my duty required me to act as I did, the necessity of the case required it, [and] self-defense permitted it" (Ammen 1864).

The five-day trial concluded with Ammen's acquittal. In reaching that verdict, the court-martial members reasoned that "the killing of John

Kelly and Alfred Bussell ... was done in the lawful discharge of the duty ... to suppress an attempted mutiny and in the opinion of the Court the same was Justifiable Homicide" (Ammen 1864).

A general court-martial held onboard the USS *Dale*, near Key West, Florida, on January 17, 1865, tested the impartiality and independence of seven officers assembled for the trial of Acting Ensign Charles H. Gaylor. Rear Admiral Cornelius K. Stribling, Commanding, East Gulf Blockading Squadron, preferred the charge of maltreatment of a landsman. The charge followed an incident on January 16, 1864, on board the USS *Proteus*, in the Key West Harbor, when the accused "maltreated Richard Shorten a landsman subject to his orders by pulling his Ear, Cursing and Kicking him" (Gaylor 1864).

Gaylor pleaded guilty except for cursing the landsman, forcing the court-martial members to briefly adjourn and consider whether to proceed with the trial. Upon returning, the court-martial directed the judge advocate to prosecute only the contested cursing. Three witnesses, a landsman, a seaman, and a private in the Marine Corps, subsequently testified. The two Navy men both denied hearing Gaylor curse Shorten, but Private Jacob Graw testified that "I heard the accused say to Richard Shorten—Damn you, I'll knock you about the deck—and when the accused kicked Shorten, he used the following expression—I'll kick you like that, damn you" (Gaylor 1864).

Gaylor called two witnesses, both of whom acknowledged that Shorten suffered no injuries because of the altercation. At the conclusion of Gaylor's defense, the judge advocate called upon Commander Robert W. Shufeldt, Commanding, USS *Proteus*, "to testify as to the previous character of the accused as well as extenuating circumstances ... which might mitigate the offense." Shufeldt praised Gaylor's zeal and general conduct but admitted that the officer was inexperienced (Gaylor 1864).

With all the evidence submitted, the court-martial members retired, deliberated, and then pronounced Gaylor guilty of maltreatment, but not guilty of cursing the man. The punishment meted out by the court-martial consisted of a 30-day suspension and a reprimand from Rear Admiral Cornelius K. Stribling (Gaylor 1864).

Admiral Stribling reviewed the trial's transcript and returned it to the court-martial's presiding officer "for revision." What rankled the senior officer was "the evidence of Jacob Graw Private Marine of the 'Proteus' was direct and established satisfactorily the charge of cursing." Stribling indirectly chastised the court-martial for dismissing Graw's testimony by favoring the two witnesses who supported the accused's defense. Stribling believed Gaylor was treated too leniently and the court-martial's actions undermined Navy law and discipline (Gaylor 1864).

In obedience to Stribling's order, the court-martial reconvened and subsequently stated "that the testimony of Jacob Graw ... was more than counterbalanced by evidence directly opposed to it ... by equally credible men ... as to the sentence the Court does not find any reason ... to change it." The court further noted that Shorten suffered no injuries and when he "reported the affair complained of none." Commander Shufeldt's positive character testimony also influenced the court's decision to spare Gaylor additional punishment. Stribling objected no further and simply dissolved the court-martial on January 20, 1864 (Gaylor 1864).

Crewmembers often traded insults, accusations, and profanity, which sometimes erupted into a violent confrontation. Such was the case when Rear Admiral Samuel Phillips Lee, Commanding, North Atlantic Blockading Squadron, convened a Navy general court-martial on board the USS *Sacramento* near Wilmington, North Carolina, on August 5, 1863. Lee preferred two charges against Coal Heaver John Murphy: assaulting and striking with murderous intent a fireman and contempt toward a senior officer (Murphy, J. 1863).

The judge advocate accused Murphy, while serving on board the USS *Chocura*, on May 19, 1863, of arming "himself with several murderous instruments, to wit, a sharp pointed Marlinspike and a knife ... and strike with intent to murder one Michael Cash 2nd Class Fireman." In the subsequent courtroom testimony, witnesses revealed that Murphy's refusal to help sweep ashes from the fireroom had been the innocuous beginning of the conflict. Heated words passed between the pair and soon boiled over, with Murphy throwing the first punch. During their altercation, Cash struck Murphy, and in the ensuing struggle, Murphy escalated the situation by wielding a marlinspike (Murphy, J. 1863).

Although he pleaded not guilty, Murphy's only defense was a plaintive request for mercy: "I am very sorry to have given the Court so much trouble ... I have a poor father and mother in Ireland and am their chief support ... and I promise to behave myself in future." The court-martial brushed Murphy's supplications aside and sentenced the accused to be confined in double irons for four months, deprived of his pay, and then dismissed with a bad conduct discharge (Murphy, J. 1863).

When the trial's transcript reached Rear Admiral Lee, he chided the court-martial and reminded the members that "the altercation originating between the parties implicated was such as often occur on shipboard." Lee further stated that Murphy's rage was not premeditated and did not justify the court-martial's sentence. The senior commander insisted that "if Murphy has been a sober well behaved man ... his service would be of value. I think forfeiture of half the pay and half the term of imprisonment would suffice" (Murphy, J. 1863).

Four. Violent Misconduct

At times, seemingly minor disagreements would turn violent, ultimately requiring resolution through a court-martial. First Class Boy Charles Bristow faced a military tribunal on board the USS *San Jacinto*, near Key West, Florida, on December 5, 1864, for assaulting First Class Boy Andrew Horn. The incident took place on Thanksgiving Day, November 24, 1864, in the yard of the Key West, Florida Contraband Headquarters. Bristow and Horn both worked for Naval Storekeeper John Philbrick (Bristow 1864).

First Class Boy Andrew Horn was placidly chopping a coconut open when the accused approached and demanded he surrender the ax. Horn refused and Bristow threatened to dump a pot of boiling water on the man. After being rebuffed once more, Bristow briefly departed but soon returned brandishing a pistol and threatening to shoot Horn. Bristow's intimidation backfired and Horn lunged at the man. As the two struggled, the pistol accidentally discharged, which caught the attention of a nearby group of contrabands, who quickly intervened and separated the combatants. The provost guard then placed the unruly pair in the "sweat box." After sorting out the facts of the fray, local authorities charged Charles Bristow with instigating the affair (Bristow 1864).

Bristow pleaded not guilty but offered no defense, relying on the court's mercy. In return, the court-martial sentenced Bristow to six months of hard labor, attached to a ball and chain, and to suffer solitary confinement at night (Bristow 1864).

Seaman Joseph Johns, attached to the USS *Mound City*, presented a novel defense at his court-martial held on board the USS *Louisville*, at Skipwith's Landing, Mississippi, on December 10, 1863. The judge advocate charged Johns with assault with intent to kill, an allegation that prompted the accused's not guilty pleading and the introduction of Seaman Patrick Sullivan as his defense counsel (Johns 1863).

The prosecution's first witness was Seaman Ambrose Garret, the victim of the assault. Garret was a lackluster witness. He acknowledged that the accused stabbed him twice in what appeared to him to be an unprovoked attack. Upon further questioning, the judge advocate discovered that Garret had reported the accused for disobedience, leading to the possibility that the attack had been motivated by revenge (Johns 1863).

Johns cross-examined Garret and quickly introduced his defense by asking, "Did something occur on the morning previous to the stabbing with me that would warrant the belief of insanity?" Garret replied, "Yes, that morning you went on the forecastle to wash and jumped overboard." Quartermaster James Smith witnessed the surprise attack on Garret and assumed that the accused was likely motivated by revenge. He also believed that Johns was not "of sound mind at the time of the stabbing" (Johns 1863).

Acting Assistant Surgeon Thomas Rice treated the victim's two wounds, neither of which was life-threatening. Rice believed that the accused was of sound mind, a conclusion likely drawn from the fact that Johns had never been under his medical care. Incredibly, Rice was unaware of Johns's jumping overboard, an opening for the accused to inquire, "As a physician do you think a man in sound mind would attempt to deprive himself of existence?" Rice simply replied, "I should not" (Johns 1863).

Johns presented a series of defense witnesses beginning with Captain of the Afterguard William Harrison, who testified, "I was on the forecastle washing myself when you came in the forecastle in double irons and jumped overboard. I caught hold of you and picked you up with the assistance of others. After you were hauled in, you made a second attempt to get overboard." Boatswain Thomas P. Parris corroborated Harrison's testimony: "I was on the forecastle when I saw you jump overboard, bidding me good-bye as you jumped." Acting Master Frederick T. Coleman believed Johns's suicide attempt was the result of a "deranged" mind (Johns 1863).

Seaman Patrick Sullivan presented a well-crafted defense statement on behalf of the accused during the trial. Sullivan argued that Johns was suffering from a mental disorder at the time of the alleged offense, citing Johns's previous suicide attempts as evidence. Sullivan quoted Johns as saying, "I was more inclined to injure myself than any other person," suggesting that Johns had no intention of harming anyone else (Johns 1863).

The three-day trial ended with the conviction of Johns for assault but without the intent to kill Garret. When deliberating on the appropriate punishment, the court reasoned that "in view of the deranged conditions of the mind of the accused ... the sentence of the court is he shall be confined in a lunatic asylum until he regains entire and complete possession of his mind" (Johns 1863).

Medical testimony was uncommon in courts-martial. Criminal trials relied on easily available eyewitness testimony, and the realities of war favored expeditious decisions. Expert witness testimony occasionally played a critical role in determining the outcome of trials, providing valuable insights into the development of military medical jurisprudence. An illustrative example involved Coal Heaver Cornelius Collins, attached to the USS *Isonomia* (Collins, C. 1864).

Rear Admiral Cornelius K. Stribling, Commanding, East Gulf Blockading Squadron, convened a Navy general court-martial on board the USS *San Jacinto*, near Key West, Florida, on December 9, 1864. Stribling preferred the charge of disobeying a lawful order and striking a superior officer. The alleged incident took place on board the USS *Isonomia* while anchored at St. George's Sound near Apalachicola, Florida, on October 18, 1864. Collins refused an order by Acting Third Assistant Francis C. Lomas

USS *Isonomia* (NH 53280, courtesy of the Naval History & Heritage Command).

"to wash out a bucket" while in the fireroom. When subsequently ordered on deck to explain his behavior, the accused "did there strike with his fist his superior officer." The accused pleaded guilty and requested the assistance of Samuel Curry for his defense (Collins, C. 1864).

There was agreement among all the prosecution witnesses that Lomas received a complaint about Collins bathing from a bucket designated for drinking water. Hollering from above, Lomas ordered the accused to scrub the bucket, but Collins resisted, complaining that other men had bathed in the water before him. Collins's refusal prompted Lomas to order the man to the main deck, where the alleged confrontation took place. Disparate testimony from both prosecution and defense witnesses made it unclear who threw the first punch. Although none of the witnesses saw Lomas strike the accused, several did observe blood trickling from Collins's lip and speculated that it was a result of Lomas hitting him (Collins, C. 1864).

Provocation was a weak defense, a reality Collins and his defense counsel probably understood. Collins's main defense rested on a tapeworm, and it was Acting Assistant Surgeon Atwood Crosby who provided the testimony to support that claim. As the first defense witness, Crosby testified that the accused had epilepsy, a condition resulting "from a tape worm in the intestine." While on board the USS *Isonomia*, Collins suffered five seizures, leading Crosby to remove "seventeen feet ... [of] common tape worm." Crosby acknowledged that epilepsy could "impair mental powers ... and long continuance of such disease tends to Mania, Dementia, and Idiocy." Crosby also agreed with the accused's contention that "these attacks visit him at any time ... depriving him of reason and making him oblivious to surrounding objects" (Collins, C. 1864).

Collins next called Fleet Surgeon Edward Gilchrist, East Gulf Blockading Squadron, who agreed that "epileptic convulsions produced by tape worm in the intestine ... is very apt to affect the soundness of any person's intellect." Despite that conclusion, Gilchrist believed that "his temper might be under his control" (Collins, C. 1864).

In his defense statement, Collins acknowledged his guilty pleading, but he also presented an argument in support of mitigation to the court-martial. Although he briefly mentioned Lomas's role in the incident, the majority of Collins's defense centered around the tapeworm. Collins contended that the unwelcome tapeworm caused his seizures and mental unsoundness. Surgeon Crosby testified that he removed seventeen feet of the tapeworm, but Collins argued "that the head, the vital part, and a portion of the body still remains ... weakening my power of self control." In a particularly novel manner, Collins's defense statement also quoted medical authorities of the time, including Dr. John Neill, who wrote that "epilepsy frequently ends in insanity" (Neill and Smith 1856, 969). When referencing the psychiatrist Jean-Étienne Dominique Esquirol, Collins added that "the great Esquirol says insanity with epilepsy is uncurable" (Collins, C. 1864).

The court-martial members dismissed Collins's assertion that Lomas instigated the altercation and instead recommended that the accused be hanged, citing the Navy law that requires appropriate punishment for the offense committed. After sentencing Collins, the court-martial members recommended mercy because "the court, however, is impressed by the testimony of Medical Officers ... and in consideration of the state of health of the accused and the probable effect that his disease of epilepsy may have had ... recommend him to the clemency of the reviewing authority" (Collins, C. 1864).

A court of inquiry convened on board the USS *Brandywine*, Hampton Roads, Virginia, on February 10, 1863, to determine the responsibility of Marine Corps Private John Britt in the death of "Negro, James Bromley." The court of inquiry's recorder presented a cross section of both officers and enlisted members to unravel the shooting death of "Contraband Bromley." Based on the evidence presented, the court discovered that Britt was cleaning a loaded musket, a practice that seemed to be commonplace but was in clear contravention of shipboard regulations. The weapon discharged, hurling a Minié ball that struck Bromley in the neck and instantly killed the man. A pale-faced Britt said it was an accident, but aside from that brief comment he remained impassive. The witnesses all agreed that Britt "was not a very good character on board ship." Orderly Sergeant Edward Sweeney testified, "I have always looked upon him as not being fit for the service—not being right in the head" (Britt 1863).

Upon careful consideration of all the testimony, the court of inquiry concluded that Bromley's death was accidental. However, the court censured Britt's disobedience due to his removal of the loaded musket and reckless handling of the weapon. With that said, the court responded to Britt's "indifferent manner throughout the investigation and the evidence before the Court induces the belief that the accused is practically idiotic" (Britt 1863).

The trial of Marine Corps Captain John C. Grayson was notable for the legal wranglings that consumed the court-martial that convened at the Marine Barracks, Brooklyn, New York, on January 18, 1864. Judge Advocate John M. Guiteau accused Grayson of drunkenness and "using provoking words to, and striking, an officer of the Marine Corps." Setting the tone for what followed, Grayson objected to one of the court members, citing the man's long-standing hostility. The court-martial countered by demanding more details, after which Grayson withdrew his objection, pleaded not guilty, and introduced Robert D. Holmes as his defense counsel (Grayson 1864).

Judge Advocate Guiteau presented only two witnesses. The first was Marine Corps Captain Clement D. Hobb, the victim of the alleged offense. Hobb testified, "I heard someone kicking violently against one of my doors—I had two rooms." After opening the undamaged door, Hobb observed Lieutenant Meeker and the accused "tussling together." When Grayson spotted Hobb he belligerently and profanely exclaimed, "I have heard you have reported me." Grayson managed to break free from the lieutenant's grip, which prompted a response from Hobb: "I then told Mr. Meeker to take him away ... that he was drunk." Grayson then hit Hobb on the arm and "the accused tried to strike me again and I threw my left hand up to fend off the blow and struck the accused in the face somewhere" (Grayson 1864).

During the trial, Grayson and the judge advocate engaged in frequent interruptions, with each man objecting to the other's line of questioning. The judge advocate was successful in blocking questions that challenged the credibility of his witnesses, whereas Grayson's objections were often overruled by the court. Grayson criticized the court's apparent bias against him in his defense statement.

Second Lieutenant George B. Haycock was the prosecution's last witness. Haycock probably disappointed the judge advocate when he failed to connect the bruise on the victim's arm to Grayson's assault. Guiteau closed his case following Haycock's brief appearance (Grayson 1864).

The first defense witness, Marine Corps Lieutenant Edward P. Meeker, contradicted critical aspects of the prosecution's case. Meeker claimed that Grayson was not drunk and that "I considered him perfectly sober." Meeker also observed Hobb push the accused, immediately after which Grayson struck the man. Hobb responded with profanity and returned the blow that sent "Captain Grayson staggering back." Meeker also refuted Hobb's contention that he "tussled" with Grayson (Grayson 1864).

A curious courtroom anomaly derailed the trial on February 2, 1864, when Grayson was absent, forcing the court-martial's premature adjournment. During the brief interlude, Grayson and his commanding officer exchanged a series of letters. When the court-martial reassembled the next day, the judge advocate sought to introduce the letters as evidence. Grayson vigorously objected, claiming "that it is irregular and wrong and may tend to prejudice the accused." After briefly considering the objection, the court-martial overruled Grayson and admitted the documents (Grayson 1864).

After the favorable ruling, the judge advocate read a letter from the commanding officer reminding Grayson that "you will not leave the Garrison until duly notified by proper authority." In his written response, Grayson complained that he had "a very important engagement with my counsel ... I was informed by the Sentry on post that he had strict orders from you not to let me go out ... Now Sir, permit me to say, that you have outraged and insulted the very delicate sensibility of my nature ... I am a gentleman and a man of honor and am ready and willing at all times to revenge an insult." In closing the letter, Grayson suggested that the commanding officer should "have informed me in private that I could not leave the quarters" (Grayson 1864).

With the derogatory documents admitted, despite Grayson's objections, the court-martial members next listened as Robert D. Holmes read the accused's defense statement. The defense statement opened respectfully: "The accused it is hoped will not be understood as in any manner censoring the rulings of the Court ... but he certainly regrets ... the rejecting of the evidence to which he has referred." Grayson then reminded the court-martial members that only three individuals participated in the quarrel; the victim, the accused, and an impartial eyewitness who contradicted Hobb's version. With that in mind, Grayson argued that the evidence tilted in his favor. The overall tone of Grayson's defense statement was pessimistic, reflecting his expectation of an unfavorable outcome, which was subsequently confirmed when the court-martial found him guilty of both charges and recommended his dismissal from the service (Grayson 1864).

Justice was delayed but not denied when Secretary of the Navy Gideon Welles disapproved of Grayson's sentence. In a rebuke to the court-martial, Welles stated that Grayson should have faced a Navy Retiring Board and not a criminal trial. As a consequence, Grayson officially retired on April 22, 1864 (Sullivan 1997, 307).

A Navy general court-martial convened on board the USS *Potomac*, in Pensacola Bay, Florida, on April 29, 1864, and charged Marine Corps Private Edward Harrington with assault. The alleged offense occurred on

April 7, 1864, at the Marine Barracks, Pensacola Navy Yard, when Harrington, "seize[d] by the beard Orderly Sergeant George Gassman ... and did kick with his feet ... in the groin" (Harrington, E. 1864).

The judge advocate presented three witnesses who collectively testified that Harrington was absent from training. A few hours later the tardy man reported to Gassman and was angry that the orderly sergeant had reported his absence. With a profane outburst, Harrington then grabbed Gassman's beard and tugged for several minutes while onlookers laughed at the orderly sergeant's plight. The ruckus continued until the sergeant of the guard arrested the accused (Harrington, E. 1864).

For his defense, Harrington called three Marine Corps privates. Their testimony differed dramatically, claiming that Gassman was the belligerent who attacked the accused. They also testified that both men were drunk. Private James H. Bonner testified that "it would be difficult to tell which was the drunkest, the Sergeant or Harrington." Harrington's arguments did not convince the court-martial members, who found the accused guilty and sentenced him to one year in prison followed by a dishonorable discharge (Harrington, E. 1864).

Enlisted members of the Marine Corps were typically subjected to military trials that emulated the Army's general court-martial format, which emphasized brevity. As a perfunctory example, Marine Corps Private Charles Barry faced a court-martial on May 23, 1863. The judge advocate charged Barry with assaulting and striking an orderly sergeant on May 6, 1863, onboard the USS *Octorara*, near Key West, Florida. Barry pleaded guilty to the charge and then, no doubt regrettably, called First Lieutenant Cornelius M. Schoonmaker as a character witness. Schoonmaker testified that Barry "has been in trouble at various times ... He has not sustained a good character on board ship previous to the matter with which he here stands charged." Schoonmaker's testimony probably sealed Barry's fate. Afterward, the court-martial found the accused guilty and imposed a six-month prison term and a dishonorable discharge (Barry 1863).

Like the Navy, the Union Army convened courts of inquiry, sometimes upon request from an officer seeking to clarify allegations of misconduct. Lieutenant Thomas E. Turner, 4th Regiment, United States Infantry, requested a court of inquiry to examine "the circumstances connected with the shooting of Private Halter, 4th Cavalry, by the said Lieutenant Turner." In response to Turner's request, a court of inquiry assembled at the Headquarters of the Army of the Potomac, in Washington, D.C., on January 13, 1862 (Turner 1862).

Based on the testimony, the court of inquiry learned that Private Halter "in managing his horse on Pennsylvania Avenue in the city of Washington" attracted the attention of a large, unruly crowd. Turner repeatedly ordered Halter to stop the disruptive behavior, to no avail. The crowd's instigation of Halter's disobedience fueled a dangerous state of anarchy, prompting Turner to decide that he "had a right, at all times, to correct any irregularity that came under his attention." Turner awaited a mounted sentry to execute his order, but Halter sensed the danger and began to leave. Seeing no alternative, Turner shot and killed the man (Turner 1862).

In judging Turner's use of deadly force, the court reasoned that "a wiser discretion might not have resorted to it, yet in time of war, the enforcement of his authority ... was paramount to any other consideration." Major General George B. McClellan agreed with the court's judgment, declaring that "it is often the duty of an officer, sword in hand, to enforce obedience to his orders ... The position of Lieutenant Turner was a very difficult one ... unless Halter was stopped he would have escaped all punishment" (Turner 1862).

A fatal error doomed a military trial but resurrected Private Louis Ahlus, Company B, "Major Backoff's Volunteer Battalion of Artillery," from certain death at a firing squad. According to the military specification, Ahlus "did this day, September 17th, 1861, willfully murder his superior officer. Lieutenant Frank Wolf." Ahlus pleaded not guilty, but the short trial ended with his conviction and the military commission sentenced the man to be shot to death. Major General Henry Halleck reviewed the trial proceedings and faulted the military commission for exceeding its legal jurisdiction when "the prisoner should have been tried by a Court Martial." Ahlus dodged a bullet when Halleck was "reluctantly compelled to disapprove the entire proceedings, and to order the release of the prisoner" (Ahlus 1861).

Private Joseph Kuhnes, Company I, 2nd Regiment, Maryland Infantry, was less fortunate when he appeared before a general court-martial held on December 12, 1861, in Baltimore, Maryland. The judge advocate charged Kuhnes with violation of the 9th Article of War for "violence against his superior officer Second Lieutenant David Whitson ... by discharging a loaded musket into the body of said Whitson and thereby causing his death" (Kuhnes 1861).

The prosecution's witnesses incontrovertibly proved that the accused wantonly fired a musket at the back of the officer, resulting in his nearly instantaneous death. It also came to light that Kuhnes nurtured a grudge and openly threatened the officer several times, with the prescient warnings dismissed by Whitson (Kuhnes 1861).

Kuhnes did not contest the murder charge. After admitting his guilt, Kuhnes relied on two intertwining arguments to avoid a death sentence. One of the witnesses provided insight into the accused's motivation, testifying that "a week before the act, that he [Kuhnes] had learned that the deceased had been too familiar with his wife." The second witness testified that Whitson had arrested the accused before and had confined him to the guardhouse. While Kuhnes was being held, the witness observed the officer "coming out of the House of the Prisoner at an early hour in the morning" (Kuhnes 1861).

The second argument put forth by the defense portrayed Kuhnes as being mentally unsound. Veterinary Surgeon James M. Donald testified about an incident related to domestic violence. "From deeds he committed I thought he was not in his right mind ... he committed strange deeds, breaking his own furniture, and I saw a pistol held eighteen or twenty inches from his head and he never moved a bit." The police officer who arrested Kuhnes testified that "in my opinion no sober or rational man could act as he did. I think he had been drinking liquor" (Kuhnes 1861).

Dr. James E. Healey treated Kuhnes for a fever a few days before the murder and considered him "a man of feeble mind." Healey noticed that Kuhnes "was also very nervous and appeared to be suffering from want of a stimulant. I considered that he had been a drinking man and had not had the usual stimulants for the twelve hours preceding my visit." To correct that deficiency, Healey prescribed brandy and morphine (Kuhnes 1861).

Kuhnes' two-pronged defense mingled a crime of passion with insanity. In closing his defense, Kuhnes proposed "an inquiry by a proper board into the mental condition of the Prisoner; for it would be a sad thing that the ultimate punishment of the law should be adjudged against one in whose case any reasonable doubt exists upon such a point." After considering the defense arguments, the court-martial rejected them and sentenced the man to death by hanging (Kuhnes 1861).

Private John Collins, Company B, 62nd Regiment, New York Infantry, faced a general court-martial, charged with conduct prejudicial to good order and military discipline. The judge advocate provided the details, alleging that on November 17, 1861, Collins "did assault a Private of said Company, who was lying asleep in his tent, in a most brutal and violent manner, without cause or provocation." Collins pleaded not guilty, but the court-martial determined otherwise and sentenced the accused to forfeit ten dollars for six months and spend 30 days in confinement with a ball and chain (Collins, J. 1862). The relatively light sentence for the "brutal" assault probably resulted from the judge advocate charging the accused with conduct prejudicial to good order and military discipline instead of assault. Collins deserted on August 15, 1862, at Harrison's Landing, Virginia ("Unit Roster 62nd Infantry Regiment" 1893).

At a general court-martial convened on May 8, 1863, at Jefferson City, Missouri, Private William Stephens, Company B, 6th Regiment, Missouri

State Militia Cavalry, listened as the judge advocate charged him for murder. According to the military specification that accompanied the charge of murder, Stephens "willfully, maliciously, and with malice aforethought, kill and murder one Barney Kennedy." Although Stephens pleaded not guilty, he implicitly acknowledged killing Kennedy by objecting only to the language claiming he acted "willfully, maliciously, and with malice aforethought." The court-martial found the accused guilty but removed the elements of premeditation, no doubt sparing the man's life. Stephens was sentenced to 25 years of hard labor at the military prison in Alton, Illinois (Stephens 1863).

Modifying a court-martial sentence was a power entrusted to the trial's convening authority and President Lincoln. Apart from the authorized means, some convicted service members managed to avoid punishment by seeking the assistance of prominent members of society, who, in turn, influenced the authorized channels. Others resorted to escaping from confinement, and unfortunately, for some, death resulted from an illness or injury. Such was the case with Private Andrew Jackson, Company A, 74th Regiment, United States Colored Infantry, charged with murder at a general court-martial convened on January 18, 1865, in New Orleans, Louisiana (Jackson 1865).

Jackson joined the Union Army in New Orleans on October 29, 1862, after which the scant records provided few additional details. Based on the information available, it appears that he was placed in a guard house in November 1864, presumably in anticipation of his upcoming court-martial (Jackson 1862). Jackson pleaded not guilty, but the court-martial found the accused guilty and on or about January 18, 1865, sentenced him "to be hanged by the neck until dead" (Jackson 1865). Less than a month later, on February 16, 1865, the Corps d'Afrique General Hospital in New Orleans reported Jackson's death from smallpox in a medical certificate sent to the "Officer in Charge, Parrish Prison, New Orleans, LA" (Jackson 1862).

The general court-martial of Colonel Michael K. Lawler, 18th Regiment, Illinois Infantry, convened at Cairo, Illinois, on December 11, 1861. There were five separate military charges accompanied by fourteen specifications, presumably reflecting the judge advocate's determination to convict the senior officer. The most serious allegation stated that Lawler "on or about the 2d day of October 1861, knowingly permit[ted] Private Robert Dickman, of Company G, 18th Regiment Illinois Volunteers, to be taken by the soldiers of his command, and, without trial or sentence by a General Court Martial, or other competent authority, to he hung by the neck until dead" (Lawler 1862).

Another specification stated that the officer "order[ed] and cause[d] tartar emetic, ipecac, or some other noxious drugs, to be put into whisky and sent to the soldiers of his command who were confined in the guard house, and said soldiers were thereby induced to drink said mixture, which caused dangerous and severe illness." The remaining specifications described Lawler's brutality, such as assaulting enlisted soldiers and threatening subordinate officers (Lawler 1862).

Lawler pleaded not guilty to all five charges and fourteen specifications. The court-martial returned mixed verdicts, but on the most serious charge of permitting a soldier's illegal hanging, he was found guilty and sentenced to be dismissed from the service (Lawler 1862).

Major General Henry W. Halleck reviewed the court-martial proceedings in Lawler's trial and conceded that "the evidence shows that irregularities have occurred in mustering, and in the way of drunkenness, punishments." After that admission, Halleck systematically deconstructed the court-martial's findings. Regarding the illegal hanging, Halleck noted, "Col. Lawler was improperly charged and found guilty of violating the 87th Article of War. The accused objected to his being tried upon said charge and specification, but the Court overruled said objection, tried and found the accused guilty." Halleck also maintained that the evidence did not support the prosecution's allegation that the whisky containing ipecac or tartar emetic caused dangerous illness among the prisoners. After citing other technical violations of military law, Halleck disapproved the sentence and returned Lawler to active duty (Lawler 1862). Colonel Lawler's career survived the general court-martial and he served with distinction throughout the remainder of the Civil War (Allen 2010, 38–39).

Union authorities seldom handed out the severest penalties to officers, and no officers were executed. Additionally, prison sentences for officers were uncommon. An exception involved the trial of First Lieutenant Isaac H. Sisson, Company D, 1st Regiment, Missouri State Militia Infantry, charged with murder by a general court-martial convened at St. Louis, Missouri. The judge advocate alleged that Sisson, on or about April 20, 1863, "without just cause or provocation, cause one John Boyle, a citizen, to be shot to death, the said Boyle being, at the time, in the pursuit of his ordinary and peaceful avocations." The court found the officer guilty but lessened the charge to fourth-degree manslaughter. Sisson's punishment included a dismissal, a one hundred dollar fine, and six months of imprisonment at the military prison in Alton, Illinois (Sisson 1863). Sisson's incarceration ended happily when President Lincoln issued a pardon on December 31, 1863, and ordered the man's release from custody (Sisson 1863).

Second Lieutenant H.A. Hawkes, 56th Regiment, New York Infantry, resorted to extreme measures to force Private Robert Cooper, of the same unit, to divulge the source of his illegal alcohol. For his efforts, Hawkes faced a general court-martial held at Hilton Head, South Carolina, on January 8, 1865. The judge advocate charged Hawkes with conduct to the prejudice of good order and military discipline and conduct unbecoming an officer and a gentleman (Hawkes 1865).

Hawkes improperly confined Cooper for 26 days and "did inflict a cruel and unusual punishment ... by confining said Cooper in an iron collar ... to the physical injury of said Cooper ... in order to make him confess where he had obtained liquor." The court-martial issued a mixed verdict, finding the accused only guilty of illegal confinement. Hawkes's punishment consisted of a reprimand with "the Court ... lenient in view of the uniform good character of the accused, and the conflicting testimony of the witnesses for the prosecution" (Hawkes 1865).

Sexual Misconduct

This section grouped rape, attempted rape, and sodomy as sexual misconduct based on the representative database analyzed in this volume. Courts-martial charged less egregious examples of sexual misconduct against officers as conduct unbecoming an officer and a gentleman. Sexual conduct unbecoming of an officer and a gentleman encompassed a range of improprieties, such as insulting a woman, making inappropriate advances, and soliciting prostitutes. Courts-martial convictions emphasized the damage to the military's reputation in cases involving sexual misconduct unbecoming an officer and a gentleman. Prosecutors charged similar examples of sexual misconduct against enlisted service members as conduct to the prejudice of good order and military discipline.

An interesting dichotomy emerged among the military services based on the representative database analyzed in this volume. The representative database identified only one example of an alleged rape in the Navy and none in the Marine Corps. Navy prosecutors charged several men with sodomy, but the representative database did not find any instances of courts-martial charging service members from the Marine Corps or Union Army with that specific offense.

The representative database analyzed for this volume identified 24 service members who faced specific allegations of rape. This group included only one officer and one Navy landsman, both of whom courts-martial found not guilty. Courts-martial convicted 20 of the remaining 22 Army soldiers. Most of the rape trials (16/24, 66.7%) in this representative database took place in 1864. Courts-martial largely convicted service members found guilty of rape (20/24, 83.3%).

To prosecute sexual misconduct, eyewitness testimony was necessary, including the alleged victim's description of the incident. Legal books available during the Civil War rarely discussed sexual misconduct. An exception was a brief entry in O'Brien's *A Treatise on American Military Laws, and the Practice of Courts Martial* that referenced the 63rd Article of War, which set forth that "for rape, the punishment will be five years' imprisonment; if committed on a girl under fourteen years of age, the punishment will be degradation, and ten years imprisonment. If violence, or the assistance of others is used, the punishment will be doubled. If death ensues from the crime, or from the violence used, the punishment will be death" (O'Brien 1846, 532).

In terms of specific criminal acts, researchers have paid more attention to desertion and murder than to rape during the Civil War. Part of that oversight stems from an assumption that "most historians, however, agree that rape during the Civil War was uncommon, although the probability [is] that a number of rapes went unreported" (Buhk 2012, 7). According to an alternate analysis, members of the Union Army were more inclined to harass Southern women, although they usually refrained from committing rape. However, Black women were less likely to receive the benefit of such restraint (Sheehan-Dean 2018, 307).

Several factors played a role in downplaying the prevalence of rapes during the Civil War. Reticence was surely paramount, as victims avoided the embarrassment and scrutiny that followed an allegation. Successful prosecution required evidence of the victim's resistance and capitulation under the threat of death. Allegations of rape were often disregarded in the absence of physical evidence that could prove the assailant's guilt, which worked in favor of the defense. In many cases, victims were intimidated by armed soldiers and could not provide sufficient physical evidence, making it difficult to arrive at a just resolution based on the prevailing rules of evidence (Sheehan-Dean 2018, 310–311).

Authors E. Susan Barber and Charles F. Ritter investigated rape in "Dangerous Liaisons: Working Women and Sexual Justice in the American Civil War" (Barber and Ritter 2015). The authors focused on women "paid and unpaid" who worked alongside Army soldiers, providing essential services in the laundry, the hospitals, and the preparation of food. This proximity increased the risk of violence, according to the authors (Barber and Ritter 2015, 3).

Based on specific examples of rape and attempted rape, the authors concluded that "the number of sexual assaults that can be documented through surviving records represents a fraction of those that actually occurred" (Barber and Ritter 2015, 5). Unfortunately, the lack of surviving records leads to a void that speculation may not accurately fill. Setting that criticism aside, the authors make an important observation from the existing records, noting that Union courts-martial took a significant step toward the evolution of military justice during the Civil War by allowing testimony from Black women who had been assaulted by White soldiers (Barber and Ritter 2015, 6).

Kim Murphy offers another scholarly work in *I Had Rather Die: Rape in the Civil War*. The author discusses the nineteenth-century approach to rape in terms of both jurisprudence and Victorian morals, the evidentiary burden rape victims encountered, an extensive review of sexual assault cases during the Civil War, and the punishments inflicted. Murphy investigated the unequal treatment of Black female victims and Black soldiers accused of rape (Murphy, K. 2014).

Murphy's research identified 450 cases of rape and attempted rape during the Civil War but admits that "with rape rarely reported during the era, any figure is meaningless" (Murphy, K. 2014, 603). According to the author, Union courts-martial punished Black soldiers severely but "few were actually executed for the crime" (Murphy, K. 2014, 44). Murphy also revealed the role alcohol misuse played among eight of the White soldiers executed for rape (Murphy, K. 2014, 61).

Soldiers accused of rape employed various strategies to rebut the military charge. Intoxication was perhaps the most common defense, often paired with testimony that described the man's typical sobriety and good character. Soldiers challenged the victim's credibility by questioning her resistance to the assault and her lack of physical injuries, and by impugning her morality (Murphy, K. 2014, 12–13). Even a court-martial conviction brought limited solace, as post-trial reviews often reversed or remitted the outcomes, although the present volume found this trend running throughout all military trials.

Judith Giesberg in *Sex and the Civil War* examined the topic by exploring the influence of pornography on the "sexual culture of the camps" (Giesberg 2017, 6). The mass publication of erotic magazines, books, and postcard-sized photographs known as cartes de visite, combined with mail delivery, ensured that every interested soldier had access to these materials. The author's central thesis suggests that female pictures, whether obscene or not, "encouraged fraternity among the men, with the images serving as unspoken communication between them of emotions barely acknowledged—homesickness, of course, but also desire" (Giesberg 2017, 52). Whether pornography reduced or enhanced tendencies toward sexual assault remained an unresolved question.

Thomas Lowry offered readers of popular history an entertaining look at *The Story Soldiers Wouldn't Tell: Sex in the Civil War* (Lowry 2012). Lowry's book is a potpourri of scholarly study infused with heaping doses of sauciness. He begins with a straw man argument that "it would appear thus far that we have an event unparalleled in history: a war free of sexual activity" (Lowry 2012, 5). Lowry then deconstructs that premise with a fusillade of facts. For example, Lowry cites the rate of venereal disease in the Union Army and the ever-present prostitutes as evidence of rampant sexual activity (Lowry 2012, 78–82). Lowry surveyed five percent of Army courts-martial records and uncovered "more than thirty trials for rape" (Lowry 2012, 123). The author also noted a proclivity to attack Black women and seemingly arbitrary courts-martial judgments that punished Black soldiers more severely (Lowry 2012, 130–131).

This volume utilized a representative database to examine instances of sexual misconduct in the Union Navy and Marine Corps, topics that modern historical researchers have largely overlooked. In a rare comment on the subject, one authoritative source declared that not one Marine faced a Navy general court-martial for rape during the Civil War (Sullivan 1997, 279).

Modern historical research on sodomy prosecution during the Civil War is limited. Furthermore, at that time, there were no specific legal procedures established for its prosecution. Richard Burg examined "Sodomy, Masturbation, and Courts-Martial in the Antebellum American Navy" (Burg 2014). Between 1805 and 1840 the Navy prosecuted only two cases of sodomy. Burg speculated "that the Navy was more discomfited than enraged by public airings of untoward sexual activity on board its ships" (Burg 2014, 68). That same analysis probably applied to the Union Navy during the Civil War, even though the representative database used for this volume revealed 16 trials involving allegations of sodomy.

During the Civil War, military officials rarely prosecuted sexual misconduct of any kind. However, research that focuses exclusively on rape overlooks the broader range of violence against women and how courts-martial managed such allegations. An early example involved Private John Ricker, Company A, 11th Regiment, Massachusetts Infantry, charged with being AWOL and conduct prejudicial to good order and military discipline. Without permission, Ricker left his unit while stationed near Bladensburg, Maryland, on September 12, 1861, and entered the nearby house of Belinda Jones. Armed with a stick he "did use threatening, insulting, and infamous language to, and did greatly terrify the said Belinda Jones" (Ricker 1861).

The court-martial members found Ricker guilty and sentenced him to "wear a barrel over his shoulders, eight hours daily, with the following placard: This is the man who insults respectable females." After reviewing the case, Major General George B. McClellan denounced the trivial sentence and remarked that "offering insults to respectable females, is one which will never be lightly passed over by the Major General

Commanding. There are few crimes calling for more condign punishment." McClellan rightly noted that without military discipline, peaceful citizens would fear the army and lawless soldiers would "bring reproach on the name and noble profession of the soldier" (Ricker 1861). With his closing comment, McClellan ordered the court-martial to reconsider Ricker's sentence. After McClellan's admonishment, the court-martial reconvened on February 3, 1862, and they reaffirmed Ricker's guilt. The court-martial members revised Ricker's punishment to six months in prison, followed by a dishonorable discharge (Ricker 1862).

A court-martial convicted Captain Thomas Radcliff, 18th Regiment, New York Infantry, of conduct unbecoming an officer and a gentleman for living with "and having the relation of man and wife with a woman of infamous reputation." Perhaps Radcliff's most unpardonable conduct involved introducing the woman as his wife to other officers throughout October 1861, an embarrassment that justified his dismissal from the Army (Radcliff 1862).

In the case of Major Theodore Lichtenheim, 58th Regiment, New York Infantry, the judge advocate charged the man with conduct unbecoming an officer and a gentleman, alleging that he "did occupy a box seat in the Theatre in company with two notorious harlots. This at Washington, DC on the evening of the 16th of November 1861." Once again, the blight on the Army's reputation convinced the court-martial to dismiss Lichtenheim (Lichtenheim 1862).

Captain George S. Merrill, Company G, Purnell Legion, Maryland Infantry, appeared before a court-martial convened at Fort Delaware, Delaware. The judge advocate charged Merrill with conduct unbecoming an officer and a gentleman for multiple occurrences of sexual misconduct spanning the period from July through early September 1863. The earliest example alleged that Merrill had "sexual intercourse with a female, name unknown, in a public and conspicuous manner." The ninth specification alleged that the officer "did induce certain females to go to his private quarters, under the pretence of sending for a friend, for whom they had enquired, and while awaiting the arrival of said friend ... did throw [one of the females] ... upon the bed and pull up her clothes, and was only prevented from further indignities by the alarm she raised." In between these two allegations, the judge advocate charged Merrill with seven counts of vulgar and indecent behavior toward other women (Merrill 1863).

Merrill's court-martial found the officer guilty of conduct unbecoming an officer and a gentleman and sentenced the man dismissed from the Army. Through unknown interventions, the War Department restored Merrill to his former command in February 1863. Upon his return, Merrill fraudulently received "pay from the thirty-first day of December 1862, knowing that he was not entitled to any part of the same previous to the fifth day of February." General Orders Number 52, published on October 21, 1863, documented Merrill's subsequent dismissal from the Army (Merrill 1863).

A general court-martial charged Second Lieutenant R. Warnick, 41st Regiment, Illinois Infantry, with conduct unbecoming an officer and a gentleman for disorderly behavior in Paducah, Kentucky, on October 6, 1861. Warnick was intoxicated and "with one or more soldiers [broke] into a dwelling house ... occupied by Mrs. Jeanes ... and committed acts of outrage therein." The court-martial found the officer guilty and sentenced him to be dismissed from the service (Warnick 1862).

One of the highest-ranking officers accused of sexual misconduct was Colonel Richard White, 55th Regiment, Pennsylvania Infantry. The judge advocate accused White of violently forcing guard while intoxicated at Camp Hamilton, Virginia, in November 1861, and with violation of the 45th Article of War for a prolonged bout of drunken behavior on August 4, 1862. The judge advocate's most serious charge alleged that White, on June 26, 1862, at Edisto Island, South Carolina, "did run after a negro woman and caught the said negro woman, and threw her on the ground, and then and there did attempt to violate her, the negro woman's person." After reviewing the evidence, the court-martial acquitted the senior officer. Major General Ormsby M. Mitchell approved the trial's proceedings, but about the alleged sexual transgression he commented "that the conduct charged upon Colonel White, and of which some unknown person appears to be guilty, richly merits the reprobation of every officer and soldier in the service" (White 1862). After the acquittal, White returned to active service and was mustered out on March 23, 1865, with the rank of Colonel (Bates 1869b, 181).

Another officer experienced a different fate. First Lieutenant George W. O'Malley, Company E, 115th Regiment, Pennsylvania Infantry, appeared before a court-martial that convened on June 3, 1863, near Falmouth, Virginia. The judge advocate charged the officer with conduct unbecoming an officer and a gentleman and "attempting to commit a rape in a military camp of the United States" (O'Malley 1863).

O'Malley received orders to escort "Mrs. Mercy M. Whippey, of Camden, New Jersey" to visit her son hospitalized at the Second Division Hospital located near Potomac Creek, Virginia. Based on an event that took place around midnight on May 31, 1863, the judge advocate accused O'Malley of "an assault with intent to commit a rape upon the person of Mercy M. Whippey ... and did attempt to ravish her by holding her down with great force and violence and kissing against her will ... his intent and purpose of having carnal connection with her person against her will." O'Malley pleaded not guilty, but the evidence considered by the court-martial resulted in a guilty verdict. The court-martial members punished the officer with a dismissal, loss of pay, and six years in prison (O'Malley 1863).

Private J.P. Ballard, Company F, 3rd Regiment, Kentucky Infantry, and Private E.M. Everett, Company F, 9th Regiment, Pennsylvania Reserve Infantry, both left the United States General Hospital at Annapolis Junction, Maryland, without permission and covertly traveled to the nearby home of Charles Haslup. The two soldiers somehow knew that Haslup was not at home on February 16, 1863, leaving his daughters Henrietta and Louisa alone in the house. Ballard and Everett forced their way into Haslup's house, determined to "take improper liberties" with the two women. When Haslup's son attempted to intervene, the two soldiers threatened "to shoot down any person" who interfered (Ballard and Everett 1863).

Ballard and Everett's court-martial convened at Baltimore, Maryland, and charged the two soldiers with AWOL and conduct to the prejudice of good order and military discipline. The court found Ballard guilty of being AWOL, but the members were unimpressed with the evidence involving sexual misconduct and extracted one month's pay as punishment. Everett was similarly found not guilty of taking "improper liberties." The court delivered a perplexing verdict, finding Everett guilty of assaulting Haslup's son, who caught the two men engaging in the alleged indecent behavior. The court-martial members sentenced Everett to four months of hard labor and the loss of ten dollars per month (Ballard and Everett 1863).

Union authorities did not execute Army officers during the Civil War even when the crimes seemingly justified its imposition. Second Lieutenant Harvey H. John appeared before a general court-martial convened at Tullahoma, Tennessee, on August 9, 1863. The judge advocate charged John with rape, assault, battery with intent to commit rape, and straggling (John 1864).

One day before his court-martial convened, on August 8, 1863, John "did assault, strike, and beat Mrs. Catherine Farmer ... and forcibly and unlawfully ravish and carnally know Mrs. Catherine Farmer." Despite his pleading not guilty, the weight of the evidence against John resulted in a guilty verdict. The court-martial sentenced the officer to be cashiered from the Army, forfeit all payments due, and be imprisoned for two years (John 1864).

A court-martial assembled at the United States Barracks, Barrancas, Florida, on June 26, 1864, to consider allegations involving conduct unbecoming an officer and a gentleman against Captain John C. Gosman, 86th Regiment, United States Colored Infantry. The judge advocate claimed that Gosman entered an enlisted man's quarters and "did get into bed with a colored woman and did remain until ordered out." He responded to the eviction with a profane outburst and then reluctantly left. Gosman pleaded not guilty, but the court-martial members focused on the "shameful example to and before the enlisted men of the Regiment" and sentenced the officer to be dismissed from the Army (Gosman 1864).

A general court-martial accused Major George Thistleton, 1st Regiment, Maryland Cavalry, with conduct unbecoming an officer and a gentleman with multiple specifications alleging theft, drunkenness, and unauthorized absence. The judge advocate additionally accused Thistleton of "associating intimately and publicly with infamous women and prostitutes during the past winter and this spring, so as to bring disgrace upon himself and the service, and to subject his encampment to scenes disgusting and disreputable to his Regiment." Thistleton's court-martial convened in Baltimore, Maryland, on May 17, 1864, and the members listened as the officer pleaded not guilty to all the specifications. The court agreed with Thistleton's pleadings except for "associating intimately and publicly with infamous women and prostitutes." Based on that amendment, the court returned a guilty verdict and sentenced the officer to be dismissed from the Army (Thistleton 1864).

The road to redemption was long and arduous for Major Alexander S. Hill, 18th Regiment Infantry, Corps d'Afrique. Hill confronted three military charges for conduct unbecoming an officer and a gentleman, conduct prejudicial to good order and discipline, and disobedience of orders. His general court-martial convened at the Headquarters of the 12th Regiment, Corps d'Afrique, on January 15, 1864. Hill pleaded guilty to conduct prejudicial to good order and discipline but announced his innocence of the two other charges. The court-martial returned guilty verdicts for all three charges and sentenced the officer to be dismissed and "publicly stripped of his insignia and rank, in presence of all the colored troops at Port Hudson, Louisiana ... and to be confined as a convict at hard labor on the Dry Tortugas." Major General Nathaniel P. Banks approved the court-martial proceedings and hinted at the offense, declaring that Hill's "attempt to effect by violence advantages over powerless women, is disgraceful to himself, and criminal in the eyes of God and man" (Hill 1864b).

On November 25, 1864, from his prison at Fort Jefferson, Florida, Hill wrote a letter imploring the inspector general of the Department of the Gulf to review his trial. His earnest appeal began by recounting his valorous Army service and severe battlefield injury. The officer's injury led military authorities to recommend that he join the Invalid Corps. Hill refused, and in its place, he accepted an assignment with the 18th Regiment Infantry, Corps d'Afrique (Hill 1864a).

Hill's letter then pivoted to the military charges that led to his confinement. Before his transgression, Hill and several other officers spent several hours reveling in rounds of beer and wine. Despite being intoxicated, Hill denied the allegation that he "visited the Laundress' camp ... and attempted to violate the person of a colored laundress." Hill argued for a new trial, claiming that the judge advocate had admitted that he had not been positively identified. To further support his request for a new trial, Hill pointed out, "I had to go to trial without counsel ... I did not know who the witnesses were until I came into Court ... I pleaded guilty to the charge of prej [udicial] conduct because I considered I was guilty of being out of camp in the condition I was in" (Hill 1864a).

The provost marshal at Key West, Florida, received notice of Hill's release from confinement on January 19, 1865, following the expiration of his four-month sentence. About a month later, President Lincoln granted a pardon to the officer, apparently influenced by Hill's commendable Army record, the flawed trial proceedings, and the four months he had unjustly spent in confinement (Hill 1864a).

Landsman Michael J. Gavican, attached to the USS *Cimarron*, was the sole Navy service member in the representative database charged with rape. The Navy general court-martial convened on board the USS *Wabash* at Port Royal Harbor, South Carolina, on June 2, 1864. Lieutenant Commander Jonathan Young, Commanding, USS *Cimarron*, preferred the charge of rape, alleging that Gavican "did on the 2nd day of April 1864 while on shore on liberty on Light House Point violate the person of a negro woman ... in a most brutal manner." When the judge advocate asked Gavican "if he desired counsel ... he replied that he did not know where to get any and that he might as well go without any," after which he pleaded not guilty (Gavican 1864).

Coal Heaver James Dolan testified for the prosecution that "as I was going up the stairs of the lighthouse, I saw Gavican and some others, and a woman standing there." After spending a few minutes walking around the lighthouse gallery Dolan descended the spiral staircase and "I saw this same woman outside the lighthouse, going to her home about fifty yards off." The other two witnesses had similar testimony. The prosecution's case was incredibly weak, with a remarkable absence of any evidence suggesting sexual misconduct. Based on the parsimonious testimony, the court-martial members had no choice but to acquit Gavican (Gavican 1864).

Commodore Andrew A. Harwood appointed two officers on August 14, 1863, to investigate "complaints [that] have been made against the Guard vessel Adolph Hugel ... stating that prostitutes have been allowed to go on board ... at all times." The two officers reported their findings to

Harwood in a letter dated September 9, 1863, and concluded that "we have carefully investigated the matter and from what we can learn ... we are of the opinion that prostitutes have been allowed to go on board the vessel ... at any and all times." Based on that report, Secretary of the Navy Gideon Welles convened a court of inquiry at the Washington Navy Yard on September 29, 1863, to "investigate alleged scandalous proceedings on board the Guard vessel Adolph Hugel." Welles assigned Acting Volunteer Lieutenant Thomas P. Ives, one of the two officers who originally investigated the matter, to also join the court of inquiry (*Adolph Hugel* 1863).

The leadership of Acting Master James Van Boskirk, Commanding, *Adolph Hugel*, was the focus of the court of inquiry, and the first witness in the investigation was Lieutenant Atwell, 1st Regiment, District of Columbia Infantry. Atwell witnessed "women of bad character go on board the Adolph Hugel ... on several occasions ... I have seen the women signal to the vessel" (*Adolph Hugel* 1863).

Most of the prosecution witnesses were civilians with various duties that involved supporting the fleet. A typical example was R. Bell, Jr., Deputy Collector of the Port of Alexandria, Virginia, who testified, "I have seen women go on the dock, and hail the Adolph Hugel who, from report, I believe were prostitutes." Bell's testimony was vague and relied on hearsay evidence, and subsequent prosecution witnesses offered no better (*Adolph Hugel* 1863).

Curiously, the court of inquiry's recorder did not call any crewmembers from the USS *Adolph Hugel*, an omission corrected by Acting Master James Van Boskirk. In his defense, Boskirk called numerous crewmembers, all of whom refuted the presence of prostitutes. Boskirk's defense statement was a rambling rebuttal, attributing the frequent presence of women on the ship to family and friends invited by the ship's commander. Boskirk admitted that on two occasions "strangers" boarded the USS *Adolph Hugel*. In one incident, Boskirk arrested two women, believing the pair were spies, and briefly detained them on board the ship. In another incident, a group of women mysteriously boarded the ship, cavorted wildly, drank whiskey with Boskirk, and then quietly left (*Adolph Hugel* 1863).

The evidence presented to the court of inquiry was often confusing and contradictory. It appeared from the record that the court of inquiry accepted Boskirk's defense of the alleged events (*Adolph Hugel* 1863). Acting Master James Van Boskirk survived the investigation and continued serving in the Navy (Van Boskirk 1863).

Seaman Peter Bourne, attached to the USS *Osage*, appeared before a Navy general court-martial on board the USS *Clara Dolsen*, near Cairo, Illinois, on October 1, 1863. Rear Admiral David D. Porter convened the trial and preferred the military charge of scandalous conduct tending to the destruction of good morals. Five specifications described the alleged misconduct, which began on July 28, 1863, when the accused approached Landsman George Legros and offered the man three dollars if "we will sleep together and do it tonight." Later that night Bourne "came to the side of Legros, who was lying by himself ... and renewed his vile solicitations." Legros rejected the initial advances, but Bourne persisted and did "commit sodomy" (Bourne 1863).

Acting Volunteer Lieutenant Joseph Pitty Couthouy, Commanding, USS *Osage*, obtained a sworn statement from Legros around September 14, 1863, describing the incident. The judge advocate read Legros's sworn statement at the court-martial, sparing the man's direct testimony, and Bourne declined the option to cross-examine the witness (Bourne 1863).

In his defense, Bourne insisted that "I gave George Legros a two dollar bill and afterward a one dollar bill to buy liquor ... and not for the purpose alleged by the charges against me." Legros did not buy the liquor and when confronted by Bourne stated, "he would tell the Captain that I had given him the money for sleeping with him." After weighing the evidence, the court-martial members rejected Bourne's defense and sentenced him to ten years in prison (Bourne 1863).

A Navy general court-martial convened on board the USS *Richmond*, located near Mobile, Alabama, on December 10, 1863, to prosecute Coal Heaver George W. Libby attached to the USS *Kennebec* for scandalous conduct tending to the destruction of good morals. The judge advocate alleged that Libby "did on the night of the 16th of November 1863 ... consent to and furnish George H. Hitchings, Officers Cook ... to commit upon his person the crime of sodomy" (Libby 1863).

Libby pleaded not guilty, after which the prosecution called seven witnesses to prove the charge. The first was Captain of After Guard Peter Campbell, USS *Kennebec*. Campbell recalled being informed by another crewmember that the accused and Hitchings were "turning in together, in a hammock on the deck." Based on that report, Campbell took a lantern and went in search of the pair "and found them turned in together." Campbell then loudly called for additional witnesses, including the master at arms and nearby crewmember Henry Waters. Hitchings attempted to leave the area but Campbell "kicked him, his privates were exposed, and the trousers of Libby were down." Campbell conceded when cross-examined that the pair were not "in an out of the way place" (Libby 1863).

Seaman Henry Waters endorsed Campbell's testimony. Landsman William H. Davis had the most damaging testimony, claiming that the day before the alleged incident he overheard "Hitchings ... ask Libby where he slept ... Hitchings said, 'why don't you come forward and sleep with me.'"

Libby demurred, fearing someone would see him, and countered by saying, "Tell me where you sleep and I'll come there" (Libby 1863).

Master at Arms John E. Holland testified in Libby's defense by endorsing the man's good conduct. At the accused's request, the judge advocate then prepared and read his defense statement. In his defense, Libby asserted, "I woke up during the night, do not know at what hour, and found some person along side of me. My trousers, I discovered, were unbuttoned. I always sleep very sound, it could easily [be] done by another and I would not wake up." Libby also rejected Davis's testimony and concluded by noting that "if I had any such intention, I should not have been so foolish as to have committed it so near the men on the berth deck" (Libby 1863).

Libby's defense neutralized the prosecution's allegations. The court-martial decided Libby was not guilty, but the members would not tolerate returning the man to active duty. Even though he was acquitted, the court-martial members stated that "in view of the heinousness of the alleged crime, the demoralizing effect of such a charge ... and of the suspicious circumstances developed by the evidence, although conflicting ... it is recommended that George W. Libby ... be discharged from the Naval service of the United States" (Libby 1863).

In a rare insight, the trial of Quarter Gunner Charles Brown, USS *Louisville*, revealed Rear Admiral David D. Porter's thoughts regarding military justice and nonconsensual sodomy. Brown's trial convened on December 7, 1863, on board the USS *Louisville*, near Skipwith's Landing, on the Mississippi River. Porter preferred the military charge of scandalous conduct tending to the destruction of good morals, alleging that the accused "did endeavor by force to have unnatural intercourse and connection with one Peter Olsen, Ordinary Seaman" (Brown, C. 1863).

The prosecution called two witnesses, Coxswain Timothy Sullivan and the victim of the attack, Peter Olsen. Sullivan testified first and recalled responding to Olsen's cry for help, and he witnessed the accused firmly holding the victim's legs. After Brown released Olsen, Sullivan "then went away and saw nothing more." On another occasion, Olsen described a more violent affray, with two other crewmembers restraining the victim at the behest of Brown. During the assault, the victim's trousers were unbuttoned. Brown decided not to defend himself at the trial, after which the court-martial reviewed the evidence and found the accused guilty "only so far as being an accessory" (Brown, C. 1863).

The attempted rape appalled Admiral Porter, who declared Brown's behavior "so unnatural that the laws of the Navy make no provision for punishment adequate to the offense." Porter referenced one other similar case during his career that resulted in harsh punishment for the perpetrators, but in Brown's case, "he is awarded a milder sentence than would be given by a summary court martial for a drunken frolic." Taking direct aim at the trial's finding, Porter criticized the court-martial members' reasoning since "the conduct of Charles Brown ... was if possible, more brutal and disgusting than that of his associate." Porter refused to approve the sentence, "as being entirely inadequate to the crime attempted by Charles Brown," and worried that doing otherwise would encourage "depraved characters to suppose that they might commit offenses of this kind with comparative impunity." Porter deeply regretted that Brown was not punished due to the disapproval (Brown, C. 1863).

Landsman George W. Curtis and First Class Boy John H. Matthews, both serving on board the USS *William G. Anderson*, faced separate courts-martial alleging scandalous conduct tending to the destruction of good morals for consensual sodomy. The trial convened on board the USS *Potomac*, in Pensacola Bay, Florida, on September 12, 1864 (Curtis 1864; Matthews 1864).

The judge advocate presented two witnesses, the principal being Master at Arms John C. Johnson. Johnson testified that another crewmember contacted him late at night on August 6, 1864, "telling me to go with him and he would show me something." Walking toward the main hatch Johnson detected two men in a passageway "in considerable motion." Johnson then "raised the blanket off the two men and saw a sight such as I never saw before. Both men were in the position of man and wife" (Curtis 1864; Matthews 1864).

Curtiss and Matthews both provided similar defense statements, denying the allegations, and insisting that their proximity resulted from a desire to talk quietly without awakening their nearby shipmates. The members of the court-martial rejected their arguments and sentenced both men to the Parish Prison in New Orleans, Louisiana, for ten years (Curtis 1864; Matthews 1864).

Roughly one month before the Civil War ended, a Navy general court-martial convened on board the USS *Dale*, Key West, Florida, on March 15, 1865, for the trial of Seaman James Conley, serving on board the USS *Neptune*. The prosecution's main witness was Landsman Joseph Morris, the victim of the accused's persistent affectionate intentions. On three separate occasions, Morris pursued the man, culminating in Conley's request "to do woman fashion towards me." Morris rebuffed the advances and ultimately reported the accused's behavior. The judge advocate called other witnesses who corroborated Morris's protestations (Conley, J. 1865).

Conley vigorously cross-examined the prosecution's witnesses. After the judge advocate's case, Conley called Master at Arms Rudolph King and Marine Corps Private John Brune. Both witnesses testified that the close confines of the ship would not permit an attempted sodomy to go unnoticed. Conley's defense statement attributed the allegation to Morris's malicious behavior, claiming, "he repeatedly said that before I left the ship, he would get me in trouble. I have many enemies in the ship ... and I believe the present charge against me to be a conspiracy." Conley's argument that he would not have risked his "unblemished character" after serving three years in the Civil War, with his enlistment expiring in just a few months, was likely more persuasive. Perhaps Conley's defense softened his punishment. The court-martial found the accused guilty and sentenced him to be dishonorably discharged, without incarceration (Conley, J. 1865).

The only instance of potential Army homoerotic behavior in the representative database analyzed for this volume was ambiguous, making it challenging to reach definitive conclusions. First Lieutenant Daniel Curran, 15th Regiment, New York Engineers, faced a general court-martial on February 19, 1863, accused of conduct unbecoming an officer and a gentleman. The judge advocate alleged that Curran "took indecent familiarities with the person of 2d Lieutenant Daniel A. Higgins ... on or about the 13th day of February 1863." The record did not provide any clarifying details. The court-martial returned a guilty verdict and sentenced Curran to be dismissed (Curran 1863).

Private William Bishop, Company H, 1st Regiment, Indiana Cavalry, had the dubious distinction of being the only service member in the representative database tried for bestiality. Bishop appeared before a general court-martial convened at Pilot Knob, Missouri, charged with "grossly immoral and unsoldierlike conduct." The judge advocate alleged that Bishop "on or about the 10th of December 1861 ... did attempt to commit bestiality, by then and there attempting to have intercourse with a mare." Fortunately for Bishop, the court-martial found him not guilty (Bishop 1862).

FIVE

Subordinate Military Crimes

General courts-martial prosecuted serious military crimes such as desertion and violence, while regimental and summary courts-martial resolved less significant infractions. Military leaders also managed an untold number of disciplinary breaches with nonjudicial actions such as verbal reprimands, extra duty, or simply ignoring the behavior. Examples of overlooked misconduct included intoxication, patronizing prostitutes, briefly overstaying an authorized absence, profanity, gambling, and malingering. This apparent indifference pitted discipline against morale, with many military leaders concluding that strict enforcement of certain military rules eroded a unit's esprit de corps. Prosecution was further constrained by the prevalence of rampant behaviors, including intoxication, among both officers and enlisted personnel. Their ubiquitous presence encouraged prosecutorial discretion, with general courts-martial reserved for the most flagrant violations or in some cases explicitly undertaken for purposes of general deterrence.

The subordinate military crimes in this chapter examine less frequent general courts-martial prosecutions. Sections include theft, forgery, consequential criticisms, malingering, gambling, and medical malfeasance. Gambling and malingering rarely resulted in a general court-martial despite their pervasive presence. General courts-martial were typically considered appropriate for cases involving theft, forgery, and other similar offenses, especially those committed by officers or when military authorities desired a deterrent effect. While rare, prosecution of medical malfeasance reinforced the military's resolve to take care of the sick and injured.

Theft

This study bundled the specific military charge of theft with instances of embezzlement, financial fraud, burglary, and robbery for a

Five. Subordinate Military Crimes

more complete picture of the misconduct. Even so, instances of general courts-martial for these offenses were rare.

The representative database analyzed for this volume included 275 trials for theft. The Army accounted for the majority with 227 courts-martial (n = 275, 82.6%), followed by 38 Navy trials (n = 275, 13.8%) and 10 Marine Corps trials (n = 275, 3.6%). In most cases, these general courts-martial considered more than one military crime. Theft was the exclusive military charge in 23 cases among Army personnel (n = 227, 10.1%), seven among the Navy (n = 38, 18.4%), and one in the Marine Corps (n = 10, 10.0%). For the remainder, the trials also considered misconduct such as assault, AWOL, desertion, and drunkenness. In terms of rank, Army officers accounted for 38 general courts-martial (n = 227, 16.7%), Navy officers eight (n = 38, 21.1%), and none for the Marine Corps. Approximately one-fifth of the courts-martial verdicts resulted in the accused being found not guilty (n = 60/275, 21.8%). Acquittal was highly likely when military authorities prosecuted theft as the sole military charge (n = 20/23, 87.0%).

Commonly stolen items included money, liquor, food, horses, clothing, and weapons. Court-martial punishments in the representative database included the imposition of the death penalty for aggravated offenses such as robbery, most of which were mitigated to incarceration. Military authorities did not mitigate the death sentences of six soldiers convicted of thefts associated with desertion or rape.

Theft was common, with apprehension and punishment less so. Military authorities responded with a variety of on-the-spot punishments for petty theft, such as extra duty, forcing the miscreant to wear a placard bearing the word "Thief," and a public display of the stolen items. Referral to a court-martial usually signaled a harsher outcome such as loss of pay, reduction in rank, and confinement (Wiley 1962, 202).

Newspapers reported the findings of military courts-martial at the beginning of the Civil War, perhaps to shame the perpetrators and constrain others, but the sheer volume precluded constant stories devoted to the subject. In the early months of the Civil War, the *Baltimore Sun* reported the outcomes of ten courts-martial, for desertion, disobedience, and drunkenness. Private Maurice Fitzgerald, Company E, 3rd Regiment, New York Light Artillery, was an exception. The judge advocate charged Fitzgerald with the theft of a blanket from another soldier. After finding the soldier guilty, the court-martial sentenced Fitzgerald to six months of hard labor with a 32-pound ball attached to his leg and ordered the man to wear a board with the word "Thief" printed on it. At the expiration of the hard labor, Fitzgerald's head was shaved and he was drummed out of the Army ("Soldiers' Duties and Punishments—Court Martial Sentences" 1861).

Frank Leslie's Illustrated Newspaper reported a scene of "great merriment" on June 20, 1861, at Fort Monroe, Virginia, when a regiment publicly humiliated two soldiers for stealing. A court-martial dishonorably discharged the men and ordered them to wear boards on their backs bearing the word "Theft." Leslie's Newspaper approved of the punishment, adding that "in this novel and ridiculous regalia, with other incidental additions unreportable," they were drummed out of the regiment ("Drumming Thieves Out of Fortress Monroe" 1861).

Private Elijah Smith, Company G, 4th Regiment, United States Artillery, appeared before a general court-martial on January 25, 1862, charged with conduct to the prejudice of good order and military discipline for stealing another soldier's coat. Smith's pilfering cost the man a week's confinement. During daylight, Smith's punishment also included marching about "wearing a knapsack weighing forty (40) pounds on his back, with the word 'Thief' plainly marked thereon." Following the one-week punishment, the court-martial ordered the man drummed out of the regiment (Smith, E. 1862).

A military proceeding met with a stern rebuke from Major General Samuel Ryan Curtis in the trial of Private W.H. Rickets, Company C, 18th Regiment, Iowa Infantry. The court's investigation took place at "the head of the Spring River, Missouri" on November 7, 1862, and charged Rickets with stealing an officer's blanket. The court found the soldier guilty and recommended a sentence "to march thirty days in charge of the Brigade Guard, with a placard on his back, with the word 'Thief' ... to receive thirty lashes on his bare back." Curtis approved the sentence except for the flogging, noting that "it is surprising that the officers of the Commission should have attempted it" since Congress eliminated that punishment on August 5, 1861 (Rickets 1862).

Private Lyman Stickney, Battery C, Massachusetts Artillery, appeared before a general court-martial on October 21, 1861, charged with three specifications alleging conduct to the prejudice of good order and military discipline. The judge advocate accused Stickney of stealing a pair of boots, a ten-dollar bill, and two dozen eggs. The court-martial found the soldier guilty of stealing the boots and the eggs and punished the transgression by confining him for "ninety days, with a thirty-two pound ball attached to his leg ... at the expiration of the ninety days his head to be shaved, the buttons torn from his coat, and that he be drummed out" (Stickney 1862).

Stealing from an officer guaranteed the general court-martial of Private Hugh Sweeney, Company E, 1st Regiment, Colorado Cavalry. Sweeney single-handedly pilfered many of the officer's personal effects, including a bed quilt, boots, uniform, and musket. The court that considered Sweeney's case met at "Denver City, Colorado Territory" on October 31, 1862, and charged the soldier with theft. After reviewing the evidence, the court found Sweeney guilty and sentenced him to four months of hard labor and loss of pay. The convening authority disapproved the trial's proceedings because "the Court neglected to enter any finding on the record. They should not have passed sentence until they had first found the accused guilty of the offence charged" (Sweeney 1863).

Private Daniel A. Conant, Company G, 17th Regiment, Maine Infantry, worked in the post office at the convalescent hospital at Camp Parole, Maryland. The judge advocate accused Conant of breaching his position of trust by opening letters, removing their contents, and discarding the empty envelopes. Additionally, Conant stole a revolver and leveraged his role to discreetly ship the weapon to his home address using the postal service. The court-martial returned a guilty verdict and sentenced Conant to six months of confinement at Fort Delaware, Delaware. The court explained the modest punishment, "believing the accused to have acted more from thoughtlessness than from a knowledge of the serious character of the offense he was committing" (Conant 1864).

The peevish side of court-martial practice occurred in the case of Corporal Michael F. Sheehan, Company G, 8th Regiment, Massachusetts Infantry. The judge advocate levied six military charges that alleged theft, insulting an officer, assault, disobedience, destruction of government property, and resisting a sentry, all occurring on October 31, 1864. All six charges arose when Sheehan allegedly stole a dog belonging to another soldier. A fight between the two soldiers followed the theft, and when an officer ordered Sheehan to return the animal, the accused, in an expletive-laden remark, declared "that he would not deliver up the dog." After hearing what was churlish testimony, the court-martial acquitted Sheehan and in a stinging rebuke professed that "the charges seem so frivolous and vexatious and unsupported by the evidence that the Court are of the opinion that they originated from the personal malice of the accuser" (Sheehan 1864).

Private George Cring, Company B, 139th Regiment, New York Infantry, was not as fortunate. The judge advocate charged Cring with stealing twenty dollars from another soldier at Camp Parole, located near Annapolis, Maryland, on February 21, 1865. After pleading guilty, Cring was summarily sentenced by the court to one year of imprisonment "at the Rips Raps or such other place" (Cring 1865). Fort Wool, otherwise known as the Rip Raps, was a small manmade island serving a role in Union coastal defenses at the Hampton Roads Harbor in Virginia (Quarstein and Mroczkowski 2000, 6–8).

A general court-martial convened at Baltimore, Maryland, and charged Private Francis Harris, Company F, 12th Regiment, New York

Cavalry, with a particularly repugnant crime. The judge advocate accused Harris of theft "on or about the 8th day of March 1865 of steal[ing] from the person or bed of Private William Doty ... said Doty being at the time in a moribund condition, one pocketbook containing at least fifty dollars, one chain with trinket attached and one pocket inkstand." Harris was the chief nurse on ward three at the General Hospital in Baltimore, making his crime even more loathsome. The court-martial found the accused guilty and lightly punished Harris with three months of hard labor and loss of pay for the same period (Harris 1865).

Courts-martial punished violent theft such as robbery more severely, as demonstrated in the case of Private Charles Reynolds, Company B, 145th Regiment, Pennsylvania Infantry. A court-martial convened in Baltimore, Maryland, on January 10, 1865, to consider the military charge of highway robbery. Reynolds participated with a small group that attacked soldiers and stole their money. The judge advocate accused Reynolds of assaulting Sergeant James Walker, Company H, 108th Regiment, New York Infantry, and stealing 262 dollars in negotiable securities. In a separate incident, the judge advocate alleged that Reynolds attacked Private John McGinnis, Company A, 69th Regiment, Pennsylvania Infantry, and robbed the soldier of 50 dollars (Reynolds 1865).

Contrary to his not guilty pleadings, the court-martial found Reynolds guilty and sentenced the soldier "to be placed at hard labor for the period of three (3) years, at the Rip Raps, or other such place." Reynolds avoided confinement at the Rip Raps by being sent to the penitentiary at Albany, New York, by Brigadier General William W. Morris, the convening authority for the case (Reynolds 1865).

Officers who were accused of theft abused their positions of trust by embezzling funds, falsifying property records, submitting fraudulent vouchers, stealing service members' bounties, and using their status to extort money. A case in point was the general court-martial of Captain David M. Stump, Company C, 6th Regiment, Iowa Infantry. The judge advocate charged Stump with two specifications of embezzlement and two specifications of swindling at a trial that convened at Otterville, Missouri, on December 31, 1861. The allegations claimed that Stump "wilfully, maliciously, and with intent ... dispose[d] of a box of shoes belonging to said Company C, containing about sixty pair shoes and convert[ed] to his own use the money arising from such sale ... and charging to divers[e] men of his company, clothing which they have never received ... thereby defrauding and swindling them out of their just pay." After Stump pleaded guilty, the court-martial members recommended that he be cashiered due to his misconduct, which had deprived his men of needed clothing (Stump 1862).

A general court-martial convened in the case of Veterinary Surgeon

Allen W. Colby, 3rd Regiment, Missouri State Militia Cavalry. The judge advocate charged Colby with robbery after the man stole 40 dollars from Private John L. Barnaby of the same unit. The robbery occurred near Springfield, Missouri, around August 24, 1862, and, unfortunately for Colby, military authorities discovered the ill-gotten gains in his possession. Colby received a particularly harsh punishment consisting of "one half of his head and whiskers shaved ... wear a ball and chain, and be exhibited on the public square two hours each day for one week, and then be confined for two years at hard labor" (Colby 1862).

First Lieutenant George W. Dobbler, 1st Indian Home Guard, faced a general court-martial convened at Camp Curtis, Arkansas, on January 22, 1863. The judge advocate charged Dobbler with two specifications of felony and fraud. The allegations contended that Dobbler "connive[d] and conspire[d] with three Indians ... to answer to the names of persons upon the muster role, and who were either dead or absent without leave." Following that deception, Dobbler pocketed the pay of the three absentee soldiers. After a brief trial, the court-martial found Dobbler guilty of abusing his authority and sentenced him to be cashiered (Dobbler 1863).

In deference to his rank, a general court-martial gingerly charged Colonel Charles H. Fox, 101st Regiment, Illinois Infantry, with embezzlement and "misapplication of money entrusted to him." During the trial held in St. Louis, Missouri, the judge advocate accused Fox of receiving three hundred and thirty-four dollars and ninety-nine cents from the Commissary of Subsistence while he oversaw a camp for paroled men at Benton Barracks. However, he did not spend the entire amount on rations, and according to official practice, he was required to return the unspent money to the commissary general. Fox did not return the money and "did appropriate to his own use." The court-martial convicted the senior officer of embezzlement but removed the language accusing him of appropriating the money to himself. They were content with Fox returning the funds to the United States Government. Fox returned to duty after reimbursing the money (Fox 1863).

Captain Cyrus H. Johnson, 9th Independent Battery, Wisconsin Light Artillery, appeared before a general court-martial in "Denver City, Colorado Territory." The judge advocate accused Johnson of three instances of embezzlement involving the theft of ammunition throughout the summer of 1862, the appropriation of two kegs of gunpowder that he sold, and selling military uniforms. Johnson faced another accusation, of plotting to trade the ordnance to the Indians. The court-martial convicted Johnson of the charges and ordered him to reimburse the value of the embezzled items. Additionally, the punishment for his crime included dismissal from the Army (Johnson, C. 1863).

Acting Provost Marshal Major Henry A. Gallup, 3rd Regiment, Missouri Cavalry, faced a staggering number of specifications alleging embezzlement when the judge advocate accused the officer of 37 violations at a general court-martial that convened in St. Louis, Missouri. The officer was accused of embezzling money and submitting fraudulent vouchers. Wading through the numerous allegations was no doubt tedious since the court-martial members had to weigh the evidence for each specification. In the end, the court-martial members determined that Gallup was guilty of 31 specifications. For punishment, the court-martial members recommended that Gallup be dismissed from the Army and that he refund to the government "nine hundred and twenty nine dollars and eighty-five cents" (Gallup 1863).

Because Major General John Schofield doubted that Gallup could repay the money, he added a further stipulation that "the Provost Marshal will hold the accused in custody until the money required to be refunded—nine hundred and twenty-nine dollars and eighty-five cents—($929.85), is paid over. And if said money is not paid within fifteen days from the date of this order, the Provost Marshal General will proceed to sell, in such manner as the best interest of the Government may require, the personal property of the accused" (Gallup 1863).

Prosecution of theft at a Navy general court-martial was not common. The representative database analyzed for this volume indicated that the court-martial cases involved several types of misconduct, including embezzlement, robbery, and petty thievery, often related to stealing money or alcohol. An example involved the trial of Second Class Boy Martin Conley, held at the New York Navy Yard on November 13, 1862. The judge advocate accused Conley of stealing "a quantity of money from the chest or safe of the Paymaster." Conley pleaded guilty, after which the court-martial, citing the accused's youth, imposed a mild punishment that included confinement on board the USS *North Carolina* for one month and no shore leave for six months (Conley, M. 1862).

A subsequent review of the trial's proceedings by the Navy Department resulted in a sternly worded rebuke, castigating the general court-martial for imposing a punishment that "is so grossly inadequate to the character of the offense committed." The Navy Department used Conley's court-martial to remind officers that punishment must match the crime. Furthermore, it was emphasized by the Navy Department that while courts-martial could suggest clemency, only the President of the United States or the convening authority had the power to pardon, remit, or lessen a sentence (Conley, M. 1862).

Rear Admiral Theodorus Bailey, Commanding, East Gulf Blockading Squadron, preferred a single military charge of stealing goods from a prize ship against Seaman Peter J. Agnew. According to the charge's specification, Agnew stole a piece of black silk while on board the captured ship Mattie. The Navy general court-martial convened near Key West, Florida, on May 1, 1863, on board the USS *Santiago de Cuba*. Agnew received the assistance of Paymaster James W. Locke for his defense counsel (Agnew 1863).

The judge advocate presented four witnesses, none of whom observed the accused stealing the black silk. Two witnesses claimed to have seen the item lying on a deck of the ship tender "Annie," but there was no evidence linking it directly to the accused. Agnew deftly cross-examined the prosecution's witnesses, and in his defense statement, he pointedly declared that their testimony was inconclusive. The court-martial agreed with Agnew's contention and found the seaman not guilty (Agnew 1863).

Seaman William McIntyre appeared before a Navy general court-martial convened at the New York Navy Yard on January 19, 1863, accused of threatening to assault his superior officer and scandalous conduct tending to the destruction of good morals. The judge advocate alleged that while onboard the USS *Patroon*, the seaman stole liquor from the ship's spirit room on September 23, 1862, and threatened to assault the commanding officer (McIntyre 1863).

Acting Master William D. Urann was the prosecution's first witness. Urann testified that about two hours after leaving Fernandina, Florida, roughly two-thirds of the crew were intoxicated. McIntyre was among the most belligerent, forcing Urann to arrest the seaman and place the man in double irons. During the arrest, McIntyre allegedly cursed Urann, the sole basis for charging the man with assault. Urann later discovered that McIntyre stole the liquor after neatly cutting a hole in the spirit room's door. McIntyre convincingly cross-examined Urann, forcing the ship's master to concede that he did not know who broke into the spirit room. The prosecution's remaining witnesses confirmed that McIntyre was drunk, but they did not provide any evidence linking the theft or profanity to the accused (McIntyre 1863).

The court-martial approved McIntyre's request for Seaman James Wallingford and Surgeon Thomas L. Smith to testify as defense witnesses. McIntyre apparently anticipated that Surgeon Smith's testimony would tarnish the reputation of the Navy officers, thereby implicitly condemning their unfeeling disregard for his well-being following the arrest. McIntyre developed typhoid fever while in double irons and insinuated that his incarceration in a dimly lit area that was poorly ventilated, and at times exposed to the weather, was the cause of the disease. Surgeon Smith's testimony was vague and provided only circumstantial evidence. He admitted that avoiding typhoid relied "upon being kept clean and well supplied with food ... and air." Wallingford testified that McIntyre was held in double irons for weeks and sometimes limited to bread and water (McIntyre 1863).

J.M. Guiteau was McIntyre's defense counsel and he read the defense statement. Guiteau challenged the allegation of assault, arguing that mere words did not establish the legal definition of a threat. He criticized the inhumane treatment of McIntyre, declaring that the "deprivations have worked as in fact as a punishment, and he feels it his duty ... on behalf of those of his fellow seaman who may be subject to ... this unwarrantable exercise of tyrannical power." Guiteau's 14-page indictment of insensitive and abusive Navy officers, combined with the prosecution's weak case, tilted the verdict in McIntyre's favor. The court-martial subsequently found McIntyre not guilty (McIntyre 1863).

Based on the representative database analyzed for this volume, Private Patrick Baker was a rare example of a member of the Marine Corps appearing before a Navy general court-martial for theft. Baker's trial convened at the Mound City, Illinois, Naval Station on May 31, 1864, and charged the man with highway robbery. The specification alleged that Baker stole the "purse and various other articles" from First Lieutenant Thomas T. Lambert, Company E, 68th Regiment, Ohio Infantry, on April 22, 1864 (Baker, P. 1864).

Lambert reported the robbery to Captain M.R. Kintzing, the post commander, and in doing so accurately described the perpetrator. Kintzing assembled the Marines on the parade ground and invited Baker to identify the thief. After a short stroll, Lambert stopped, scrutinized Baker, and accused him of the robbery (Baker, P. 1864).

Kintzing stood as the sole witness for the prosecution due to unforeseen military operations that prevented Lambert from attending the court-martial, leaving Kintzing as the only one able to testify. Baker had no witnesses and relied on the judge advocate to transcribe his oral comments. His defense statement pointedly claimed, "I have to say that I am innocent of any crime, that I never saw Lieutenant Lambert until he picked me from the ranks." The court-martial members were not impressed and sentenced the guilty man to imprisonment at hard labor for the remainder of his enlistment, six months attached to a ball and chain, and to be dishonorably discharged (Baker, P. 1864).

Forgery

The estimated incidence of nonmonetary forgery is unknown and there is scant historical research on the subject. Only 21 examples emerged from the representative database used for this volume. This tiny number nonetheless hints at a widespread practice, or concerns about it becoming such, as the justification for empaneling a general court-martial. In 13 cases (n = 21, 61.9%), courts-martial accused service members of forging passes and furloughs, six (n = 21, 28.6%) of forged paperwork for sick leave, and two of forged documents (n = 21, 9.5%) to get alcohol.

Second Lieutenant C.J. Snyder, Company A, 1st Regiment, Michigan Cavalry, and Second Lieutenant J.I. Daniels, Company E, 1st Regiment, Michigan Cavalry, faced separate courts-martial for "presenting an altered pass" and conduct unbecoming an officer. Both officers stood accused of falsifying a pass on November 18, 1861, and using their ill-gotten time "in company with lewd women ... at a house of prostitution in Washington, D.C." The courts-martial proceedings found both officers guilty and sentenced them to be dismissed from the Army (Snyder and Daniels 1862).

A court-martial convened at Port Hudson, Louisiana, for the trial of Captain Andrew J. Mulhern, "17th Regiment Infantry, Corps d'Afrique." The judge advocate charged the officer with disobedience and conduct unbecoming an officer and a gentleman for transgressions that occurred in mid–March 1864. Mulhern resolutely refused an order from his commanding officer to take command of a detached unit, declaring that "it is not my turn, and before I will go, I will report myself on the sick list." Following through on the threat, Mulhern reported to the surgeon, who refused to place the officer on the sick list. After meeting with the surgeon, Mulhern misrepresented the results of the encounter with a forged note saying "excused by the Doctor." The court-martial found Mulhern guilty and sentenced him to be dismissed from the Army (Mulhern 1864).

Private John Setright, Company K, 2nd Regiment, Michigan Infantry, fabricated a pass for a visit to Washington, D.C., on November 30, 1861, by forging the names of four approving officials. He pleaded guilty, and for his creative writing, the court-martial punished the soldier with fourteen days of confinement on bread and water, after which he worked at hard labor with a 12-pound ball and chain attached to his left leg (Setright 1862).

In a similar case, Private Jesse T. Nichols, Company M, 20th Regiment, Pennsylvania Cavalry, forged a pass on February 21, 1865, while working at Camp Parole, Maryland. The court-martial sentenced Nichols to three months of hard labor at Fort Delaware, Delaware (Nichols 1865).

Private Frank H. Folsom, Company B, 16th Regiment, New York Infantry, appeared before a general court-martial that convened on December 9, 1861, charged with conduct prejudicial to good order and military discipline. The judge advocate claimed that the soldier on September 24, 1861, "did knowingly present at the Sutler's store ... an order for a bottle of brandy with the forged signature of Dr. Horatio Pine, of said 16th Regiment." In a shrewd move immediately after his arrest, Folsom refused to talk when confronted by his commanding officer, ultimately depriving the prosecution of incriminating evidence. The judge advocate's case fizzled and the court-martial members subsequently acquitted the soldier (Folsom 1862).

Corporal Richard Lloyd, Company F, 25th Regiment, Missouri Infantry, suffered a different fate at a general court-martial that convened at New Madrid, Missouri. The judge advocate charged Lloyd with conduct prejudicial to good order and military discipline after he forged an order for a gallon of whiskey on August 18, 1863. The accused soldier falsified the name of an officer and then presented the document to the post commissary. Lloyd pleaded guilty to the military charge, after which the court-martial sentenced the soldier to be reduced in rank, perform hard labor for 30 days, and then be returned to active duty (Lloyd 1863).

Private Edward E. Young, Company C, 71st Regiment, Pennsylvania Infantry, leveraged his position as a clerk at the military headquarters in Philadelphia, Pennsylvania, to earn some extra money. Young forged the adjutant's name for a discharge certificate and then sold the prize to Private John Harberger, Company D, 2nd Regiment, Pennsylvania Reserve Infantry. The scheme unraveled and a general court-martial convicted

Soldier in a barrel labeled "Too fond of whiskey; forged an order on the surgeon," with one soldier saying to him, "How are you Monitor?" and another saying to him, "Where's the Merrimac?" (LC-USZ62–96119, Library of Congress Prints and Photographs Division, Washington, D.C.).

Young. For his efforts, Young was forced to remain in the Army, without pay, for the duration of his enlistment, and then be dishonorably discharged (Young 1863).

Landsman Robert Sherman, attached to the USS *Mount Washington*, appeared at a Navy general court-martial on board the USS *Roanoke*, Newport News, Virginia, on November 16, 1863. Rear Admiral Samuel P. Lee preferred the charge of "attempting to desert upon presenting a forged pass in time of war." According to the specification, Sherman attempted to desert on September 6, 1863, while en route to Baltimore, Maryland. To achieve his objective, the landsman allegedly presented a forged pass to the provost marshal at Fort Monroe, Virginia. Sherman pleaded not guilty after hearing the charges read by the judge advocate (Sherman 1863).

The prosecution's first witness was the provost marshal, who testified that Sherman, along with two other seamen, presented a pass to the clerk. The provost marshal immediately suspected forgery and questioned the three men. Despite the accusation of forging the document, Sherman maintained his innocence, and the provost marshal admitted that the clerk had suspected someone else of submitting the fake pass (Sherman 1863).

Sherman had no witnesses and asked the judge advocate to transcribe his defense statement. The landsman denied attempting to desert, claiming instead that "I came back to the Navy Yard and the boat had left." As Sherman waited for another boat, he spent his time drinking, and it was during this interlude that he met the other two sailors. One of the sailors gave Sherman a pass and "I didn't know what was on the pass until the Provost Marshal called me in." Sherman emphasized to the court-martial members that his 18-month tenure on board the USS *Mount Washington* was free of any wrongdoing (Sherman 1863).

The prosecution's failure to link Sherman to the falsified pass torpedoed the judge advocate's case. The defense statement may have also tilted the case in Sherman's favor. After reviewing the evidence, the court-martial found Sherman not guilty (Sherman 1863).

Consequential Criticisms

Consequential criticisms are a section devoted to the limits of free speech among service members in the Civil War. As might be imagined, profanity was exceedingly common and beyond the capacity of the military to prosecute in every instance. Exceptions occurred when subordinate service members swore at their leaders, usually in the context of some form of disobedience. Drunkenness also loosened lips.

Consequential criticisms provided examples of general

courts-martial involving offenses other than profanity. This section was broadly interpreted to include cases in which service members openly criticized military leaders and government policies, particularly with regard to denouncing President Lincoln's Emancipation Proclamation.

The representative database studied for this volume revealed 25 examples of consequential criticisms. Since this offense required literacy, judge advocates primarily targeted officers (n = 19/25, 76.0%). Conviction rates were high, with 21 service members (n = 25, 84.0%) found guilty.

The mental stability of Captain Louis Weiderhold, Company D, 27th Regiment, Pennsylvania Infantry, was a central issue in one of the earliest trials. Weiderhold appeared at a general court-martial on November 19, 1861, charged with conduct unbecoming an officer and a gentleman. The accused officer wrote a letter in German to Brigadier General Louis Blenker "intended to irritate, injure, and provoke his superior officer." Weiderhold threatened to publish his grievances in a newspaper if Blenker ignored his letter (Weiderhold 1862).

Weiderhold was displeased with Blenker's decision to promote certain officers, and he claimed that one of them was "accused of bank swindle." Furthermore, in the case of two other officers, Weiderhold insinuated that "this accusation should not be made behind their backs." During Weiderhold's trial, his unpredictable and suspicious behavior was a focal point, and medical testimony concluded that his "illness ... is chronic, and during its attacks, he is not responsible for his actions." The medical testimony proved to be compelling, and as a result, the court-martial acquitted Weiderhold and recommended his honorable discharge from the Army (Weiderhold 1862).

Based on the representative database, the highest-ranking officer involved in a newspaper controversy was Brigadier General Erastus B. Tyler. A general court-martial convened on March 2, 1863, to consider seven military charges, all stemming from Tyler's report of military operations that took place on December 13, 1862, at the Battle of Fredericksburg, Virginia. The judge advocate alleged that Tyler "did thus permit and connive at the publication of what purported to be an official report ... and without proper authority; the said report having been published in a daily newspaper in Harrisburg, PA" (Tyler 1863).

The court absolved Tyler of all charges except for conduct deemed prejudicial to good order and military discipline. The court-martial recommended that Tyler be reprimanded for this offense. Major General Joseph Hooker concurred with the court-martial's sentence and reprimanded Tyler for the unauthorized publication of military operations. Hooker further remarked "that high rank brings with it duties ... one of the most important is the setting an example of exact obedience of orders and regulations" (Tyler 1863).

First Lieutenant Demmon S. Decker, Company F, 56th Regiment, New York Infantry, also ran afoul of the edict precluding unauthorized publications. Decker's general court-martial convened at Beaufort, South Carolina, on March 2, 1864, and charged the officer with conduct unbecoming an officer and a gentleman, disobedience, and disrespect. The judge advocate accused Decker of submitting a letter that was published in the *Republican Watchman* and *Jeffersonian Democrat* newspapers on December 2, 1863 (Decker 1864).

In his lengthy letter, Decker lamented that Colonel Charles H. Van Wyck's "reputation as a military man is as bad as ever ... Every day we see more of the unworthiness of this mock statesman ... he had committed the unpardonable sin of dismissing officers without a trial, and ruined one of the best regiments in the service." The incident that incited Decker's defamatory letter was Van Wyck's alleged dismissal of the regiment's adjutant without a trial. Decker's letter claimed that Van Wyck had imprisoned the adjutant on a minor charge and had denied him the opportunity to clear his name at a court-martial, which resulted in several months of confinement. Decker's letter concluded with a perceptive note: "This letter may result in my dismissal. Let it come!" (Decker 1864).

President Lincoln's Emancipation Proclamation inflamed the sentiments of six Army officers and one Army sergeant, all of whom could not contain their disdain and subsequently found themselves facing courts-martial. It is unclear whether this small group represented a larger but silent group, but the Army's zealous prosecution of outspoken critics was likely an attempt to suppress any overt dissent.

An example of this group was the case of Captain Josiah W. McCuddon, Company D, 37th Regiment, Iowa Infantry. The officer penned a scathing diatribe in which he vehemently denounced President Lincoln's Emancipation Proclamation. McCuddon's general court-martial took place at Schofield Barracks, St. Louis, Missouri, on February 6, 1863. Based on the testimony, McCrudden strongly criticized the Emancipation Proclamation, characterizing it "as a very weak and foolish move, and if it was carried out, it would perfectly destroy this Government and ... that all free blacks of the Northern Government should be slaves." McCuddon's invective attacked Lincoln as "vacillating in his course, and had suffered himself to be nosed around by the Cabinet, and his Cabinet being all fanatics ... that he had never any confidence whatever in the efforts of the Government to suppress the rebellion ... and that he held that the South had a perfect right to secede" (McCuddon 1863).

McCrudden's use of intemperate language led to his general court-martial. The judge advocate charged him with violating the 5th Article of War, which prohibited reproachful language against the president, as well as conduct unbecoming of an officer and a gentleman. The court found the officer guilty and recommended that he be cashiered from the Army "and that he be utterly disabled from having or holding any office or employment in the service of the Unites States" (McCuddon 1863).

With the help of senior officers, Chief Engineer Joshua Follansbee refuted charges brought by Secretary of the Navy Gideon Welles. Judge Advocate H.H. Goodman read the single charge of "being disrespectful in language to his superior officer." Follansbee's Navy general court-martial convened at the Philadelphia, Pennsylvania, Navy Yard on May 29, 1863, and he listened as Goodman provided the details (Follansbee 1863).

According to the specification, Follansbee sent an insulting letter to Welles, which began with a cautious complaint: "My orders to Key West received on Saturday, so soon after being ordered to duty in this city [Philadelphia] took one by surprise … I had already made up my mind that my orders were distasteful to the steam engine contractors in this city." Follansbee speculated that the contractors in Philadelphia resented his presence and maliciously maneuvered to remove him. To soften that criticism, Follansbee concluded, "Let me not be misunderstood. I distinctly disdain any intention of finding fault with the Hon. Secretary of the Navy." Welles bristled at the insinuation that he bowed to the contractors, and not the interests of the Navy, when he reassigned Follansbee to Key West, Florida (Follansbee 1863).

Upon pleading not guilty, Follansbee, with the assistance of legal counsel, requested testimony from Commodores Thomas A. Dornin, Cornelius K. Stribling, and Frederick Engle. The prosecution solely relied on reading Follansbee's letter to the members of the court-martial. At the conclusion of the prosecution's case, Commodore Engle testified in favor of the accused. Engle's brief comments described Follensbee as an excellent officer. Commodore Dornin praised the officer's "character for subordination and discipline" but he was more ambiguous about "perusing" Follansbee's letter. Before submitting the letter to Secretary of the Navy Welles, Follansbee requested Commodore Dornin to review the document. However, Dornin clarified, "I gave no indication of my approval in words to him." Commodore Stribling followed Dornin and testified that "I have never been associated with a man more uniformly respectful to his superior officer" (Follansbee 1863).

During the court-martial proceedings, Follansbee's legal counsel delivered a 25-page defense statement highlighting the accused's 21-year Navy service. The counsel urged the court-martial members to read the letter dispassionately and reflect on the testimony of his witnesses. At the conclusion of Follansbee's defense, the court-martial retired to consider the case. Challenging an assertion made by the Secretary of the Navy must have weighed on their deliberations, but the unimpeachable testimony of three Commodores supported Follansbee's good conduct. In balancing those factors, the court-martial found Follansbee guilty and sentenced him to forfeit half pay during a three-month suspension and to receive a reprimand from the Secretary of the Navy (Follansbee 1863).

Malingering

To combat malingering, the military focused on improving recruitment practices, as well as detecting and preventing fraudulent medical claims. Although common, malingering was rarely prosecuted at a general court-martial. Malingerers were known for their inventive dodges, assuming nearly every conceivable medical imposture after donning a uniform in an attempt to avoid duty (Lande 2005, 131–157).

Malingering's corrosive effects on enlistment and retention did not escape the attention of newspapers, at least in the early years of the Civil

CANDIDATES FOR THE EXEMPT BRIGADE.—

Candidates from the exempt brigade. A woman mutilated a man's right hand with a hammer and a knife. "Oh Lord! Oh Lord! how it hurts," screams the man. Another man with an amputated finger reassures him, "'Twont hurt but a minute, and then you can get one of those" exemption certificates (C-USZ62–8385, Library of Congress Prints and Photographs Division, Washington, D.C.).

War. An article in the *Chicago Tribune* on August 27, 1862, began with a sarcastic reproach: "We have been almost equally amused and disgusted with the shifts to which the cowards have resorted ... at the idea of making any sacrifice to support their country." To emphasize the point, the newspaper reported that men flee to Canada, engage in self-mutilation, feign illness and injuries, convert to the Quaker religion, and in one case a man "was detected in an attempt to slip across the lines [Canada] in women's clothes" ("Schemes of the Shirks" 1862).

The implementation of the Union draft further accelerated the occurrence of fraud. *Frank Leslie's Illustrated Newspaper* dripped with acerbic wit, chastising "editors who have been writing the most ferocious articles against those who have hesitated to rush to the field, now find out that they themselves are exempt. One has no courage, another has weak knees, a third has no front teeth." To further dramatize the deceptions, Leslie's newspaper observed the panoply of pretenders at a recruitment site in New York City. One man feigned deafness while another whined about his weak eyes: "Although he has been known to see a pretty woman ... half a mile off, he protests he has lately become ... seriously shortsighted that he cannot see the nose on his face." Beyond the parody, the article condemned the lot as "unheroic" ("The Draft—Who Escaped, and Who Didn't" 1862).

The exit ramp from the draft forced the War Department to issue a new order limiting medical exemptions. Circular Number 100 from the Provost Marshal General's Office issued on November 9, 1863, directed surgeons on boards of enrollment to list the number of men rejected along with the disqualifying conditions. In recognizing the ease of fabrication, pain "is a symptom of disease so easily pretended that it is not to be admitted as a cause for exemption, unless accompanied with manifest derangement of the general health," deafness "must not be admitted on the mere statement of the drafted man," and "nearsightedness does not exempt" ("The Diseases and Infirmities Exempting from the Draft" 1863).

The representative database analyzed for this volume only identified ten examples of malingering that resulted in general courts-martial. Those small numbers nonetheless provide insights into the factors motivating the constitution of these courts-martial. Of the ten cases, eight involved Army officers. The remaining cases involved a Navy surgeon's steward and an Army private. In every case, malingering was a supplemental accusation that accompanied more serious charges of drunkenness, unauthorized absences, and misbehavior before the enemy. Three out of the ten cases, including that of the Army private, ended in acquittals.

Lieutenant Benjamin Brownell, Company E, 2nd Regiment, Michigan Infantry, faced a general court-martial on August 1, 1861. The court-martial charged Brownell with "unofficerlike conduct" for abandoning his command on July 18, 1861, when the unit was engaged with the enemy. Just before deserting Company E, Brownell "pretend[ed] to be sick ... when a few moments before he was to all appearances in excellent health" (Brownell 1861).

Brownell pleaded not guilty, and the court-martial agreed in part. The court-martial members acquitted Brownell on the malingering allegation but found the man guilty of leaving his command, resulting in a trivial 15-day suspension from rank and pay. Major General George B. McClellan disapproved the sentence and no doubt regretfully returned the officer to duty because the punishment "is entirely inadequate to the offense and is calculated to impair proper respect for Courts-martial" (Brownell 1861).

Second Lieutenant Oliver Walton, Company D, 1st Regiment, Massachusetts Infantry, appeared at a general court-martial convened on May 28, 1862, at the camp of the 1st Regiment located near New Bridge, Virginia. The judge advocate accused Walton of "cowardice and misbehavior before the enemy" when he left his company and went "to the rear while the battle was raging." Assistant Surgeon F. Lebron Monroe, 1st Regiment, Massachusetts Infantry, approached the officer during the battle and asked, "where are you going?," prompting Walton to complain that "I fell between two trees and hurt my knee." The surgeon's testimony minimized Walton's professed disability, as suggested by the court-martial convicting the officer of misbehavior before the enemy and sentencing him to be dismissed. After reviewing the case, Major General George B. McClellan condemned the sentence, stating that "the penalty for such conduct is Death" (Walton 1862).

Private Robert McBride, Company H, 2nd Regiment, Colorado Infantry, ran afoul of military discipline for habitual drunkenness and avoiding duty "on the pretense of being sick." The judge advocate maintained that the accused perpetually avoided work and was intoxicated whenever liquor was available. After considering the evidence, the court-martial members were unimpressed and acquitted the soldier. The convening authority criticized the legal proceedings for its lack of specific details about the soldier's drunkenness, but the senior officer did not return the case for further consideration (McBride 1863).

The representative database identified only one example of malingering in the Navy. Surgeon's Steward Alexander Browne, attached to the USS *Chocura*, appeared at a Navy general court-martial on board the USS *Portsmouth* located near New Orleans, Louisiana, on January 20, 1865. Commodore James S. Palmer, Commanding, West Gulf Blockading Squadron, preferred the military charges of scandalous conduct tending to the destruction of good morals, disobedience, and treating with contempt his superior officer (Browne 1865).

George W. Reynolds served as judge advocate and alleged that

Browne, while working at the United States Naval Hospital in New Orleans since December 26, 1863, "has been guilty since that date at various times of feigning disease ... having been ordered by Surgeon Samuel J. Jones ... to discontinue the use of tobacco did disobey that order ... and when admonished by the said Surgeon Jones ... he [Browne] wanted to see what consequences would follow from his disobedience." After Reynolds read the charges Browne pleaded not guilty and declined the assistance of defense counsel (Browne 1865).

The prosecution's first witness was Surgeon Samuel J. Jones, in charge of the New Orleans Naval Hospital. Jones testified that officials transferred Browne from the USS *Chocura* to the naval hospital on December 26, 1863, after Browne repeatedly complained of "night blindness and chronic inflammation of the bladder." Assistant Surgeon Thomas Hiland investigated Browne's complaints over the course of two days and concluded "that the patient was not suffering from those diseases." Hiland reported his findings to Jones and at the same time criticized the patient's disrespect (Browne 1865).

Browne justified his rude behavior by arguing that a surgeon's steward should have the privilege to dine with the officers in the hospital. Jones denied the request, but he moved Browne to a private room and arranged for his meals to be delivered there to alleviate the patient's discomfort. Jones also "took him as my individual patient. Wishing also to satisfy myself that the assistant surgeon was not mistaken in his opinion of him. I then prescribed for him as though he was really suffering from an inflammation of the bladder." Browne's complaint of night blindness also faded when testimony revealed that "he went to the theatre with Corpl McLaughlin ... who said that while in passing along the street and whilst at the theatre, no evidence of imperfect vision was manifested" (Browne 1865).

Initially, Browne refused the medications prescribed by Jones, claiming that the mild doses were causing him pain.

Surgeon Samuel J. Jones, USN (NH 48670, courtesy Naval History & Heritage Command).

Dr. Jones ordered Browne to comply with the prescribed medications, and he eventually resumed taking them. However, a few days later, Browne complained that the medications were not alleviating his pain. Jones prescribed bedrest and instructed Browne to abstain from using tobacco, both intended to alleviate bladder irritation. The unruly patient did neither, and staff members frequently observed Browne in the smoking room (Browne 1865).

Feeling increasingly frustrated with Browne's lack of cooperation, Jones requested that Assistant Surgeon Thomas Hiland examine the patient again. After examining the patient, Hiland found nothing wrong, and Jones subsequently informed Browne "that he was no longer considered a patient but as a prisoner to be brought to trial by a Court-martial. I ordered him confined in double irons" (Browne 1865).

During the trial, Browne chose to defend himself and summoned several witnesses from the USS *Augusta Dinsmore*, the ship responsible for transporting him to the hospital in New Orleans. Acting Assistant Surgeon Ezra Pray and Surgeon's Steward J.S. Murray both remembered Browne and his medical complaints, but both considered him fit for duty. The defense witnesses' lackluster testimony did not support Browne, leaving the defense statement as his last hope to influence the court-martial members (Browne 1865).

In his defense statement, Browne asserted that his duty on board the USS *Chocura* was enjoyable and that he was not motivated to feign illness. He rejected Hiland's testimony, arguing that "he tested my urine and found it healthy, it was not until the third day that I had been in the Hospital that he tested it, and in the intervening [period] I had been taking medicine that would materially alter the state of my urine." Browne also claimed that he chose not to request treatment while on board the USS *Augusta Dinsmore*, opting instead to wait for admission to the hospital. In his closing statement, Browne expressed dissatisfaction with the proceedings and suggested that his defense was hindered by the judge advocate's failure to provide his requested witnesses. The court-martial convicted Browne of all three charges, sentenced him to three months of confinement at the New Orleans Parish Prison, and dishonorably discharged him (Browne 1865).

Gambling

Next to alcohol, gambling was probably the most pervasive leisure activity, and like the beverage, it was officially denounced and informally permitted. To maintain discipline within the Army of the Potomac, Major

General George B. McClellan strategically appointed Brigadier General Andrew Porter as the provost marshal. With his new role, Porter was able to effectively expand his authority by installing a provost marshal in each division of the Army. These provost marshals played a crucial role in policing the Army, and among their specific duties was "suppression of gambling houses, drinking houses, or bar-rooms and brothels" (General Orders Number 69, 1862).

Stamping out vices was an impossible task and even "suppression" was aspirational. Gambling suffused military life, and, like alcohol, relieved boredom and tempered the sharp realities of a lethal war. It was a pastime pursued by enlisted service members and officers, with the latter group's participation implicitly approving the practice.

In *The Life of Billy Yank*, author Bell I. Wiley examined gambling's pervasive influence. Playing card games, such as poker, faro, and twenty-one, was common. Dice games, such as chuck-a-luck, were exceedingly popular. Less common forms of wagering included horse racing, cock fighting, and raffling of personal possessions. Gambling peaked during paydays, but the soldiers' meager wages ensured that bets were small. Firsthand accounts amply document Civil War gambling, with one soldier marveling that "so far as my observation goes, nine out of ten play cards for money" (Wiley 1962, 249–252).

Various periodicals in the early years of the Civil War bemoaned the prevalence of gambling. Soon after the Civil War began, the *New York Times* published an inspection of camp conditions conducted by the Sanitary Commission that noted "serious mischief from gambling." Professional gamblers were among those causing trouble when they fleeced unsuspecting soldiers of their hard-earned dollars. The Sanitary

Soldiers playing cards (LC-DIG-ppmsca-33088, Library of Congress Prints and Photographs Division, Washington, D.C.).

Commission recommended wholesome activities such as reading, attending religious services, and writing letters to loved ones ("The Sanitary Commission" 1862).

The *New York Times* sounded incredulous after observing half the soldiers in an encamped regiment gambling, with some hapless soldiers losing all their pay within minutes. The newspaper lauded the Army's crackdown, rejoiced that several soldiers were arrested, and assured their readers that " the evil will soon be entirely removed" ("The Routine of Camp Life" 1862).

Harper's Weekly begrudgingly acknowledged that curbing gambling was impossible. In a short article published in 1863, the magazine opened the subject by describing an unusual punishment. Military officials forced a pair of inveterate gamblers from the 93rd Regiment, New York Infantry, to spend an entire day, without breaks or meals, playing cards and dice. The soldiers also sported placards neatly lettered "Gambler." It was a humiliating punishment, but as *Harper's Weekly* astutely concluded, "It is useless to punish the men while it is so prevalent a vice with the officers" ("Gamblers in the Army" 1863).

The representative database analyzed for this volume identified 27 examples of gambling that resulted in general courts-martial. Army officers were the primary subjects, with 23 (n = 27, 85.2%) charged with either gambling or playing cards. There were no examples of gambling

General Patrick's punishment for gamblers (LC-DIG-ppmsca-21212, Library of Congress Prints and Photographs Division, Washington, D.C.).

prosecuted by Navy general courts-martial. Army courts-martial invariably charged service members with more than one offense (n = 25/27, 92.6%). The most common supplemental charge was drunkenness (n = 11/27, 40.7%). Courts-martial considered five gambling charges in 1861 (n = 27, 18.5%), eight in 1862 (n = 27, 29.7%), 10 in 1863 (n = 27, 37.0%), and four in 1864 (n = 27, 14.8%). In 22 cases, the courts-martial returned guilty verdicts (n = 27, 81.5%), after which the convening authority reversed three (n = 22, 13.6%).

Officers gambling with enlisted soldiers undermined command authority, and this was a common justification for convening a general court-martial. Second Lieutenant Timothy F. Lee, Company E, 9th Regiment, Massachusetts Infantry, learned that lesson the hard way. Lee's trial took place at Fort Corcoran, Virginia, and charged the officer with conduct unbecoming an officer and a gentleman and embezzlement. The judge advocate alleged that Lee played cards and drank with enlisted soldiers on September 24, 1861, and pocketed 60 dollars in winnings. After weighing the evidence, the court-martial found Lee guilty of gambling and sentenced him to be dismissed from the Army (Lee, T. 1861).

A general court-martial assembled to consider the case of First Lieutenant Allen Varner, 25th Regiment, Illinois Infantry. The judge advocate accused Varner of three military offenses: disobedience, conduct prejudicial to good order and military discipline, and subversive conduct. The judge advocate accused Varner of violating a military edict issued in October 1861, which expressly outlawed the playing of cards. Contrary to this order, Varner reportedly participated in gambling with enlisted men at the Lamine Bridge encampment in Missouri that precipitated a series of disciplinary issues within the unit. In an inexplicable finding, the court-martial determined that Varner was not guilty of disobedience but was guilty of gambling and sentenced him "to be severely reprimanded by the Commanding General." Major General Henry Halleck reviewed the proceedings and considered Varner "lucky in receiving so mild a sentence" (Varner, A. 1862).

Private Charles Weidner, Company A, 5th Regiment, Wisconsin Infantry, was one of the very few enlisted soldiers in the representative database accused of gambling by a general court-martial. The judge advocate charged Weidner with disobedience of orders when the trial convened on October 22, 1861. The court-martial subsequently convicted Weidner of violating a regimental order forbidding gambling and sentenced the soldier to five days of hard labor. Without any explanation, Major General George B. McClellan remitted the sentence, perhaps realizing the futility of punishing the soldier for the rampant behavior (Weidner 1862).

Colonel John McCluskey, 15th Regiment, Maine Infantry, was among the highest-ranking officers accused of overlooking gambling. McCluskey's trial assembled at Ship Island, Mississippi, on April 15, 1862, to consider three military charges: conduct unbecoming an officer and a gentleman, violation of the 24th Article of War that prohibited disrespectful language and gestures, and neglect of duty. The crux of the charges developed while McCluskey and his regiment were on board a transport ship. On the journey from Portland, Maine, to Ship Island, the judge advocate alleged that McCluskey was frequently drunk, neglected his duties, and permitted gambling between officers and enlisted service members. The prosecutor's case was weak, and as a result, the court-martial acquitted McCloskey (McCluskey 1862).

The fate of Captain William W. Miller, Company C, 7th Regiment, Missouri Cavalry, turned on a procedural error. Miller's general court-martial convened at Cross Hollows, Arkansas, on October 20, 1862, and charged the officer with disobedience and conduct prejudicial to good order and military discipline. Miller refused an order to move his company, insulted another officer, and "at various other times, and places, [did] engage at and play the game of cards in his own tent, and those of others, with the Privates of his own Company." The trial concluded with Miller's conviction and sentence to be dismissed from the Army. Major General Samuel Ryan Curtis disapproved of the sentence because "only half of the Court met at its first session, and only five at the time the sentence was passed" (Miller, W. W. 1862).

Captain William F. Cardiff, Company B, 3rd Regiment, Maryland Infantry, Potomac Home Brigade, appeared before a general court-martial at Baltimore, Maryland, on October 27, 1863. The judge advocate charged Cardiff with eight specifications of drunkenness on duty. Attesting to Cardiff's serious alcohol problem was a prolonged period of drinking that culminated in "mania-a-potu" and necessitated a five-day hospitalization. Another specification alleged that Cardiff while "in a drinking house, engage[d] in a game of cards with enlisted men of his command." The court rendered a mixed verdict, finding Cardiff guilty of four specifications, including playing cards, and sentenced the officer to be cashiered from the Army (Cardiff 1863).

Major Napoleon B. Knight faced military charges that included drunkenness on duty, AWOL, and conduct prejudicial to good order and military discipline at a general court-martial held in Baltimore, Maryland, on January 30, 1864. The judge advocate accused Knight of 14 separate incidents of intoxication and one specification alleging that he "did play at cards for money, with an enlisted man, or men, of his command." The court convicted Knight of gambling and one specification of intoxication and imposed the forfeiture of one day's pay for punishment.

The lenient sentence resulted from the court-martial's opinion that "the charges approach very nearly to such as come under the head of frivolous and vexatious." Brigadier General Henry Hayes Lockwood disagreed with the court's opinion and blamed the trial's outcome on "charges and specifications which seem to have been imperfectly developed by the Judge advocate" (Knight 1864).

An unusual trial unfolded when Colonel Charles Carroll Tevis, 3rd Regiment, Maryland Cavalry, appeared before a general court-martial empaneled at Morganza, Louisiana. The judge advocate accused Tevis of conduct to the prejudice to good order and military discipline and conduct unbecoming an officer and a gentleman. The judge advocate's first military charge accused the officer of organizing a horse race at a public venue in New Orleans, Louisiana, on March 19, 1864. The second charge alleged that Tevis permitted "private soldiers of his command to be present and to bet on the result of the same." The court found Tevis only guilty of conduct to the prejudice to good order and military discipline and punished the officer with a reprimand (General Orders Number 81, 1864).

Tevis wrote a letter on July 26, 1864, to Major General Edward Canby expressing his dissatisfaction with the court-martial proceedings. In the letter, Tevis voiced his frustration and concerns regarding the fairness and impartiality of the trial. Not only did Tevis spend 107 days in confinement awaiting the court-martial, but he was also upset because he strongly believed that the trial was unfair. He bitterly complained, "Surely the authority which judged a horse race worthy of so severe an action, should have taken cognizance of charges against another officer where drunkenness [and] incapacity ... were the offenses alleged: but on six different occasions have these charges been suppressed." Tevis's subsequent resignation was a response to the unfair trial and reprimand he received, which he believed were the result of disparate treatment and therefore unconscionable (Tevis 1864).

Medical Malfeasance

Historical research has thoroughly examined the intricacies of Civil War medicine. Military surgeons documented their observations and provided practical advice for treating the vast array of wounds and illnesses in Civil War medical journals. After the war, their experiences contributed to the wealth of knowledge that propelled the innovative growth of medicine.

There is a vast body of research on Civil War medicine that covers a wide range of topics. However, there are still areas of inquiry that remain relatively unexplored, such as medical malfeasance. Although this topic has attracted the attention of some historians, there is still much to be learned about it. Thomas P. Lowry stands out as one of the few historians who have delved into the subject of medical malfeasance during the Civil War, and readers seeking an in-depth exploration of this topic will find value in his research.

Lowry's *Tarnished Scalpels: The Court-Martials of Fifty Union Surgeons* rates as the first modern research exploring medical malfeasance (Lowry and Welsh 2000). The author's narrative style recognized the laissez-faire nineteenth-century approach to healthcare, which lacked uniform requirements for medical education and had virtually nonexistent rules regulating the delivery of quality care. Additionally, the author identified the concept of dual agency, where surgeons had obligations as military officers and physicians, sometimes resulting in conflicting responsibilities. The distinguishing factor was how the surgeon managed the conflict (Lowry and Welsh 2000, 18–29).

The authors asserted that "newly appointed officers knew little of military rules and regulations, but the doctors seem to have known even less" (Lowry and Welsh 2000, 24). This comment cannot excuse medical malfeasance since surgeons and newly appointed officers did not require intimate familiarity with the Articles of War, as Lowry suggested, to avoid behaviors such as drunkenness, theft, assault, rape, or the provision of substandard care. Lowry's *Tarnished Scalpels* would also seem to suggest that all 50 courts-martial ended with an ignominious conviction, but some surgeons were acquitted while several others received minor punishments (Lowry and Welsh 2000).

Tarnished Scalpels devoted a chapter to the trial of Assistant Surgeon Warren Webster (Lowry and Welsh 2000, 177–185). His general court-martial convened in New York City on December 14, 1863, and charged the surgeon with disobedience of orders and conduct prejudicial to good order and military discipline. The gist of the charges claimed that Webster refused an order from General Harvey Brown, Commanding, Fort Schuyler, to permit the arrest and incarceration of Private Phillip Fitzsimmons, Company F, 40th Regiment, New York Infantry, a patient under the doctor's care (*Letter of The Secretary of War* 1864).

Webster oversaw the McDougall Hospital, located on the grounds of Fort Schuyler in New York City. He refused Brown's order, insisting that with "general hospitals to be under the sole control of the Surgeon General of the army, he considered himself duty bound to obey orders relating to the transfer of patients from the hospital only when coming through the Surgeon General." Webster's principled stand led to his court-martial (*Letter of The Secretary of War* 1864).

The evidence presented at the trial clearly showed that Webster was justified in refusing the order without the Surgeon General's concurrence.

The witnesses also lauded the surgeon's character and superb administration of the hospital. Webster found himself in a difficult position, torn between his duty as a surgeon and his obligation as a military officer. He was caught in a conflict of dual agency, where obeying one order potentially put him at odds with the other. In this case, complying with General Brown's order would have meant going against the Surgeon General's control over the hospitals, while refusing the order resulted in the court-martial. Webster's principled stand ultimately led to his court-martial.

The court-martial found Webster guilty and sentenced him to six months of confinement at Fort Schuyler. However, due to his outstanding military record, the members recommended clemency. Major General John A. Dix refused to remit the sentence, "believing, with the court, that the offence was founded in some degree on a misconception of duty, which, however, would have been more pardonable in an officer of less intelligence, the sentence of confinement to the limits of the post at which Assistant Surgeon Webster is employed is reduced from six months to sixty days" (*Letter of The Secretary of War* 1864).

Lowry added a comment in *Tarnished Scalpels* that acknowledged the injustice in Webster's case (Lowry and Welsh 2000, 183). At the same time, including his court-martial among the 50 trials designated by the sobriquet *Tarnished Scalpels* downplays the complexity of Webster's dilemma.

Thomas P. Lowry and Terry Reimer co-authored *Bad Doctors: Military Justice Proceedings Against 622 Civil War Surgeons*. This concise book covers the topic in 126 pages, with an additional 19 pages dedicated to ten "special cases." The remaining 612 courts-martial, which included 30 Confederate trials, consisted of the surgeon's name and one or two sentences describing the trial. *Bad Doctors* ran out of steam describing Navy courts-martial, devoting only three pages to the subject. Despite its brevity, *Bad Doctors* is a useful reference for historians since it occupies a relatively unoccupied niche in exploring the intersection between medicine and the law during the Civil War (Lowry and Reimer 2011).

Both of Lowry's books annotated instances of medical malpractice, but lawsuits alleging physician's negligence were on the rise before the Civil War (De Ville 1992, 25–64). The surge in malpractice litigation captured the attention of John J. Elwell, a physician and lawyer, whose 1860 treatise on malpractice filled a void as it "sets forth and maintains the rights of the medical and surgical practitioner, not shielding the culpable and guilty, and at the same time bringing the two professions into closer union" (Elwell 1860, 6).

Before his presidency, Lincoln practiced law and handled several cases related to legal medicine (Eckley 2012, 43–48). Lincoln's experience

Five. Subordinate Military Crimes 213

with medical jurisprudence probably influenced his decision to stay the execution of Private Lorenzo C. Stewart, 14th Regiment, New York Heavy Artillery, following the soldier's conviction for desertion and murder. Stewart's lawyer, family, and friends launched an aggressive campaign after his conviction, insisting that the condemned man was insane. Lincoln ordered a court of inquiry to investigate Stewart's mental state, but after weeks of testimony, the anxious Stewart escaped from confinement. Years later Stewart resurfaced, appealed his case to President Rutherford B. Hayes, and received a pardon (Lande 1988).

During the Civil War 12,343 physicians, with widely disparate skills and training, supported the Union cause (Griffiths 1966, 207). Soldiers endlessly complained about their medical care and a small number of surgeons faced courts-martial, but the vast majority did their best under dreadful conditions. As a testament to the perils of a doctor's life, "the death rate among them, both from enemy action and from disease, was higher than that in any other staff corps" (Griffiths 1966, 207).

The author of this volume analyzed a list of Navy officers from 1775 to 1900 and identified 698 surgeons who served varying amounts of time between the dates of April 12, 1861, and April 9, 1865. Out of those 698 surgeons who served during the Civil War, Navy officials dismissed 30 Navy surgeons from their positions. Slightly more than half were dismissed in 1861 (n = 17/30, 56.6%), three in 1862 (n = 3/30, 10.0%), six in 1863 (n = 6/30, 20.0%), two in 1864 (n = 2/30, 6.7%), and two in 1865 (n = 2/30, 6.7%) (Callahan 1901). The high number of dismissals in 1861 was likely due to factors such as some surgeons' aversion to combat, President Lincoln's mandate for officers to sign loyalty oath forms, or their southern sympathies (Dudley 1981, 10–13).

The representative database analyzed for this volume identified 50 general courts-martial involving Army surgeons and 10 Navy surgeons. Among the Army group, nearly half were surgeons (n = 22/50, 44.0%) while the remainder were assistant surgeons (n = 28/50, 56.0%). In the Navy, almost the entire group consisted of acting assistant surgeons (n = 9/10, 90.0%).

Surgeons often faced multiple charges in general courts-martial, encompassing various military-specific offenses. The most common charges involved allegations of being AWOL (n = 18), being drunk (n = 15), neglect of their duties (n = 7), and alcohol-fueled assaults (n = 4). Navy general courts-martial convicted six of the surgeons (n = 10, 60.0%), while Army general courts-martial found 40 surgeons guilty (n = 50, 80.0%). Punitive discharges were common, with the Navy dismissing four surgeons while the Army dismissed 25 surgeons and sentenced another five surgeons to be cashiered. Postconviction reviews remitted the sentences in five Army courts-martial.

An example of a surgeon's trial was the case of David Little, 13th Regiment, New York Infantry. The judge advocate charged Little with neglect of duty and AWOL at a general court-martial that convened on October 21, 1861. The court-martial members heard the judge advocate allege that Little wantonly neglected his duties as a physician and "at one time he did not visit the Hospital tent or prescribe for any sick, for ten or twelve consecutive days." Little also overstayed a furlough, which led to the AWOL charge (Little 1862).

Little's court-martial returned a not guilty verdict, which resulted in a blistering rebuke from Major General George B. McClellan. The surgeon's defense relied on a claim of illness, an excuse that McClellan eviscerated because Little never sought medical treatment. Little also asserted ignorance of military law, which McClellan rejected out of hand. McClellan savaged the surgeon, declaring that "it is hard to imagine anything more unpardonable than negligence or procrastination on the part of a Surgeon." Despite his disgust, McClellan reluctantly returned the surgeon to active duty (Little 1862).

Assistant Surgeon Ferdinand Guenste, 35th Regiment, Pennsylvania Infantry, appeared before a general court-martial charged with drunkenness, conduct to the prejudice of good order and military discipline, and breach of arrest. On December 8, 1861, Guenste was intoxicated and

Mansion House Hospital, Alexandria, Virginia (LC-DIG-ppmsca-33628, Library of Congress Prints and Photographs Division, Washington, D.C.).

incapable of performing his duties. Adding to the charges were his belligerent tirade and refusal to remain in his tent. The surgeon pleaded guilty, and the court-martial subsequently sentenced the man to be dismissed from the Army. At the same time, the court-martial members recommended mercy, perhaps considering the solitary incident unworthy of dismissal. Major General George B. McClellan disagreed and insisted that "habits of strict temperance are eminently demanded of the Surgeon, upon whose clearness of judgement, and steadiness of hand, the lives of brave men must often depend" (Guenste 1862).

Surgeon John B. Porter requested a court of inquiry after a group of patients complained of care received at the Mansion House Hospital in Alexandria, Virginia. In a lurid headline titled "The Horrors of the Alexandria Hospital," a newspaper willingly published letters from 14 soldiers who indicated their willingness to testify if needed. Eleven letters faulted the food, with complaints such as "I do not get sufficient [food] to eat"; "some of the patients of this hospital dip from the slop barrel soup"; "rations for breakfast and supper being nothing but dry bread, without butter, and tea or coffee, without milk or sugar"; and "I have suffered for the want of food many times." Porter faced additional complaints, accusing him of physically assaulting a patient and unjustly withholding the discharge of others ("The Horrors of the Alexandria Hospital" 1862).

Porter's court of inquiry took place on March 1, 1862, in Alexandria, Virginia. In an unusual move, the court of inquiry only took testimony from the complaining soldiers and declined Porter's proffered witnesses. After considering the testimony of the soldiers, and reviewing their published letters, the court of inquiry determined that "the evidence has failed to substantiate the statements." The court of inquiry acknowledged that the demands of war created shortages and provided an example of one month's supply of substandard flour that officials sent to the hospital. When queried under oath, none of the witnesses recalled Porter striking a patient, and the only disciplinary actions imposed by the surgeon involved a drunk and disorderly patient and those who violated hospital rules (Porter, J. 1862).

The court of inquiry concluded with an unequivocal endorsement that "this meritorious officer is ... out of the mouths of those who were published as his accusers, not only completely exculpated, but shown to have been throughout exemplary in the discharge of his arduous and responsible duties." Concerning Porter's accusers, the court denounced that "charges of the most injurious character were, with perverse industry circulated" (Porter, J. 1862).

Surgeon James M. Hoffman, 155th Regiment, Pennsylvania Infantry, took inappropriate advantage of his official position. At a general court-martial convened on February 24, 1863, near Falmouth, Virginia, the judge advocate charged the surgeon with conduct prejudicial to good order and military discipline and embezzlement. The specifications accused Hoffman of procuring supplies, including whiskey, by using hospital funds and then selling the ill-gotten items to soldiers. Hoffman's entrepreneurial activities went even further when he started selling medical discharge certificates to the officers. The court-martial found Hoffman not guilty of selling discharge certificates, but guilty of distributing the alcohol to the soldiers. For punishment, the court-martial required restitution of the embezzled funds and then sentenced Hoffman to be dismissed from the Army (Hoffman, J. 1863).

A general court-martial convened at Baltimore, Maryland, on January 30, 1863, for the trial of Assistant Surgeon Andrew McLetchie, 79th Regiment, New York State Militia. The judge advocate accused the surgeon of drunkenness while in charge of the hospital at Camp Parole, Maryland. McLetchie's disruptive behavior and unauthorized absences while intoxicated added to the surgeon's woes. The court-martial found the surgeon guilty and sentenced him to be dismissed from the Army (McLetchie 1864).

Surgeon James W. Pettinos, United States Volunteers, lost his job in the Army due to his baseless accusations and drunkenness. The judge advocate charged the surgeon with five specifications of conduct unbecoming an officer and a gentleman, 12 specifications of drunkenness, and three specifications for disobedience at a general court-martial that convened in Baltimore, Maryland (Pettinos 1864).

The cascade of crimes began with the judge advocate's allegation that Pettinos was intoxicated when summoned for unknown reasons to the office of Colonel Adrian R. Root, 94th Regiment, New York Infantry, Commanding, Camp Parole, Maryland, on February 18, 1864. Root momentarily left his office and the idled surgeon cast his gaze across the room and noted "a lady's hairpin." As he examined the hairpin, Pettinos asked Colonel Root's orderly if "Miss H.D. Williams, the agent of the United States Sanitary Commission" had visited the senior officer. The orderly confirmed the visit but was not present when the pair met. According to the orderly's subsequent testimony, Pettinos immediately concluded "it was just as he supposed, intimating and intending thereby, that improper intimacy and relations existed between the said Miss H.D. Williams and said Col. A.R. Root." The surgeon acted on his suspicions and demanded through the orderly that Williams only be admitted to Camp Parole with the express approval of Colonel Root or himself, thereby escalating the situation. The judge advocate insisted that this additional step was intended "to injure them in their good name and reputation for virtue and chastity" (Pettinos 1864).

During the trial, the judge advocate further accused Pettinos of assaulting a patient named Private Joseph W. McCue from the 106th Regiment, New York Infantry, while he was receiving treatment at Camp Parole's hospital. What provoked Pettinos is unknown, but the surgeon then "tied [McCue] up by his thumbs to the flag-staff for four hours ... gagged with a rope tied through the mouth ... and ordered an enlisted man to shoot the said private." Assistant Surgeon B.F. Berkeley witnessed the barbarism and interceded, sparing the man's life (Pettinos 1864).

After listening to the testimony, the court-martial concluded that Pettinos was guilty of conduct unbecoming an officer and a gentleman, not guilty of all 12 counts of drunkenness, and guilty of disobedience. Despite the mixed verdicts, the court-martial sentenced Pettinos to be dismissed from the Army (Pettinos 1864).

The case of Surgeon Joshua B. Treadwell, 5th Regiment, Massachusetts Militia, was unusual. A court-martial assembled at Baltimore, Maryland, on January 6, 1865, to hear the judge advocate accuse the surgeon of conduct to the prejudice of good order and military discipline. The single specification alleged that Treadwell, while in charge of the hospital at Fort Marshall, Maryland, conspired with a hospital steward "to receive and exact money from soldiers ... in consideration for the procurement of discharges ... from the military service" (Treadwell 1865).

Treadwell argued that the general court-martial lacked jurisdiction to consider the charges because he was "fully and honorably discharged from the service ... before any charges were preferred against him." The court-martial members accepted Treadwell's defense, and Brevet Brigadier General William W. Morris released the surgeon from arrest but recommended his subsequent trial by a military commission (Treadwell 1865). Treadwell apparently avoided any further legal entanglements, based on records that indicated a brief period of service with the 62nd Regiment, Massachusetts Infantry, from February 28,

Surgeon Joshua Brackett Treadwell (LC-DIG-ppmsca-86049, Library of Congress Prints and Photographs Division, Washington, D.C.).

1865, through May 5, 1865 (*Massachusetts Soldiers, Sailors, and Marines in the Civil War* 1932, 166).

Navy surgeons appeared before military tribunals less frequently than their Army counterparts, but they faced similar allegations. An example involved a court of inquiry convened on board the USS *R.R. Cuyler*, at Tampa Bay, Florida, on May 5, 1862. Assistant Surgeon David T. Lewis, attached to the USS *Ethan Allen*, contributed to a tempest that blew an ill wind over a senior Navy officer. Lewis wrote a derogatory letter to Flag Officer William W. McKean in which he complained about a fellow officer who "habitually uses profane oaths and blasphemous language," threatened crewmembers, and assaulted one. The surgeon assigned much of the man's behavior to "the very frequent use of stimulating drinks, from which I have in vain professionally advised him to abstain entirely" (Lewis 1862).

The officer who was the target of Lewis's complaint fiercely responded with a two-page letter to McKean. Dripping with insinuation, the officer stated "I consider his [Lewis's] conduct in writing such a report as he has, is highly improper for the reason that he has sought an intimate acquaintance with my steward. He has been closeted with him in his own room day and night." The officer's broadside volley also accused Lewis of interfering with the ship's discipline and overseeing a filthy dispensary (Lewis 1862).

McKean assembled the court of inquiry to unravel the dueling officers' allegations. The testimony confirmed the relationship between the surgeon and the steward, but it also revealed that the steward had previously worked with Lewis as a nurse. Witnesses described the dispensary's cleanliness as no different from the rest of the ship except for permanent stains on a shelf caused by various medications. Similarly, the accusations made by Lewis against an officer for being intoxicated and exhibiting despotic behavior did not receive any supporting evidence. After weighing all the testimony, the court of inquiry exonerated both men. With regard to Lewis, the court of inquiry found no evidence that he interfered with the ship's discipline "nor any impropriety in his intercourse with the Cabin Steward" (Lewis 1862).

An incredibly weak investigation unfolded in a court of inquiry held on board the USS *Conestoga*, at Skipwith's Landing, on the Mississippi River, on December 14, 1863. Rear Admiral David D. Porter ordered the court of inquiry in the matter of Thomas Rice, Acting Assistant Surgeon, attached to the USS *Mound City*. Porter alleged that the surgeon "did participate in the pillaging and burning of a house or houses, and did take therefrom certain articles of china plate, furniture, books, oil paintings, and other articles, too numerous to mention." The court of inquiry's recorder also investigated alleged occurrences of unspecified disorderly conduct (Rice 1863).

The recorder presented two witnesses, both of whom denied any knowledge of pillaging or any instances of disorderly conduct. Rice explained that the questionable items in his possession were either purchased or accepted as gifts. The court of inquiry summarily concluded "that none of the charges were proven" (Rice 1863).

Bibliography

Adolph Hugel. 1863. Records of General Courts Martial and Courts of Inquiry of the Navy Department, 1799–1867, Volume 103, Record Group 125, Publication Number M273. Washington, D.C.: National Archives and Records Administration. (Courts-martial records lack uniform pagination.)
Agnew, Peter J. 1863. Records of General Courts Martial and Courts of Inquiry of the Navy Department, 1799–1867, Volume 96, Record Group 125, Publication Number M273. Washington, D.C.: National Archives and Records Administration.
Ahlus, Louis. 1861. General Orders Number 16. Department of the Missouri. St. Louis, MO. Washington, D.C.: Government Printing Office.
Allen, John W. 2010. *It Happened in Southern Illinois*. Carbondale: Southern Illinois University Press.
Alotta, Robert I. 1989. *Civil War Justice: Union Army Executions Under Lincoln*. Shippensburg, PA: White Mane Publishing Company.
Ammen, Daniel. 1864. Records of General Courts Martial and Courts of Inquiry of the Navy Department, 1799–1867, Volume 118, Record Group 125, Publication Number M273. Washington, D.C.: National Archives and Records Administration.
Anderson, Charles W. 1862. General Orders Number 9. Department of the Missouri. St. Louis, MO. Washington, D.C.: Government Printing Office.
Andrie, William. 1862. General Orders Number 40. Department of the Missouri. St. Louis, MO. Washington, D.C.: Government Printing Office.
Ashley, B.J. 1864. General Orders Number 97. Middle Department. Baltimore, MD. Washington, D.C.: Government Printing Office.
Atkinson, Paul. 1862. Records of General Courts Martial and Courts of Inquiry of the Navy Department, 1799–1867, Volume 92, Record Group 125, Publication Number M273. Washington, D.C.: National Archives and Records Administration.
_____. 1864. Navy Officers' Letters 1802–1884. M148. Record Group 45. Washington, D.C.: National Archives and Records Administration.
Baker, David L. 1862. General Orders Number 23. Department of the Missouri. St. Louis, MO. Washington, D.C.: Government Printing Office.
Baker, Lafayette C. 1894. *Spies: Traitors and Conspirators of the Late Civil War*. Philadelphia, PA: John E. Potter.
Baker, Patrick. 1864. Records of General Courts Martial and Courts of Inquiry of the Navy Department, 1799–1867, Volume 120, Record Group 125, Publication Number M273. Washington, D.C.: National Archives and Records Administration.
Ballard, J.P., and E.M. Everett. 1863. General Orders Number 29. Middle Department. Baltimore, MD. Washington, D.C.: Government Printing Office.
Barber, E. Susan, and Charles F. Ritter. 2015. "Dangerous Liaisons: Working Women and Sexual Justice in the American Civil War." *European Journal of American Studies*. 10–1, Special Issue: Women in the USA.
Barrett, Wallace W., Edwin L. Hayes, and John B. Stoner. 1862. General Orders Number 21. Department of the Missouri. St. Louis, MO. Washington, D.C.: Government Printing Office.

Barry, Charles. 1863. Records of General Courts Martial and Courts of Inquiry of the Navy Department, 1799–1867, Volume 97, Record Group 125, Publication Number M273. Washington, D.C.: National Archives and Records Administration.
Bateman, Newton, and Paul Selby. 1912. *Historical Encyclopedia of Illinois*. Vol. 2. Chicago: Munsell Publishing Company.
Bates, Samuel P. 1869a. *History of Pennsylvania Volunteers, 1861–5; Prepared in Compliance With Acts of the Legislature*, 5 vols., Vol. 1. Harrisburg, PA: B. Singerly, State Printer.
———. 1869b. *History of Pennsylvania Volunteers, 1861–5; Prepared in Compliance With Acts of the Legislature*, 5 vols., Vol. 2. Harrisburg, PA: B. Singerly, State Printer.
Bath, William L. 1862. General Orders Number 17. Army of the Potomac. Washington, D.C.: Government Printing Office.
"Before The Court." 1896. *San Francisco Chronicle*, May 14.
Benedict, Augustus W. 1863. Compiled Military Service Records of Volunteer Union Soldiers Who Served the United States Colored Troops: 56th-138th USCT Infantry, 1864–1866. Record Group 94. Roll RG94-USCT-076-Bx05.
Benét, Stephen V. 1862. *A Treatise on Military Law and the Practice of Courts-Martial*. New York: D. Van Nostrand.
Bennett, Kevin B. 1991. "The Jacksonville Mutiny." *Military Law Review* 134 (Fall): 157–172.
Biggs, George. 1862. General Orders No. 31. Department of the Missouri. St. Louis, MO. Washington, D.C.: Government Printing Office.
Bishop, William. 1862. General Orders Number 11. Department of the Missouri. St. Louis, MO. Washington, D.C.: Government Printing Office.
Bourne, Peter. 1863. Records of General Courts Martial and Courts of Inquiry of the Navy Department, 1799–1867, Volume 104, Record Group 125, Publication Number M273. Washington, D.C.: National Archives and Records Administration.
Bowden, Joseph. 1863. Records of General Courts Martial and Courts of Inquiry of the Navy Department, 1799–1867, Volume 105, Record Group 125, Publication Number M273. Washington, D.C.: National Archives and Records Administration.
Boyd, Richard. 1862. Records of General Courts Martial and Courts of Inquiry of the Navy Department, 1799–1867, Volume 90, Record Group 125, Publication Number M273. Washington, D.C.: National Archives and Records Administration.
Boyle, John. 1863. General Orders Number 55. Army of the Potomac. Washington, D.C.: Government Printing Office.
Boyles, John A. 1862. General Orders Number 45. Department of the South. Hilton Head, SC. Washington, D.C.: Government Printing Office.
Breese, Samuel L. 1863. Records of General Courts Martial and Courts of Inquiry of the Navy Department, 1799–1867, Volume 103, Record Group 125, Publication Number M273. Washington, D.C.: National Archives and Records Administration.
Bright, George S. 1863. Records of General Courts Martial and Courts of Inquiry of the Navy Department, 1799–1867, Volume 99, Record Group 125, Publication Number M273. Washington, D.C.: National Archives and Records Administration.
Bristow, Charles. 1864. Records of General Courts Martial and Courts of Inquiry of the Navy Department, 1799–1867, Volume 132, Record Group 125, Publication Number M273. Washington, D.C.: National Archives and Records Administration.
Britt, John. 1863. Records of General Courts Martial and Courts of Inquiry of the Navy Department, 1799–1867, Volume 94, Record Group 125, Publication Number M273. Washington, D.C.: National Archives and Records Administration.
Brown, Charles. 1863. Records of General Courts Martial and Courts of Inquiry of the Navy Department, 1799–1867, Volume 108, Record Group 125, Publication Number M273. Washington, D.C.: National Archives and Records Administration.
Brown, James F. 1864. Proceedings of U.S. Army Courts-Martial and Military Commissions of Union Soldiers Executed by U.S. Military Authorities, 1861–1866. M1523, Roll 1. Washington, D.C.: National Archives and Records Administration.
Browne, Alexander. 1865. Records of General Courts-Martial and Courts of Inquiry of the Navy Department, 1799–1867, Volume 91, Record Group 128, Publication Number M273. Washington, D.C.: National Archives and Records Administration.

Brownell, Benjamin. 1861. General Orders Number 11. Army of the Potomac. Washington, D.C.: Government Printing Office.
Budy, Anderson. 1861. General Orders Number 43. Army of the Potomac. Washington, D.C.: Government Printing Office.
Buhk, Tobin T. 2012. *True Crime in the Civil War: Cases of Murder, Treason, Counterfeiting, Massacre, Plunder & Abuse*. Mechanicsburg, PA: Stackpole Books.
Burg, B.R. 2014. "Sodomy, Masturbation, and Courts-Martial in the Antebellum American Navy." *Journal of the History of Sexuality* 23 (1): 53–78.
Butterfield, David. 1862. *Camp and Outpost Duty for Infantry*. New York: Harper & Brothers.
Byrne, Bernard M. 1855. *An Essay to Prove the Contagious Character of Malignant Cholera: With Brief Instructions for Its Prevention and Cure*, second ed. Philadelphia: Childs and Peterson.
_____. 1859. *Proceedings of a Court Martial for the Trial of Surgeon B.M. Byrne*. Charleston, SC: Steam Power Press of Walker, Evans and Co.
Callaghan, Daniel. 1861. General Orders Number 33. Army of the Potomac. Washington, D.C.: Government Printing Office.
Callahan, Edward W. 1901. *List of Officers of the Navy of the United States and of the Marine Corps, from 1775 to 1900,.Comprising a Complete Register of All Present and Former Commissioned, Warranted, and Appointed Officers of the United States Navy, and of the Marine Corps, Regular and Volunteer. Comp. from the Official Records of the Navy Department*. New York: L.R. Hamersly and Company.
Callan, John F. 1863. *The Military Laws of the United States*. Philadelphia: George W. Childs.
Cardiff, William F. 1863. General Orders Number 62. Middle Department. Baltimore, MD. Washington, D.C.: Government Printing Office.
Carmichael, Peter S. 2018. *The War for the Common Soldier: How Men Thought, Fought, and Survived in Civil War Armies*. Chapel Hill: University of North Carolina Press.
Carrigan, James. 1863. Records of General Courts Martial and Courts of Inquiry of the Navy Department, 1799–1867, Volume 107, Record Group 125, Publication Number M273. Washington, D.C.: National Archives and Records Administration.
Carter, H. 2018. *A Cavalryman's Reminiscences of the Civil War (Classic Reprint)*. London: Fb&c Limited.
Casstevens, Frances H. 2015. *Edward A. Wild and the African Brigade in the Civil War*. Jefferson, NC: McFarland.
Catlin, Isaac S. 1862. General Orders Number 62. Army of the Potomac. Washington, D.C.: Government Printing Office.
Chandler, William. 1861. Records of General Courts Martial and Courts of Inquiry of the Navy Department, 1799–1867, Volume 89, Record Group 125, Publication Number M273. Washington, D.C.: National Archives and Records Administration.
Cheever, Susan. 2015. *Drinking in America: Our Secret History*. New York: Grand Central Publishing.
Christie, William P. 1862. General Orders Number 13. Army of the Potomac. Washington, D.C.: Government Printing Office.
"Clerk." 1891. *Brooklyn Daily Eagle,* May 10.
Colby, Allen W. 1862. General Orders Number 16. Department of the Missouri. St. Louis, MO. Washington, D.C.: Government Printing Office.
Cole, Henry, and George Adams. 1863. General Orders Number 32. Department of the South. Hilton Head, SC. Washington, D.C.: Government Printing Office.
Collins, Cornelius. 1864. Records of General Courts Martial and Courts of Inquiry of the Navy Department, 1799–1867, Volume 123, Record Group 125, Publication Number M273. Washington, D.C.: National Archives and Records Administration.
Collins, John. 1862. General Orders Number 32. Army of the Potomac. Washington, D.C.: Government Printing Office.
Conant, Daniel A. 1864. General Orders Number 130. Middle Department. Baltimore, MD. Washington, D.C.: Government Printing Office.
"Confirms Kershner's Conviction." 1896. *Chicago Tribune,* March 27.

Conley, James. 1865. Records of General Courts Martial and Courts of Inquiry of the Navy Department, 1799–1867, Volume 133, Record Group 125, Publication Number M273. Washington, D.C.: National Archives and Records Administration.
Conley, Martin. 1862. Records of General Courts Martial and Courts of Inquiry of the Navy Department, 1799–1867, Volume 93, Record Group 125, Publication Number M273. Washington, D.C.: National Archives and Records Administration.
Connell, Francis. 1864. Records of General Courts Martial and Courts of Inquiry of the Navy Department, 1799–1867, Volume 110, Record Group 125, Publication Number M273. Washington, D.C.: National Archives and Records Administration.
Conway, John. 1863. Records of General Courts Martial and Courts of Inquiry of the Navy Department, 1799–1867, Volume 102, Record Group 125, Publication Number M273. Washington, D.C.: National Archives and Records Administration.
Coppée, Henry. 1864. *Field Manual of Courts-Martial.* Philadelphia: J.B. Lippincott and CO.
Cornelius, Richard. 1863. Records of General Courts Martial and Courts of Inquiry of the Navy Department, 1799–1867, Volume 102, Record Group 125, Publication Number M273. Washington, D.C.: National Archives and Records Administration.
"Correspondence." 1863. *Sunday Dispatch,* January 11.
Cottrell, John. 1863. General Orders Number 4. Army of the Potomac. Washington, D.C.: Government Printing Office.
Cring, George. 1865. General Orders Number 48. Middle Department. Baltimore, MD. Washington, D.C.: Government Printing Office.
Curran, Daniel. 1863. General Order Number 23. Army of the Potomac. Washington, D.C.: Government Printing Office.
Curtis, George W. 1864. Records of General Courts Martial and Courts of Inquiry of the Navy Department, 1799–1867, Volume 120, Record Group 125, Publication Number M273. Washington, D.C.: National Archives and Records Administration.
Decker, Demmon S. 1864. General Orders Number 48. Department of the South. Hilton Head, SC. Washington, D.C.: Government Printing Office.
De Freest, William H. 1863. General Orders Number 83. Department of the Missouri. St. Louis, MO. Washington, D.C.: Government Printing Office.
De Hart, William C. 1863. *Observations on Military Law, and the Constitution and Practice of Courts Martial.* New York: D. Appleton & Co.
"Department of the Gulf, The Mutiny in Fort Jackson." 1864. *New York Times,* January 6.
"Desertion." 1862. *Frank Leslie's Illustrated Newspaper,* May 31.
De Ville, Kenneth. 1992. *Medical Malpractice in Nineteenth-Century America: Origins and Legacy.* New York: NYU Press.
Devlin, James, alias Pat Diamond and Frank Tully. 1865. Proceedings of U.S. Army Courts-Martial and Military Commissions of Union Soldiers Executed by U.S. Military Authorities, 1861–1866. M1523, Roll 1. Washington, D.C.: National Archives and Records Administration.
"The Diseases and Infirmities Exempting from the Draft." 1863. *New York Times,* November 15.
Dobbler, George W. 1863. General Orders Number 76. Department of the Missouri. St. Louis, MO. Washington, D.C.: Government Printing Office.
"The Draft—Who Escaped, and Who Didn't." 1862. *Frank Leslie's Illustrated Newspaper,* November 15.
Draper, Theodore W. 1863. Records of General Courts Martial and Courts of Inquiry of the Navy Department, 1799–1867, Volume 104, Record Group 125, Publication Number M273. Washington, D.C.: National Archives and Records Administration.
"Drumming Thieves Out of Fortress Monroe." 1861. *Frank Leslie's Illustrated Newspaper,* June 29.
Dudley, William S. 1981. *Going South: U.S. Navy Officer Resignations and Dismissals on the Eve of the Civil War.* Washington, D.C.: Naval Historical Foundation.
Duyckinck, Evert A. 1866. *Supplement to the Cyclopædia of American Literature.* New York: Charles Scribner and Company.
Eagan, Edward. 1865. Records of General Courts Martial and Courts of Inquiry of the Navy

Department, 1799–1867, Volume 133, Record Group 125, Publication Number M273. Washington, D.C.: National Archives and Records Administration.
Eckley, Robert S. 2012. *Lincoln's Forgotten Friend, Leonard Swett*. Carbondale: Southern Illinois University Press.
Eldridge, Charles. 1862. Records of General Courts Martial and Courts of Inquiry of the Navy Department, 1799–1867, Volume 90, Record Group 125, Publication Number M273. Washington, D.C.: National Archives and Records Administration.
Elwell, John J. 1860. *A Medico-legal Treatise on Malpractice and Medical Evidence*. Cleveland: J.S. Voorhies.
English, Michael. 1862. General Orders Number 40. Department of the Missouri. Washington, D.C.: Government Printing Office.
Eutwistle, James. 1865. General Orders Number 36. Department of the South. Hilton Head, SC. Washington, D.C.: Government Printing Office.
Evans, Frank E. 1916. "The Corps One Hundred Years Ago." *Marine Corps Gazette* 1 (1).
Everson, Alfred. 1863. Records of General Courts Martial and Courts of Inquiry of the Navy Department, 1799–1867, Volume 96, Record Group 125, Publication Number M273. Washington, D.C.: National Archives and Records Administration.
Everts, Morgan. 1865. General Orders Number 112. Department of the Gulf. New Orleans, LA. Washington, D.C.: Government Printing Office.
Fader, David. 1864. Records of General Courts Martial and Courts of Inquiry of the Navy Department, 1799–1867, Volume 123, Record Group 125, Publication Number M273. Washington, D.C.: National Archives and Records Administration.
———. 1866. Navy Officers' Letters 1802–1884, Volume 675, Publication M148, Record Group 45. Washington, D.C.: National Archives and Records Administration.
Fahey, Bryan. 1862. General Orders Number 14. Army of the Potomac. Washington, D.C.: Government Printing Office.
Fallon, Martin. 1862. General Orders Number 57. Army of the Potomac. Washington, D.C.: Government Printing Office.
Fannin, John F. 2010. "The Jacksonville Mutiny of 1865." *Florida Historical Quarterly* 88 (3): 368–396.
Fantina, Robert. 2006. *Desertion and the American Soldier, 1776–2006*. New York: Algora Publishing.
Field, Ron. 2004. *American Civil War Marines 1861–65*. Oxford, UK: Osprey Publishing.
"First of its Kind." 1896. *The Constitution*, May 1.
Fleming, Christopher, and Aleck Barnett. 1862. General Orders Number 6. Army of the Potomac. Washington, D.C.: Government Printing Office.
Follansbee, Joshua. 1863. Records of General Courts Martial and Courts of Inquiry of the Navy Department, 1799–1867, Volume 97, Record Group 125, Publication Number M273. Washington, D.C.: National Archives and Records Administration.
Folsom, Frank H. 1862. General Orders Number 41. Army of the Potomac. Washington, D.C.: Government Printing Office.
Foote, Lorien. 2013. *The Gentlemen and the Roughs: Violence, Honor, and Manhood in the Union Army*. New York: NYU Press.
Ford, James. 1864. Records of General Courts Martial and Courts of Inquiry of the Navy Department, 1799–1867, Volume 113, Record Group 125, Publication Number M273. Washington, D.C.: National Archives and Records Administration.
Forshay, Charles H. 1863. General Orders Number 86. Army of the Potomac. Washington, D.C.: Government Printing Office.
Fox, Charles H. 1863. General Orders Number 104. Department of the Missouri. St. Louis, MO. Washington, D.C.: Government Printing Office.
French, Anthony. 1863. Records of General Courts Martial and Courts of Inquiry of the Navy Department, 1799–1867, Volume 94, Record Group 125, Publication Number M273. Washington, D.C.: National Archives and Records Administration.
"From the Sixteenth Vermont Regiment." 1863. *The Daily Green Mountain Freeman*, June 5.
Gallagher, Gary, Stephen Engle, Robert Krick, and Joseph T. Glatthaar. 2003. *The American Civil War: This Mighty Scourge of War*. Oxford, UK: Osprey Publishing.

Gallup, Henry A. 1863. General Orders Number 77. Department of the Missouri. St. Louis, MO. Washington, D.C.: Government Printing Office.
"Gamblers in the Army." 1863. *Harper's Weekly,* November 7.
Garrison, Webb B. 2001. *Mutiny in the Civil War.* Shippensburg, PA: White Mane Books.
Gatewood, Richard. 1861. Proceedings of U.S. Army Courts-Martial and Military Commissions of Union Soldiers Executed by U.S. Military Authorities, 1861–1866. M1523, Roll 1. Washington, D.C.: National Archives and Records Administration.
Gaul, William. 1864. Records of General Courts Martial and Courts of Inquiry of the Navy Department, 1799–1867, Volume 121, Record Group 125, Publication Number M273. Washington, D.C.: National Archives and Records Administration.
Gavican, Michael J. 1864. Records of General Courts Martial and Courts of Inquiry of the Navy Department, 1799–1867, Volume 117, Record Group 125, Publication Number M273. Washington, D.C.: National Archives and Records Administration.
Gaylor, Charles H. 1864. Records of General Courts Martial and Courts of Inquiry of the Navy Department, 1799–1867, Volume 132, Record Group 125, Publication Number M273. Washington, D.C.: National Archives and Records Administration.
General Orders Number 81. 1864. Department of the Gulf. Washington, D.C.: Government Printing Office.
General Orders Number 51. 1864. Department of the South. Washington, D.C.: Government Printing Office.
General Orders Number 40. 1863. Army of the Potomac. Washington, D.C.: Government Printing Office.
General Orders Number 9. 1859. *War Department, A Collection of Miscellaneous General Orders and Circulars,* September 22, 1856 to October 20, 1861. Washington, D.C.: Government Printing Office.
General Orders Number 90. 1863. Department of the Gulf. Washington, D.C.: Government Printing Office.
General Orders Number 1. 1864. War Department. Adjutant General's Office. Washington, D.C.: Government Printing Office.
General Orders Number 136. 1862. Army of the Potomac. Washington, D.C.: Government Printing Office.
General Orders Number 6. 1862. Army of the Potomac. Washington, D.C.: Government Printing Office.
General Orders Number 69. 1862. Army of the Potomac. Washington, D.C.: Government Printing Office.
General Orders Number 38. 1863. Middle Department. Washington, D.C.: Government Printing Office.
General Orders Number 391. 1863. War Department. Adjutant General's Office. Washington, D.C.: Government Printing Office.
General Orders Number 376. 1863. War Department. Adjutant General's Office. Washington, D.C.: Government Printing Office.
General Orders Number 279. 1864. War Department. Adjutant General's Office. Washington, D.C.: Government Printing Office.
General Orders Number 206. 1864. War Department. Adjutant General's Office. Washington, D.C.: Government Printing Office.
Giesberg, Judith. 2017. *Sex and the Civil War: Soldiers, Pornography, and the Making of American Morality.* Chapel Hill: University of North Carolina Press.
Gillies, Donald. 1864. General Orders Number 29. Army of the Potomac. Washington, D.C.: Government Printing Office.
Gosman, John C. 1864. General Orders Number 149. Department of the Gulf. New Orleans, LA. Washington, D.C.: Government Printing Office.
Grayson, John C. 1864. Records of General Courts Martial and Courts of Inquiry of the Navy Department, 1799–1867, Volume 109, Record Group 125, Publication Number M273. Washington, D.C.: National Archives and Records Administration.
Green, Daniel. 1863. Records of General Courts Martial and Courts of Inquiry of the Navy

Department, 1799–1867, Volume 100, Record Group 125, Publication Number M273. Washington, D.C.: National Archives and Records Administration.
Griffiths, D.L. 1966. "Medicine and Surgery in the American Civil War." *Proceedings of the Royal Society of Medicine* 59 (3): 204–208.
Guenste, Ferdinand. 1862. General Orders Number 17. Army of the Potomac. Washington, D.C.: Government Printing Office.
Guilford, Elbridge W. 1864. General Court Martial Orders Number 20. Army of the Potomac. Washington, D.C.: Government Printing Office.
Hamilton, Frank H. 1865. *A Treatise on Military Surgery and Hygiene*. New York: Baillière Brothers.
Hamilton, Thomas. 1862. Records of General Courts Martial and Courts of Inquiry of the Navy Department, 1799–1867, Volume 91, Record Group 125, Publication Number M273. Washington, D.C.: National Archives and Records Administration.
Hamlin, Elbin L. 1863. General Orders Number 5. Army of the Potomac. Washington, D.C.: Government Printing Office.
Hammond, William A. 1863. *A Treatise on Hygiene: With Special Reference to the Military Service*. Philadelphia: J.B. Lippincott & Company.
Hanna, William F. 1990. "The Boston Draft Riot." *Civil War History* 36 (3): 262–273.
Harrington, Edward. 1864. Records of General Courts Martial and Courts of Inquiry of the Navy Department, 1799–1867, Volume 114, Record Group 125, Publication Number M273. Washington, D.C.: National Archives and Records Administration.
Harrington, Fred H. 1942. "The Fort Jackson Mutiny." *Journal of Negro History* 27 (4): 420–431.
Harris, Francis. 1865. General Orders Number 76. Middle Department. Baltimore, MD. Washington, D.C.: Government Printing Office.
Harrison, William H. 1864a. General Orders Number 117. Department of the South. Hilton Head, SC. Washington, D.C.: Government Printing Office.
_____. 1864b. General Orders Number 86. Department of the South. Hilton Head, SC. Washington, D.C.: Government Printing Office.
Hawkes, H.A. 1865. General Orders Number 32. Department of the South. Hilton Head, SC. Washington, D.C.: Government Printing Office.
Heliker, Henry. 1863. Records of General Courts Martial and Courts of Inquiry of the Navy Department, 1799–1867, Volume 108, Record Group 125, Publication Number M273. Washington, D.C.: National Archives and Records Administration.
Hill, Alexander S. 1864a. Compiled Military Service Records of Volunteer Union Soldiers Who Served the United States Colored Troops: 56th-138th USCT Infantry, 1864–1866. Record Group 94. Washington, D.C.: National Archives and Records Administration.
_____. 1864b. General Orders Number 29. Department of the Gulf. New Orleans, LA. Washington, D.C.: Government Printing Office.
Hoegenauer, Charles. 1862. General Orders Number 87. Army of the Potomac. Washington, D.C.: Government Printing Office.
Hoffman, Gustav. 1864. General Orders Number 50. Department of the South. Hilton Head, SC. Washington, D.C.: Government Printing Office.
Hoffman, James M. 1863. General Orders Number 33. Army of the Potomac. Washington, D.C.: Government Printing Office.
Holden, J. Albert. 1862. General Orders Number 35. Army of the Potomac. Washington, D.C.: Government Printing Office.
Holliday, Fleming. 1863. General Orders Number 4. Army of the Potomac. Washington, D.C.: Government Printing Office.
Hoppin, James M. 1874. *Life of Andrew Hull Foote Rear Admiral United States Navy*. New York: Harper and Brothers.
"The Horrors of the Alexandria Hospital." 1862. *National Republican*, February 3.
"How to Preserve the Health of the Soldier." 1861. *Cleveland Morning Leader*, August 27.
Howell, David M. 1863. Records of General Courts Martial and Courts of Inquiry of the Navy Department, 1799–1867, Volume 101, Record Group 125, Publication Number M273. Washington, D.C.: National Archives and Records Administration.

Hudson, Henry W. 1863a. General Orders Number 54. Army of the Potomac. Washington, D.C.: Government Printing Office.

_____. 1863b. New York Civil War Muster Roll Abstracts 1861–1900, New York Adjutant General's Office, Albany, NY.

Hyman, Robert. 1864. Records of General Courts Martial and Courts of Inquiry of the Navy Department, 1799–1867, Volume 109, Record Group 125, Publication Number M273. Washington, D.C.: National Archives and Records Administration.

"Interesting From New Orleans." 1863. *Utica Daily Observer*, December 21.

Ives, Rollin A. 1879. *A Treatise on Military Law: And the Jurisdiction, Constitution, and Procedure of Military Courts, with a Summary of the Rules of Evidence as Applicable to Such Courts*. New York: D. Van Nostrand.

Jackson, Andrew. 1862. Compiled Military Service Records of Volunteer Union Soldiers Who Served the United States Colored Troops: 56th-138th USCT Infantry, 1864–1866, Record Group 94. Washington, D.C.: National Archives and Records Administration.

_____. 1865. General Orders Number 28. Department of the Gulf. New Orleans, LA. Washington, D.C.: Government Printing Office.

Jansen, Henry. 1864. General Orders Number 81. Department of the Gulf. New Orleans, LA. Washington, D.C.: Government Printing Office.

John, Harvey H. 1864. General Orders Number 140. War Department, Adjutant General's Office. Washington, D.C.: Government Printing Office.

Johns, Joseph. 1863. Records of General Courts Martial and Courts of Inquiry of the Navy Department, 1799–1867, Volume 108, Record Group 125, Publication Number M273. Washington, D.C.: National Archives and Records Administration.

Johnson, Cyrus H. 1863. General Orders Number 122. Department of the Missouri. St. Louis, MO. Washington, D.C.: Government Printing Office.

Johnson, Edward C., Gail R. Johnson, and Melissa J. Williams. 1997. *All Were Not Heroes: A Study of the List of U.S. Soldiers Executed by U.S. Military Authorities During the Late War*. Chicago: E.C. Johnson.

Johnson, William H. 1861. Proceedings of U.S. Army Courts-Martial and Military Commissions of Union Soldiers Executed by U.S. Military Authorities, 1861–1866. M1523, Roll 2. Washington, D.C.: National Archives and Records Administration.

Jordan, Daniel. 1863. Records of General Courts Martial and Courts of Inquiry of the Navy Department, 1799–1867, Volume 97, Record Group 125, Publication Number M273. Washington, D.C.: National Archives and Records Administration.

Kane, William. 1864. Compiled Service Records of Volunteer Union Soldiers Who Served in Organizations from the State of Maryland, M384. Record Group 94, Maryland Roll 170. Washington, D.C.: National Archives and Records Administration.

Kane, William, alias William Carter. 1864. Proceedings of U.S. Army Courts-Martial and Military Commissions of Union Soldiers Executed by U.S. Military Authorities, 1861–1866. M1523, Roll 2. Washington, D.C.: National Archives and Records Administration.

Kavenaugh, Richard. 1862. General Orders Number 36. Department of the Missouri, St. Louis, MO. Washington, D.C.: Government Printing Office.

Kennedy, Francis H. 1998. *The Civil War Battlefield Guide*, second ed. Boston: Houghton Mifflin Company.

Kennedy, John. 1864. Records of General Courts Martial and Courts of Inquiry of the Navy Department, 1799–1867, Volume 126, Record Group 125, Publication Number M273, Record Group 153. Washington, D.C.: National Archives and Records Administration.

Kershner, Edward. 1863. Records of General Courts Martial and Courts of Inquiry of the Navy Department, 1799–1867, Volume 98, Record Group 125, Publication Number M273. Washington, D.C.: National Archives and Records Administration.

Knight, Napoleon B. 1864. General Orders Number 10. Middle Department. Baltimore, MD. Washington, D.C.: Government Printing Office.

Kuhnes, Joseph. 1861. Proceedings of U.S. Army Courts-Martial and Military Commissions of Union Soldiers Executed by U.S. Military Authorities, 1861–1866. M1523, Roll 2. Washington, D.C.: National Archives and Records Administration.

Kynoch, Gary. 1997. "Terrible Dilemmas: Black Enlistment in the Union Army During the American Civil War." *Slavery and Abolition* 18 (2): 104–127.
Lamb, William. 1861. Records of General Courts Martial and Courts of Inquiry of the Navy Department, 1799–1867, Volume 89, Record Group 125, Publication Number M273. Washington, D.C.: National Archives and Records Administration.
Lande, R. Gregory. 1988. "Madness, Malingering and Malfeasance." *Lincoln Herald* 90 (1): 17–20.
Lande, R. Gregory. 1997. "The History of Forensic Psychiatry in the U.S. Military." In R.G. Lande and D.T. Armitage (Eds.), *Principles and Practice of Military Forensic Psychiatry* (pp. 3–27). Springfield, IL: Charles C. Thomas Publisher, Ltd.
_____. 2005. *Madness, Malingering, and Malfeasance: The Transformation of Psychiatry and the Law in the Civil War Era*. Washington, D.C.: Potomac Books.
_____. 2012. *The Abraham Man: Madness, Malingering, and the Development of Medical Testimony*. New York: Algora Publishing.
_____. 2017. *Psychological Consequences of the American Civil War*. Jefferson, NC: McFarland.
_____. 2020. *Spiritualism in the American Civil War*. Jefferson, NC: McFarland.
Lane, Roger. 1997. *Murder in America: A History*. Columbus: Ohio State University Press.
Langley, Harold D. 2015. *Social Reform in the United States Navy, 1798–1862*. Annapolis, MD: Naval Institute Press.
Lardner, J. 1864. Letters Received from Commissioned Officers Below the Rank of Commander and from Warrant Officers, 1802–1886. Record Group 45: Naval Records Collection of the Office of Naval Records and Library, 1691–1945. Department of the Navy. Office of the Secretary. 1798–9/1947. Washington, D.C.: National Archives and Records Administration.
Lardner, John. 1864. Records of General Courts Martial and Courts of Inquiry of the Navy Department, 1799–1867, Volume 91, Record Group 125, Publication Number M273. Washington, D.C.: National Archives and Records Administration.
Laven, John. 1863. Records of General Courts Martial and Courts of Inquiry of the Navy Department, 1799–1867, Volume 104, Record Group 125, Publication Number M273. Washington, D.C.: National Archives and Records Administration.
Lawler, Michael K. 1862. General Orders Number 12. Department of the Missouri. St Louis, MO. Washington, D.C.: Government Printing Office.
Lee, Charles E., James Ward, and John Wallace. 1862. General Orders Number 53. Department of the South. Hilton Head, SC. Washington, D.C.: Government Printing Office.
Lee, Timothy F. 1861. General Orders Number 39. Army of the Potomac. Washington, D.C.: Government Printing Office.
Leighton, George. 1861. General Orders Number 24. Army of the Potomac. Washington, D.C.: Government Printing Office.
Leslie, Frank. 1861. Records of General Courts Martial and Courts of Inquiry of the Navy Department, 1799–1867, Volume 89, Record Group 125, Publication Number M273. Washington, D.C.: National Archives and Records Administration.
"Letter From the Navy." 1861. *Cedar Falls Gazette*, October 18.
Letter of The Secretary of War. 1864. *In answer to a resolution of the Senate of the 9th instant, copy of the proceedings of the general court-martial for the trial of Assistant Surgeon Webster*. Senate Documents, 38th Congress, Volume 188. Washington, D.C.: Government Printing Office.
Lewis, David T. 1862. Records of General Courts Martial and Courts of Inquiry of the Navy Department, 1799–1867, Volume 90, Record Group 125, Publication Number M273. Washington, D.C.: National Archives and Records Administration.
Libby, George W. 1863. Publisher: Records of General Courts Martial and Courts of Inquiry of the Navy Department, 1799–1867, Volume 108, Record Group 125, Publication Number M273. Washington, D.C.: National Archives and Records Administration.
Library of Universal Knowledge. 1880. New York: American Book Exchange.
Lichtenheim, Theodore. 1862. General Orders Number 17. Army of the Potomac. Washington, D.C.: Government Printing Office.

Lieber, Francis. 1863. *General Orders Number 100.* Adjutant General's Office. *Instructions for the Government of Armies of the United States in the Field.* New York: D. Van Nostrand.
Little, David. 1862. *General Orders Number 18.* Army of the Potomac. Washington, D.C.: Government Printing Office.
Livermore, Thomas L. 1901. *Numbers and Losses in the Civil War in America, 1861–65.* New York: Houghton, Mifflin and Company.
Lloyd, Richard. 1863. *General Orders Number 125.* Department of the Missouri. St. Louis, MO. Washington, D.C.: Government Printing Office.
Lonn, Ella. 1928. *Desertion During the Civil War.* New York: Century Company.
Lowry, Thomas P. 2003. *Curmudgeons, Drunkards, and Outright Fools: Courts-Martial of Civil War Union Colonels.* Lincoln: University of Nebraska Press.
_____. 2010. *Merciful Lincoln: The President and Military Justice.* Scotts Valley, CA: CreateSpace Independent Publishing Platform.
_____. 2011. *Irish and German—Whiskey and Beer: Drinking Patterns in the Civil War.* Scotts Valley, CA: CreateSpace Independent Publishing Platform.
_____. 2012. *The Story the Soldiers Wouldn't Tell: Sex in the Civil War.* Mechanicsburg, PA: Stackpole Books.
Lowry, Thomas P., and Jack D. Welsh. 2000. *Tarnished Scalpels: The Court-Martials of Fifty Union Surgeons.* Mechanicsburg, PA: Stackpole Books.
Lowry, Thomas P., and Terry Reimer. 2011. *Bad Doctors.* Frederick, MD: National Museum of Civil War Medicine.
Lutton, Morgan. 1864. Records of General Courts Martial and Courts of Inquiry of the Navy Department, 1799–1867, Volume 132, Record Group 125, Publication Number M273. Washington, D.C.: National Archives and Records Administration.
Macomb, Alexander. 1809. *A Treatise on Martial Law, and Court Martial: As Practised in the United States of America.* Charleston, SC: J. Hoff.
Martin, Scott C. 2011. "A Soldier Intoxicated Is Far Worse Than No Soldier At All: Intoxication and the American Civil War." *Social History of Alcohol and Drugs* 25: 66–87.
Massachusetts Soldiers, Sailors, and Marines in the Civil War. 1932. Vol. 5. Norwood, MA: Norwood Press.
Matthews, John H. 1864. Records of General Courts Martial and Courts of Inquiry of the Navy Department, 1799–1867, Volume 127, Record Group 125, Publication Number M273. Washington, D.C.: National Archives and Records Administration.
McBride, Robert. 1863. *General Orders Number 21.* Department of the Missouri. St. Louis, MO. Washington, D.C.: Government Printing Office.
McCann, Felix. 1863. Records of General Courts Martial and Courts of Inquiry of the Navy Department, 1799–1867, Volume 107, Record Group 125, Publication Number M273. Washington, D.C.: National Archives and Records Administration.
McCarthy, Jeremiah. 1863. Records of General Courts Martial and Courts of Inquiry of the Navy Department, 1799–1867, Volume 101, Record Group 125, Publication Number M273. Washington, D.C.: National Archives and Records Administration.
McClain, Edward. 1864. Records of General Courts Martial and Courts of Inquiry of the Navy Department, 1799–1867, Volume 125, Record Group 125, Publication Number M273. Washington, D.C.: National Archives and Records Administration.
McCluskey, John. 1862. *General Orders Number 26.* Department of the Gulf. New Orleans, LA. Washington, D.C.: Government Printing Office.
McCuddon, Josiah W. 1863. *General Orders Number 121.* Department of the Missouri. St. Louis, MO. Washington, D.C.: Government Printing Office.
McDonald, John. 1863. Records of General Courts Martial and Courts of Inquiry of the Navy Department, 1799–1867, Volume 101, Record Group 125, Publication Number M273. Washington, D.C.: National Archives and Records Administration.
McFadden, Jackson. 1862. *General Orders Number 81.* Army of the Potomac. Washington, D.C.: Government Printing Office.
McGee, Benjamin F. 1882. *History of the 72d Indiana Volunteer Infantry of the Mounted Lightning Brigade,* Vol. 72, pt. 4. Edited by William R. Jewell. LaFayette, IN: S. Vater & Company.

McIntyre, William. 1863. Records of General Courts Martial and Courts of Inquiry of the Navy Department, 1799–1867, Volume 93, Record Group 125, Publication Number M273. Washington, D.C.: National Archives and Records Administration.
McLetchie, Andrew. 1864. General Orders Number 14. Middle Department. Baltimore, MD. Washington, D.C.: Government Printing Office.
McMenamin, Patrick. 1861. Records of General Courts Martial and Courts of Inquiry of the Navy Department, 1799–1867, Volume 89, Record Group 125, Publication Number M273. Washington, D.C.: National Archives and Records Administration.
McPherson, James M. 1997. *For Cause and Comrades: Why Men Fought in the Civil War.* New York: Oxford University Press.
McVaugh, Edmund. 1863. Records of General Courts Martial and Courts of Inquiry of the Navy Department, 1799–1867, Volume 96, Record Group 125, Publication Number M273. Washington, D.C.: National Archives and Records Administration.
"A Meeting of Sailors." 1863. *Cleveland Morning Leader,* December 24.
Merrill, George S. 1863. General Orders Number 52. Middle Department. Baltimore, MD. Washington, D.C.: Government Printing Office.
"Military and Naval." 1864. *New York Herald,* August 28.
Miller, William, alias James Craig. 1864. Proceedings of U.S. Army Courts-Martial and Military Commissions of Union Soldiers Executed by U.S. Military Authorities, 1861–1866. M1523, Roll 3. Washington, D.C.: National Archives and Records Administration.
Miller, William W. 1862. General Orders Number 31. Department of the Missouri. St. Louis, MO. Washington, D.C.: Government Printing Office.
Mindrup, Alexander H. 2021. "The Lieber Code: A Historical Analysis of the Context and Drafting of General Orders No. 100." *The Cardinal Edge* 1 (1): 1–11.
Mitchell, James. 1864. Records of General Courts Martial and Courts of Inquiry of the Navy Department, 1799–1867, Volume 124, Record Group 125, Publication Number M273. Washington, D.C.: National Archives and Records Administration.
Moore, Charles H. 1864. Records of General Courts Martial and Courts of Inquiry of the Navy Department, 1799–1867, Volume 123, Record Group 125, Publication Number M273. Washington, D.C.: National Archives and Records Administration.
Morgan, Walter J. 1864. General Court Martial Orders Number 25. Army of the Potomac. Washington, D.C.: Government Printing Office.
Morgan, William. 1865. Records of General Courts Martial and Courts of Inquiry of the Navy Department, 1799–1867, Volume 132, Record Group 125, Publication Number M273. Washington, D.C.: National Archives and Records Administration.
Mulhern, Andrew J. 1864. General Orders Number 62. Department of the Gulf. New Orleans, LA. Washington, D.C.: Government Printing Office.
Murphy, John. 1863. Records of General Courts Martial and Courts of Inquiry of the Navy Department, 1799–1867, Volume 101, Record Group 125, Publication Number M273. Washington, D.C.: National Archives and Records Administration.
Murphy, Kim. 2014. *I Had Rather Die: Rape in the Civil War.* Batesville, VA: Coachlight Press.
Neill, John, and Francis G. Smith. 1856. *An Analytical Compendium of the Various Branches of Medical Science: For the Use and Examination of Students.* Philadelphia: Blanchard and Lea.
"News From Port Royal." 1862. *New York Herald,* September 8.
"News Summary." 1860. *The Anderson Intelligencer,* September 11.
Nichols, Jesse T. 1865. General Orders Number 48. Middle Department. Baltimore, MD. Washington, D.C.: Government Printing Office.
O'Brien, John P.J. 1846. *A Treatise on American Military Laws, and the Practice of Courts Martial: With Suggestions for Their Improvement.* Philadelphia: Lea & Blanchard.
O'Malley, George W. 1863. General Order 249. War Department. Adjutant General's Office, Washington, D.C.: Government Printing Office.
Oliver, Willard M., and James F. Hilgenberg. 2018. *A History of Crime and Criminal Justice in America,* third ed. Durham, NC: Carolina Academic Press.

Bibliography

Overin, Henry C. 1865. General Court Martial Orders Number 12. Army of the Potomac. Washington, D.C.: Government Printing Office.
Parker, Albert D. 1865. Records of General Courts Martial and Courts of Inquiry of the Navy Department, 1799–1867, Volume 133, Record Group 125, Publication Number M273. Washington, D.C.: National Archives and Records Administration.
Pennock, Alexander Mosely. 1864. Letters Received by the Secretary of the Navy from Commanding Officers of Squadrons. Publication Number M89. Record Group 45. The Washington, D.C.: National Archives and Records Administration.
Pension Number 28669. Numerical Index to Pensions, 1860–1934. Publication Number A1158. Record Group 15. Washington, D.C.: National Archives and Records Administration.
Perdue, John B. 1863. General Court Martial Orders Number 52. Middle Department. Baltimore, MD. Washington, D.C.: Government Printing Office.
Perry, David A., John Evans, and Michael McGrath. 1864. General Orders Number 28. Department of the South. Hilton Head, SC. Washington, D.C.: Government Printing Office.
Pettinos, James W. 1864. General Orders Number 66. Middle Department. Baltimore, MD. Washington, D.C.: Government Printing Office.
Polhill, Charles. 1863. Records of General Courts Martial and Courts of Inquiry of the Navy Department, 1799–1867, Volume 100, Record Group 125, Publication Number M273. Washington, D.C.: National Archives and Records Administration.
Porter, David D. 1864. Letters Received by the Secretary of the Navy from Commanding Officers of Squadrons,. Publication Number M89. Washington, D.C.: National Archives and Records Administration.
Porter, John B. 1862. General Orders Number 85. Army of the Potomac. Washington, D.C.: Government Printing Office.
Postwiller, William. 1863. General Orders Number 28. Department of the Missouri. St. Louis, MO. Washington, D.C.: Government Printing Office.
Proceedings of U.S. Army Courts-Martial and Military Commissions of Union Soldiers Executed by U.S. Military Authorities, 1861–1866, M1523, Rolls 1–8. Washington, D.C.: National Archives and Records Administration.
Quarstein, John V., and Dennis P. Mroczkowski. 2000. *Fort Monroe: The Key to the South.* Mount Pleasant, SC: Arcadia Publishing.
Radcliff, Thomas. 1862. General Orders Number 6. Army of the Potomac. Washington, D.C.: Government Printing Office.
Ramold, Stephen. J. 2010. *Baring the Iron Hand: Discipline in the Union Army.* DeKalb: Northern Illinois University Press.
Randall, Francis V. 1861. General Orders Number 65. Army of the Potomac. Washington, D.C.: Government Printing Office.
"Recent Execution at Fort Lafayette." 1865. *New York Herald,* April 2.
Registry of Prisoners Incarcerated at the Joliet Correctional Center. Image 1–0055. 1864. Springfield, IL: Illinois Department of Corrections and Predecessor Agencies, Joliet Correctional Center, Volume 1, Register of Illinois Prison Records (Illinois Digital Archives).
Reid, Richard M. 1990. "Black Experience in the Union Army: The Other Civil War." *Canadian Review of American Studies* 21 (2): 145–156.
Reis, Ronald A. 2009. *African Americans and the Civil War.* New York: Chelsea House, an Imprint of Infobase Publishing.
Rerick, Rowlan H., and Francis P. Fleming. 1902. *Memoirs of Florida: Embracing a General History of the Province, Territory and State; and Special Chapters Devoted to Finances and Banking, the Bench and Bar, Medical Profession, Railways and Navigation, and Industrial Interests,* 2 vols., Vol. 2. Atlanta, GA: Southern Historical Association.
Reynolds, Charles. 1865. General Orders Number 52. Middle Department. Baltimore, MD. Washington, D.C.: Government Printing Office.
Rice, Thomas. 1863. Records of General Courts Martial and Courts of Inquiry of the Navy

Department, 1799–1867, Volume 108, Record Group 125, Publication Number M273. Washington, D.C.: National Archives and Records Administration.
Ricker, John. 1861. General Orders Number 36. Army of the Potomac. Washington, D.C.: Government Printing Office.
———. 1862. General Orders Number 76. Army of the Potomac. Washington, D.C.: Government Printing Office.
Rickets, W.H. 1862. General Orders Number 31. Department of the Missouri, St. Louis, MO. Washington, D.C.: Government Printing Office.
Riley, Owen. 1863. Records of General Courts Martial and Courts of Inquiry of the Navy Department, 1799–1867, Volume 96, Record Group 125, Publication Number M273. Washington, D.C.: National Archives and Records Administration.
Roberts, Edward A.L. 1863. General Orders Number 2. Army of the Potomac. Washington, D.C.: Government Printing Office.
Rohrer, John W., Benjamin Nannah, and Thomas K. Hill. 1863. Records of General Courts Martial and Courts of Inquiry of the Navy Department, 1799–1867, Volume 104, Record Group 125, Publication Number M273. Washington, D.C.: National Archives and Records Administration.
Rooney, James E. 1865. Records of General Courts Martial and Courts of Inquiry of the Navy Department, 1799–1867, Volume 132, Record Group 125, Publication Number M273. Washington, D.C.: National Archives and Records Administration.
Roscommons, Thomas. 1862. Records of General Courts Martial and Courts of Inquiry of the Navy Department, 1799–1867, Volume 92, Record Group 125, Publication Number M273. Washington, D.C.: National Archives and Records Administration.
Rothrauff, Samuel. 1862. Records of General Courts Martial and Courts of Inquiry of the Navy Department, 1799–1867, Volume 91, Record Group 125, Publication Number M273. Washington, D.C.: National Archives and Records Administration.
"The Routine of Camp Life." 1862. *New York Times,* July 27.
Rush, Richard, and Robert H. Woods. 1894. *Official Records of the Union and Confederate Navies in the War of the Rebellion,* Volume 5, Series 1. Washington, D.C.: Government Printing Office.
———. 1896. *Official Records of the Union and Confederate Navies in the War of the Rebellion,* Volume 3, Series 1. Washington, D.C.: Government Printing Office.
Samito, Christian G. 2007. "The Intersection Between Military Justice and Equal Rights: Mutinies, Courts-Martial, and Black Civil War soldiers." *Civil War History* 53 (2): 170–202.
"The Sanitary Commission." 1862. *New York Times,* January 9.
"Schemes of the Shirks." 1862. *Chicago Tribune,* August 27.
Scoby, Gilbert W. 1864. Records of General Courts Martial and Courts of Inquiry of the Navy Department, 1799–1867, Volume 124, Record Group 125, Publication Number M273. Washington, D.C.: National Archives and Records Administration.
Scovill, Samuel G. 1864. Records of General Courts Martial and Courts of Inquiry of the Navy Department, 1799–1867, Volume 121, Case Number 3673, Publication Number M273. Washington, D.C.: National Archives and Records Administration.
"Seeing a Ghost." 1863. *New York Herald,* October 9, 1863.
Setright, John. 1862. General Orders Number 33. Army of the Potomac. Washington, D.C.: Government Printing Office.
Shea, John G. 1890. *History of the Catholic Church in the United States.* New York: John G. Shea.
Sheehan, Michael F. 1864. General Orders Number 125. Middle Department. Baltimore, MD. Washington, D.C.: Government Printing Office.
Sheehan-Dean, Aaron. 2018. *The Calculus of Violence: How Americans Fought the Civil War.* Cambridge, MA: Harvard University Press.
Sheridan. Edward E. 1861. General Orders Number 27. Army of the Potomac. Washington, D.C.: Government Printing Office.
Sherman, Robert. 1863. Records of General Courts Martial and Courts of Inquiry of the Navy Department, 1799–1867, Volume 106, Record Group 125, Publication Number M273. Washington, D.C.: National Archives and Records Administration.

"The Ship's Writer." 1893. *San Francisco Call,* April 9, 1893.
Shivers, Nicholas. 1863. General Orders No. 23. Middle Department. Baltimore, MD. Washington, D.C.: Government Printing Office.
Siegel, Jay M. 1997. *Origins of the Navy Judge Advocate General's Corps: A History of Legal Administration in the United States Navy, 1775 to 1967.* Washington, D.C.: U.S. Navy, Judge Advocate General's Corps.
Sisson, Isaac. 1863. Compiled Service Records of Volunteer Union Soldiers Who Served in Organizations From the State of Missouri. Record Group 94. Roll 0383. Washington, D.C.: National Archives and Records Administration.
Sisson, Isaac H. 1863. General Orders Number 140. Department of the Missouri. St. Louis, MO. Washington, D.C.: Government Printing Office.
Smalley, Eugene A. 1862. Records of General Courts Martial and Courts of Inquiry of the Navy Department, 1799–1867, Volume 91, Record Group 125, Publication Number M273. Washington, D.C.: National Archives and Records Administration.
Smart, Charles. 1888. *The Medical and Surgical History of the War of the Rebellion,* Vol. 1, Part 3. Washington, D.C.: Government Printing Office.
Smith, Charles N. 1863. General Orders Number 48. Department of the Gulf. New Orleans, LA. Washington, D.C.: Government Printing Office.
Smith, Elijah. 1862. General Orders Number 55. Army of the Potomac. Washington, D.C.: Government Printing Office.
Smith, George E. 1864. Records of General Courts Martial and Courts of Inquiry of the Navy Department, 1799–1867, Volume 113, Record Group 125, Publication Number M273. Washington, D.C.: National Archives and Records Administration.
Snyder, C.J., and J.I. Daniels. 1862. General Orders Number 77. Army of the Potomac. Washington, D.C.: Government Printing Office.
"Soldiers' Duties and Punishments—Court Martial Sentences." 1861. *The Sun,* November 18.
"A Solemn Warning to Wives." 1863. *Spirit of the Age,* March 23.
Southwick, William. 1863. Records of General Courts Martial and Courts of Inquiry of the Navy Department, 1799–1867, Volume 107, Record Group 125, Publication Number M273. Washington, D.C.: National Archives and Records Administration.
Spear, Thomas. 1862. General Orders Number 6. Army of the Potomac. Washington, D.C.: Government Printing Office.
Squires, William J. 1864. Records of General Courts Martial and Courts of Inquiry of the Navy Department, 1799–1867, Volume 124, Record Group 125, Publication Number M273. Washington, D.C.: National Archives and Records Administration.
_____. 1891. Case Files of Approved Pension Applications of Civil War and Later Navy Veterans (Navy Survivors' Certificates), 1861–1910. M1469. Record Group 15, Records of the Department of Veterans Affairs, 1773–2001. Washington, D.C.: National Archives and Records Administration.
"Startling Disclosures in New York in Regard to Bounty Jumping." 1865. *Cleveland Morning Leader,* February 11.
Stephens, William. 1863. General Orders Number 70. Department of the Missouri. St. Louis, MO. Washington, D.C.: Government Printing Office.
Stewart, Charles W. 1901. *Official Records of the Union and Confederate Navies in the War of the Rebellion. Volume 12, Series 1.* Washington, D.C.: Government Printing Office.
_____. 1905. *Official Records of the Union and Confederate Navies in the War of the Rebellion. Volume 19, Series 1.* Washington, D.C.: Government Printing Office.
_____. 1911. *Official Records of the Union and Confederate Navies in the War of the Rebellion, Volume 24, Series 1.* Washington, D.C.: Government Printing Office.
_____. 1912. *Official Records of the Union and Confederate Navies in the War of the Rebellion. Volume 25, Series 1.* Washington, D.C.: Government Printing Office.
Steyn, R.W. 1976. "Drink, Doctors, and Seadogs." *U.S. Navy Medicine* 67 (7).
Stickney, Lyman. 1862. General Orders Number 18. Army of the Potomac. Washington, D.C.: Government Printing Office.
Stillwell, Daniel M, Walter Allen, and Edward Adams. 1861. General Orders Number 25. Army of the Potomac. Washington, D.C.: Government Printing Office.

Strachan, William. 1863. Government Orders Number 70. Army of the Potomac. Washington, D.C.: Government Printing Office.
Stump, David M. 1862. General Orders Number 35. Department of the Missouri. St. Louis, MO. Washington, D.C.: Government Printing Office.
Sturgeon, E.B. 1863. Records of General Courts Martial and Courts of Inquiry of the Navy Department, 1799–1867, Volume 105, Record Group 125, Publication Number M273. Washington, D.C.: National Archives and Records Administration.
Sullivan, David M. 1997. *The United States Marine Corps in the Civil War: The Third Year.* Shippensburg, PA: White Mane Publishing Company.
Sweeney, Hugh. 1863. General Orders Number 18. Department of the Missouri. St. Louis, MO. Washington, D.C.: Government Printing Office.
Taylor, Alfred W. 1862. General Orders Number 88. Army of the Potomac. Washington, D.C.: Government Printing Office.
Taylor, William B. 1864. Records of General Courts Martial and Courts of Inquiry of the Navy Department, 1799–1867, Volume 123, Record Group 125, Publication Number M273. Washington, D.C.: National Archives and Records Administration.
Tevis, Charles. 1864. Compiled Service Records of Volunteer Union Soldiers Who Served in Organizations from the State Of Maryland. Publication Number M384, Roll 0038. Washington, D.C.: National Archives and Records Administration.
Thistleton, George. 1864. General Orders Number 42. Middle Department. Baltimore, MD. Washington, D.C.: Government Printing Office.
Thompson, Edward R. 1861. Records of General Courts Martial and Courts of Inquiry of the Navy Department, 1799–1867, Volume 89, Record Group 125, Publication Number M273. Washington, D.C.: National Archives and Records Administration.
_____. 1879. *The Journal of the Armed Forces: (1878–1879).* New York: Army and Navy Journal Incorporated, 16 (495).
Thornton, James S. 1862. Records of General Courts Martial and Courts of Inquiry of the Navy Department, 1799–1867, Volume 91, Record Group 125, Publication Number M273. Washington, D.C.: National Archives and Records Administration.
Tighe, Richard F. 1864. General Court Martial Orders Number 32. Army of the Potomac. Washington, D.C.: Government Printing Office.
Tomblin, Barbara B. 2009. *Bluejackets and Contrabands: African Americans and the Union Navy.* Lexington: University Press of Kentucky.
Treadwell, Joshua B. 1865. General Orders Number 43. Middle Department. Baltimore, MD. Washington, D.C.: Government Printing Office.
Tucker, Spencer. 2000. *Andrew Foote: Civil War Admiral on Western Waters.* Annapolis, MD: Naval Institute Press.
Turner, Thomas E. 1862. General Orders Number 46. Army of the Potomac. Washington, D.C.: Government Printing Office.
Tyler, Erastus B. 1863. General Orders Number 29. Army of the Potomac. Washington, D.C.: Government Printing Office.
"Unit Roster 62nd Infantry Regiment." 1893. New York State Military Museum and Veteran Research Center. https://museum.dmna.ny.gov/unit-history/infantry-1/62nd-infantry-regiment.
US Sanitary Commission. 1866. *Documents of the US Sanitary Commission,* Vol. 1. New York: Sanitary Commission.
_____. 1867. *Contributions Relating to the Causation and Prevention of Disease, and to Camp Diseases.* Edited by Austin Flint. New York: Hurd and Houghton.
Van Boskirk, James. 1863. US Navy Officers' Letters 1802–1884, Publication Number M148, Record Group 45. Washington, D.C.: National Archives and Records Administration.
Van Buren, William H. 1861. *Rules for Preserving the Health of the Soldier,* 5th ed. Washington, D.C.: United States Sanitary Commission.
Varhola, Michael J. 2011. *Life in Civil War America.* Cincinnati, OH: Family Tree Books.
Varner, Allen. 1862. General Orders Number 21. Department of the Missouri. St. Louis, MO. Government Printing Office, Washington, D.C.

Varner, Van. 1951. *The Medical Corps of the United States Navy from the Revolution Through the Civil War*. Oakland: University of California Press.

Wade, Eugene J. 1862. Records of General Courts Martial and Courts of Inquiry of the Navy Department, 1799–1867, Volume 91, Record Group 125, Publication Number M273. Washington, D.C.: National Archives and Records Administration.

Walton, Oliver. 1862. General Orders Number 130. Army of the Potomac. Washington, D.C.: Government Printing Office.

Warnick, R. 1862. General Orders Number 2. Department of the Missouri. St. Louis, MO. Washington, D.C.: Government Printing Office.

Weiderhold, Louis. 1862. General Orders Number 16. Army of the Potomac. Washington, D.C.: Government Printing Office.

Weidner, Charles. 1862. General Orders Number 48. Army of the Potomac. Washington, D.C.: Government Printing Office.

Wells, Philip. 1862. General Orders Number 30. Army of the Potomac. Washington, D.C.: Government Printing Office.

Westwood, Howard C. 1985. "The Cause and Consequence of a Union Black Soldier's Mutiny and Execution." *Civil War History* 31: 222–236.

"What Shall be Done with Deserters?" 1862. *Frank Leslie's Illustrated Newspaper* August 30.

White, Richard. 1862. General Orders Number 41. Department of the South. Hilton Head, SC. Washington, D.C.: Government Printing Office.

Whittier, Andrew J. 1864. General Orders Number 68. Department of the Gulf. New Orleans, LA. Washington, D.C.: Government Printing Office.

Wiley, Bell I. 1962. *The Life of Billy Yank, the Common Soldier of the Union*. Newport, RI: Charter Books.

Williams, Aleck. 1864. General Orders Number 95. Department of the South. Hilton Head, SC. Washington, D.C.: Government Printing Office.

Williams, Jackson. 1862. General Orders Number 45. Department of the South. Hilton Head, SC. Washington, D.C.: Government Printing Office.

Wills, William. 1862. General Orders Number 34. Army of the Potomac. Washington, D.C.: Government Printing Office.

Will-Weber, Mark. 2017. *Muskets and Applejack: Spirits, Soldiers, and the Civil War*. Washington, D.C.: Regnery History.

Wilson, Joseph. 1870. *Naval Hygiene*. Washington, D.C.: Government Printing Office.

Winterfield. 1862. General Orders Number 35. Army of the Potomac. Washington, D.C.: Government Printing Office.

Wistar, Isaac J. 1914. *Autobiography of Isaac Jones Wistar, 1827–1905*. Vol. 2. Philadelphia: Wistar Institute of Anatomy and Biology.

Wood, Mersereau. 1862. General Orders Number 44. Army of the Potomac. Washington, D.C.: Government Printing Office.

Young, Edward E. 1863. General Orders Number 35. Middle Department. Baltimore, MD. Washington, D.C.: Government Printing Office.

Index

abolitionist 66
Adams, Edward 136
Adams, George 144, 223
Adams, Samuel L. 69
USS *Adolph Hugel* 180–81
African Brigade 223
Agnew, Peter J. 193
alcohol
  benefits 69
  as a defense 22, 82, 147
  mortality data 71
  onboard ship 76, 124
  poisoned 74
  prohibitionists 68
  related to crime, database 81
  Sanitary Commission report 78
  smuggled 115
  sutlers 86, 100
  theft 77, 107, 110
alcoholism, incidence 70
Alden, James M. 60
Alexandria Hospital 215
Allen, Walter 136
Ammen, Daniel 156
Anderson, Charles W. 101
Anderson, James A. 60
Andrie, William 107
Apalachicola, Florida 162
Articles of War
  defined 12–13
  55th, death penalty 21
  45th, drunkenness 68, 177
  preferring charges 18
  punishments 23
  63rd, rape 173
  24th, disrespect 209
Ashley, B.J. 45
Atkinson, Paul 108
AWOL
  database 28, 30

  as lesser charge 43, 45, 57, 63
  surgeons 213–14

Baily's Crossroads, Virginia 111
Baker, David L. 85
Baker, Joseph F. 43
Baker, Lafayette C. 38
Baker, Patrick 194
Baldwin, Augustus S. 75
Ball, Henry H. 116
Ball, John B. 101
Banks, John M. 137
Banks, Nathaniel P. 150, 179
Banning, Edmund P. 105
Barnaby, John L. 191
Barrancas, Florida 178
Barrett, Edward 82, 84
Barrett, Wallace W. 149
Barry, Charles 167
Barry, David 57
Bath, William L. 87
Battle of Fredericksburg 198
Battle of Gettysburg 55, 132
Battle of Missionary Ridge 112
Battle of Nashville 130
Battle of Stones River 130
Bell, Thomas 157
Benedict, Augustus W. 145–47
Benét, Stephen Vincent 18
Benton Barracks, Missouri 101, 191
bestiality 185
Biggs, George 62
Bishop, William 185
Black service members
  abused 135
  draft riots 131
  mutiny 144
  not commissioned 135
  prejudice in sentencing 135
  rape 173–75, 177, 180

237

Blaney, James A. 43
Bonner, James H. 167
Boskirk, James Van 181
Boudro, Julius 146
bounties
 brokers 36–38
 federal 39
 jumpers 36, 38, 44
 Marine Corps 39
Bourne, Peter 181
Boyd, Richard 34
Boyle, John 171
Boyles, John A. 138
branding 30, 131
brandy 73–74, 98, 100, 169, 195
Breese, Samuel L. 88, 117, 154
Bright, George S. 82
Bristow, Charles 161
British military law 18
Britt, John 164
Bromley, James 164
Brooklyn Navy Yard 56–57, 117, 119
Brown, Charles 184
Brown, Daniel R. 49
Brown, Harvey 211
Brown, James F. 41
Brown, Robert Eden 84, 89
Brownell, Benjamin 202
Brune, John 184
Brunt, Gershom Jacques Van 109
Burg, Richard 175
Burnside, Ambrose E. 101
Bussell, Alfred 156–59
Byrne, Bernard M. 13–14

Cady, Lewis 146
Caldwell, John C. 86
Callaghan, Daniel 137
Campbell, Peter 182
Camp Carroll, Maryland 45
Camp Cross Timbers, Arkansas 149
Camp Curtis, Arkansas 191
Camp Hamilton, Virginia 177
Camp Lake Springs, Missouri 86
Camp Parole, Maryland 189, 195, 216–17
Canada 40, 202
Canby, Edward 210
Cape Girardeau, Missouri 62, 107
capital punishment 9
Cardiff, William F. 209
Carrigan, James 114
Cash, Michael 160
cashiering 16, 106
Cassard, Lewis 40
Catlin, Isaac S. 91
Chadwick, William 51

Chandler, William 151–53
charges
 against surgeons, database 213
 lesser 133
 multiple, database 130
 preferred 14, 18
Charleston Navy Yard, Massachusetts 34, 108
USS *Cherokee* 124–26
Childs, George W. 223
chloral hydrate 74
USS *Choctaw* 98, 119
USS *Chocura* 160, 203–5
Christie, William P. 100
Christmas 145
chuck-a-luck 206
church, forced attendance 17
Churchill, William H. 143
Cincinnati Naval Rendezvous 28
City Point, Virginia 39–40, 44, 47
City Point Hospital, Virginia 44
Civil War Medical Department 69
civilian attorneys 24
USS *Clara Dolsen* 60, 114, 147, 151, 181
clemency 23–24, 31–32, 192
Cline, George W. 114
coaling 123, 154
coffee 70–71, 73
Colby, Allen W. 191
Cole, Henry 144
Coleman, Frederick T. 162
Collins, Cornelius 162
Collins, John 169
command authority 6, 151
Commissary of Subsistence 191
Conant, Daniel A. 189
USS *Conestoga* 151, 218
condition
 deranged 162
 mental 169
 moribund 190
 wretched 109
conduct
 abusive 154
 belligerent 98
 insubordinate 145, 150
 riotous 116
 scandalous 82, 92, 113, 126–27, 182–84
 subversive 208
 tyrannical 150
 unofficerlike 202
 unpardonable 176
 unsoldierlike 185
 valorous 140
confession 44, 57
Conley, James 184

Index

Connecticut
  cavalry 44–45
  infantry 62, 110, 144
Connell, Francis 147
conscription 36, 131–32
conspiracies 89, 95, 185
consultation, medical 69, 73, 96
Continental Army 12
contrabands 147, 161
contributory negligence 119
Conway, John 141
Coppée, Henry 22–24
Cornelius, Richard 147
court-martial
  addressing members 20
  compulsion 22
  convening authority 23, 30
  cross-examination 20, 24
  defense statement 20
  defense witnesses 19
  deliberate muteness 19
  earliest, database 7
  errors 14–15, 62, 139
  mandatory death sentences 21
  Marine Corps 167
  membership 15, 17, 19–21
  peremptory challenges 19
  president 15, 19
  punishments 15
  regimental 15
  right to counsel 20
  summary 24, 140, 143
  supernumerary member 101
  voting 21
court of inquiry, database 7
Crabbe, Thomas 74
Craig, James B. 154
Craven, Thomas T. 73
credibility, rape victim 174
crew
  intoxicated 127
  quarrelsome 155
  rebellious 117, 141
Cring, George 189
cruelty 145, 154
Curry, Samuel 163
Curtis, George W. 184
Curtis, Samuel Ryan 139, 188, 209
Curtis, Willis 146
customs of the sea 25

Dahlgren, John A. 76, 93, 127
database
  alcohol related offenses 80
  assault 155
  cavalry 9
  desertion, not guilty 29–30, 39
  engineers 8–9, 81, 129
  enlisted personnel 7–9, 30, 133–34, 136, 156
  forgery 194–95
  gambling 207
  guilty 8–9, 30, 81, 208
  landsmen 7, 81
  malingering 202
  manslaughter 129–30
  marauding 129–30
  Marine Corps 7–8, 80
  mitigation 30, 82
  murder 130, 156
  mutiny 133–34, 147
  Navy 7
  officers guilty 80
  punishments 9, 81
  rank distribution 7
  rape 130, 172, 180
  sexual misconduct 175
  theft 187, 192
  unauthorized absences 30
Davidson, Richard 62
Davis, Kent D. 102
Davis, William H. 182
Dawes, Richard C. 122
USS *Dawn* 151–52
deafness, feigned 202
Deemer, Samuel W. 56
defense
  legal ignorance 22
  witnesses 19
De Freest, William H. 86
De Hart, William C. 14
delirium tremens
  cases 74, 94, 96–97
  incidence 70
De Luce, Theodore F. 124–25
Dennison, William E. 124
desertion
  apprehended 27
  estimates 27
  Navy 28
  trend in punishments 34
Devlin, James 44–45
dice games 206
Dickinson, John R. 113
Dickman, Robert 170
Dinneny, Owen 144
discharge certificates, selling 196, 216
diseases
  feigning 204
  venereal 175
District of Columbia Infantry 181
Dix, John A. 44, 91, 212

Dobbler, George W. 191
doctors, death rate 213
Donald, James M. 169
Dornin, Thomas A. 200
Dorsey, John 100
Doty, William 190
Doyle, James A. 117
draft boards 36
draft riots 131–32, 140
Draper, Theodore W. 57
Dred Scott v. Sandford 96
Drew, Charles W. 146
Dripps, William A. 83
Driscoll, Patrick H. 35
drumming out 33, 131, 188
drunkenness
  Army regulations 68
  on duty 87, 110
  frequency 79
  punishment 106
Dry Tortugas, Florida 12, 30, 99, 122, 138, 179
Dulany, William 102–5
Dulany, William, Jr. 103–4
Duncan, William W. 84

Eagan, Edward 51
Eagle, Henry 117
East Gulf Blockading Squadron 49, 123, 159, 162–63, 192
Edisto Island, South Carolina 177
Eldridge, Charles 113
Elwell, John J. 212
Emancipation Proclamation, denounced 61, 198
embezzlement 113, 186, 190–92, 208, 216
Emerson, George A. 88
Engle, Frederick 200
English, Michael 107
English Mutiny Act and Articles of War 12
Enrollment Act of 1863 36, 131
epilepsy 163–64
erotic magazines 174
Esquirol, Jean-Étienne Dominique 164
USS *Ethan Allen* 123–24, 218
Eutwistle, James 86
Evans, John 110, 232
Evers, Michael 108
Everts, Morgan 100
Excelsior Brigade 31
excessive fines 16
execution
  by the Army 30
  firing squad 23, 168
  murder, database 156

  mutiny, database 134
  by the Navy 65
  types 23

Fahey, Bryan 31
Fair, Isaac C. 61
Fallon, Martin 110
Falmouth, Virginia 47, 86, 100, 177, 216
falsifying records 190
Farquhar, Norman H. 48
Farragut, David G. 42, 49, 65, 93, 140, 142
Felix, Ambrose 51
Fernandina, Florida 72, 138, 144, 193
Field, Stephen Johnson 158
Field, Thomas Y. 105
Fisher, Lucius 51
Fitzgerald, Maurice 187
Fitzsimmons, Phillip 211
Flagg, Samuel 69
Fleming, Christopher 112
flogging 16, 23–24, 188
Florida Contraband Headquarters 161
Floyd, John B. 14
Foland, John T. 60, 62
Folsom, Frank H. 195–96
Foltz, Jonathan M. 96
Foote, Andrew Hull 71
Ford, Thomas 143
Formhoff, Augustus 114
Forshay, Charles H. 54
Fort Cass, Virginia 100
Fort Columbus, New York 45
Fort Ellsworth, Virginia 137
Fort Ethan Allen, Virginia 87
Fort Jackson, Louisiana 144–45, 147
Fort Jefferson, Florida 99–100, 139, 146, 179
Fort Marcy, Virginia 52–53
Fort Marshall, Maryland 217
Fort Monroe, Virginia 17, 31, 66, 188, 197
Foster, John G. 53
Foster, Robert S. 41
Fox, Charles H. 191
Frank Leslie's Illustrated Newspaper 32, 36, 188, 202
fraternization 100–101
Fredericksburg, Virginia 70, 100, 198
Freeman, Nathaniel C. 124
furloughs
  forged, database 195
  regulations 64
Fyffe, Joseph P. 66

Gabaudan, Edward 94, 96–97
Gallup, Henry A. 192

gambling
  database 207
  horse race 210
  overlooked 186
Garret, Ambrose 161
Gavican, Michael J. 180
Gaylor, Charles H. 159
ghost 34
Gibbs, Edwin H. 158
Gill, Henry Z. 69
Gillmore, Quincy A. 62, 86
Gilmartin, Peter P. 98
Glynn, James 117
Glynn, John 66
Goldsborough, Louis M. 72
Gosman, John C. 178
Grafton, Edward C. 109
Graw, Jacob 159–60
Grayson, John C. 165
Green, Daniel 123
grievances 34, 40, 132, 198
grog 71–73, 76, 155
guard
  forcing 177
  provost 86, 161
  quitting 8
Guiteau, John M. 165, 194

Hagan, James 146
Halleck, Henry W. 86, 101, 168, 171, 208
hallucinations 95–96
Hamilton, Thomas 153
Hammond, William A. 68–69
Handle, Theodore 62
Harberger, John 196
Hargous, Peter J. 89
Harrington, Daniel C. 59
Harris, George 34
Harrison, Napoleon B. 108
Harrison, William 162
Harrison, William H. 53
Harwood, Andrew A. 28, 180–81
Haskins, William 108
Haslup, Charles 178
Haycock, George B. 165
Hayes, Edwin L. 149, 221
head shaving 131
Healey, James E. 169
Henderson, Andrew A. 96
Henry, Michael 113
Higbee, John H. 105
Higgins, Daniel A. 185
Hill, Alexander S. 179
Hill, Thomas K. 150, 233
Hillman, John 113
Hillman, William 113

Hilton Head, South Carolina 62, 138, 172
Hinsdale, Theodore 73
Hitchings, George H. 182
Hobb, Clement D. 165
Hobbs, George H. 119
Hoben, John 108
Hoegenauer, Charles 111
Hoffman, James M. 215
Holden, J. Albert 31
Holland, John E. 183
Holmes, Robert D. 165–66
Hoofan, Gustav 62
Hooker, Joseph 47, 198
Howell, David M. 97
Hudson, Henry W. 86
Hyman, Robert 116

idiocy 65, 163
idleness 17, 130, 132
Illinois
  cavalry 150
  infantry 85, 149, 170, 177, 191, 208
illness
  chronic 65, 198
  as excuse for desertion 53
  feign 109, 202, 205
  physician neglect 214
incitement 113, 136, 138
indecent behavior 176, 185
Indian Home Guard 191
Indiana
  cavalry 185
  infantry 131
inebriation 70, 79, 82, 92
insanity
  cases 65, 161, 164, 169
  legal 19, 21–22
insolence 134–35, 142–43
USS *Isonomia* 162–63
inspection report, false 102–03
insubordination
  cases 98, 123, 139, 143, 149
  legal 17, 28
insults, to females 175
intemperance 71, 85, 108–09
intent, criminal 18
Invalid Corps 179
Iowa
  cavalry 86
  infantry 188, 190, 199
Ireland 44, 154, 160
iron
  collar 172
  gag 117
  neck yoke 131

irons
  double 51, 56, 59, 123, 140, 160
  red-hot 131
  single 59, 143
  wrist 147
Ives, Thomas P. 181

Jack, Charles 51
Jackson, Andrew 170
Jackson, Henry 114
Jacksonville Mutiny 144
James, Hiram H. 97
USS *James Adger* 92–93
Jansen, Henry 150
Jefferson City, Missouri 169
Jewell, Harvey 34
Johns, Joseph 161
Johnson, Cyrus H. 191
Johnson, John C. 184
Johnson, William H. 30
Jones, Hugh 50
Jones, James H. 32
Jones, Robert 96
Jordan, Daniel 115
judge advocate, role 18–22
jumping overboard 162
justifiable homicide 159

Kane, William 40
Kavenaugh, Richard 106
Kelly, John 156
Kenealy, Patrick 56
Kennedy, Barney 170
Kennedy, Jacob 146
Kent, Stephen C. 61
Kentucky Infantry 31, 178
Key West, Florida 48, 55, 90, 124, 184, 193
King, Frederick T. 92
King, Rudolph 184
Kitchen, John S. 59, 109
Knight, Napoleon B. 209
Knobelsdorff, Charles 149
Kuhnes, Joseph 168

USS *Lackawanna* 123, 142
Lafayette Barracks, Maryland 63
Lamb, William 31
Lambert, Thomas T. 194
Lamine Bridge, Missouri 208
USS *Lancaster* 50–51
Lande, R. Gregory 1, 34, 201, 213
language
  abusive 81, 117, 147, 152
  blasphemous 218
  disloyal 60–61, 140
  disrespectful 61, 138, 142, 199–200
  infamous 175
  mutinous 127, 141, 158
  profane 90, 101, 144
Laven, John 57
Lawler, Michael K. 170
lawyers
  civilian 56
  complaint 146
  ship's 157
Lee, Charles E. 139
Lee, Samuel Phillips 59, 67, 116, 118, 197
Lee, Timothy F. 208
legal proceedings, reviewed 102, 112, 127, 144
Legros, George 182
Leighton, George 136
Leslie, Frank 33–34, 75
Lewis, Charles 49
Lewis, David T. 218
Libby, George W. 182–83
Lichtenheim, Theodore 176
Lieber, Francis 26
Light House Point, South Carolina 180
Lincoln, Abraham 11, 23, 25, 27, 76, 170–71
liquor
  before combat 79
  obtaining 77, 157
  poisoned 101, 119
  to prisoners 111
  to quell anger 157
  stealing 93, 187, 193
Little, David 214
Little, George D. 64
Lloyd, Richard 196
Locke, James W. 193
Lockwood, Henry H. 45
Lockwood, Samuel 72
Lomas, Francis C. 162
USS *Louisville* 161, 183
lunatic asylum 162

Macomb, Alexander 17–18
Maine Infantry 32, 189, 208
malingering 109, 201–3
Mallow, John H. 114
Maloney, Walter C. 124
mania-a-potu 209
Mansion House Hospital, Virginia 215
manslaughter 156, 171
USS *Marblehead* 126–27
Marine Corps
  bringing liquor on board 115
  draft riots 141
  grog 76
  mutinous conduct 147

Marine Corps Barracks
  Brooklyn, New York 56, 115, 165
  Cairo, Illinois 60
  Norfolk, Virginia 43, 102
  Pensacola, Florida 167
  Washington, D.C. 32, 147
Martin, James 34
Martin, William E. 14
Maryland
  cavalry 179, 210
  infantry 40, 63, 168, 176, 209
Massachusetts
  artillery 47, 132, 188
  infantry 55, 110, 175, 189, 203, 208
Matthews, John H. 184
McBride, Robert 203
McCarthy, Jeremiah 55
McClain, Edward 119–22
McCleery, Robert W. 83
McClellan, George B. 45–47, 52–53, 87, 111–13, 175–76, 214–15
McClelland, James 142
McCluskey, John 208
McCrea, Edward P. 50
McCuddon, Josiah W. 199
McCue, Joseph W. 217
McCutcheon, John F. 48
McDonald, John 58
McGrath, Michael 110, 232
McIntyre, William 193
McKean, William W. 218
McMahon, Bernard J. 156
McMenamin, Patrick 32
McVaugh, Edmund 43
Meade, George B. 55
Meade, George G. 40, 48
Meade, Richard W. 141
  medical care refused 64
  education 211
  exemptions 202
  malpractice 212
Meeker, Edward P. 165
Meley, James H. 64
Memphis Naval Hospital, Tennessee 121
mental incompetency 19
mental intent 18
mental stability 198
mental state 213
mental unsoundness 164
Merchant, Clark 89
mercy
  denied 45, 93, 121
  Lincoln 65
  recommended 45, 58, 122, 147, 164, 215
Merrill, George S. 176

Michigan
  cavalry 195
  infantry 195, 202
military law, defined 12
Miller, William W. 209
USS *Minnesota* 66, 108–10
Minor's Hill, Virginia 45
Mississippi River Squadron 116, 121
Missouri
  cavalry 139, 192, 209
  infantry 62, 101, 107, 196
mistreatment 151, 154
Mitchell, Ormsby M. 177
Monroe, F. Lebron 203
Moore, James H. 146
Moore, John 116
Morgan, Walter J. 55
Morgan, William 126
Morong, John C. 150
Morris, Henry W. 152
Morris, Joseph 184
Morris, William W. 190, 217
Morris Island, South Carolina 127
USS *Mound City* 161, 218
Mowry, George W. 62
Mulhern, Andrew J. 195
Mullan, Dennis W. 122
muskets
  accidental death 164
  shot to death with 54, 112
Myers, William H. 153

Naval Appropriations Act of 1862 24
Navy justice, administration 24
Navy officers
  abusive 194
  in database 129
  many charges, database 187
  mutiny, database 136
  surgeons, database 213
  unauthorized absences, database 30
  violence, database 129
Navy personnel
  alcohol-related offense, database 80
  numbers during war 24
Navy regulations, judge advocate 123
Navy surgeons, debating alcohol 73
nearsightedness 202
negligence, physician's 212
Neill, John 164
New Bridge, Virginia 203
New Hampshire Infantry 39, 41–42
New Jersey Infantry 87, 112
New Madrid, Missouri 196
New Orleans
  courts-martial 114, 116, 122, 126, 170

Naval Hospital 204
Parish Prison 205
New York
  artillery 45, 187, 213
  cavalry 30
  engineers 139, 185
  infantry 54–55, 86–87, 101, 132, 190, 214
  Naval Rendezvous 75
Newcomb, Henry S. 73
Nichols, Jesse T. 195
Nicholson, William C. 117
Norfolk Hospital, Virginia 155
Norfolk Naval Station, Virginia 102, 105
North Atlantic Blockading Squadron 59, 66, 72, 160

O'Brien, Henry F. 132
O'Brien, John 17
USS *Ocean Queen* 156–58
O'Connor, Frederick A. 66
USS *Octorara* 55, 167
officers
  cashiered for drunkenness 68
  convicted, database 9
  gambling 208
  inebriated 77
  resignation 55, 72, 92, 97, 210
  sentenced to prison 47
Ohio Infantry 53, 60–62, 194
Olsen, Peter 183
O'Malley, George W. 177
O'Neill, James 154
O'Neill, William 40
opiates 74, 95
orders
  disobeying 12, 107
  illegal as a defense 22
USS *Osage* 119, 121, 181–82
Otterville, Missouri 85, 106, 190
Overin, Henry C. 47–48
overstaying leave 28, 186

Pacific Squadron 50
Paducah, Kentucky 177
Palmer, James S. 122, 140, 203
Parker, Albert D. 124
Parker, James 156, 158
Parris, Thomas P. 162
Pass, Charles W. 152
Patten, David 153
Patterson, Edward 73
Patterson, Thomas H. 92
Paulding, Hiram 97, 140
USS *Pawnee* 72, 127
Pearson, George F. 50
Peck, George 74

Pendergrast, Garrett J. 152
Pennell, Isaac A. 124
Pennsylvania
  cavalry 87, 195
  infantry 39, 100, 177, 196, 198, 214–15
Pensacola, Florida 42, 123, 166, 184
Pensacola Navy Yard 167
Perdue, John B. 63
perjury 105, 121, 143
Perkins, Samuel C. 154, 156
Perley, Charles S. 92
Perry, David A. 110
Pettinos, James W. 216
Phelps, Elisha R. 157
Philadelphia
  Naval Asylum 71
  Navy Yard 75, 82, 88, 97
physicians, dual agency 211
Pilot Knob, Missouri 185
playing cards 101, 206–9
Plunkett, George 94–95
Point Lookout, Maryland 52
Polhill, Charles 142
Porter, David D. 60, 65, 150, 183–84, 218
Porter, John B. 215
Postwiller, William 139
Praxton, Albert 120
Prentiss, George A. 117
Prickett, James M. 137
profanity
  charged 197
  overlooked 186
prostitution
  courts-martial 179–81, 195
  overlooked 186
punishments
  Articles of War 23
  barrel suit 77
  common 131
  extrajudicial 133
  hard labor 16, 23, 81
  remitted 32, 86–87, 116
  sweat box 152, 161
  theft 187
  wearing knapsack 188

racial prejudice 135, 144
Randall, Francis V. 52
rape
  courts-martial 177–78, 180, 183
  Marine Corps 175
  not reported 173
  threats 173
  wartime law 26
Read, John H. 140
reduction to the ranks 23

regulations 12–13
reprimand 23, 81, 138, 156
revenge 161, 166
Reynolds, Charles 190
Reynolds, George W. 203
Rice, Thomas 218
Ricker, John 175
Riley, Owen 123
Roberts, Edward A.L. 87
Rodgers, Christopher Raymond Perry 28
Rohrer, John W. 150–51
Rooney, James E. 50
Root, Adrian R. 216
Roscommons, Thomas 140
Ross, John 117
Rothrauff, Samuel 107
Russel, William 150
Rutter, George H. 48

St. Augustine, Florida 18, 110
St. George's Sound, Florida 162
St. Inigoes Navy Yard, Maryland 51
St. Phillips, Louisiana 146
Sanborn, John E. 69
Sands, Joshua R. 75
USS *San Jacinto* 161–62
USS *Santiago de Cuba* 123, 193
Sartori, Louis C. 34
Schenck, Robert C. 62
Schermerhorn, John 57
Schley, Winfield Scott 94
Schofield, John 192
Schoonmaker, Cornelius M. 167
Scoby, Gilbert W. 92
Scovill, Samuel G. 42
Selfridge, Thomas O. 151
sentence, lenient 32, 38, 47, 87, 93, 210
Setright, John 195
sexual intercourse 176, 183, 185
sexual misconduct, Navy 175
Shannon, Thomas 143
Sheehan, Michael F. 189
Sheerin, John 125
Sheridan, Edward E. 106
Sherman, Robert 197
Shivers, Nicholas 63
Shorten, Richard 159
Shufeldt, Robert W. 159
sick list 69, 109, 195
Singleton, Abram 146
Sisson, Isaac H. 171
Smalley, Eugene A. 31
Smith, Charles N. 90
Smith, Edward B. 146
Smith, Elijah 188
Smith, George E. 65

Smith, James 161
Smith, Thomas L. 193
sodomy 172, 175, 182, 185
Southwick, William 60
Spear, Thomas 112
Spicer, William F. 35
Spitler, William 100
Squires, William J. 102–6
Stephens, William 169
Stewart, Lorenzo C. 213
Stillwell, Daniel M. 136
Stoner, John B. 149
straggling 28, 55, 178
Stribling, Cornelius K. 159–60, 162, 200
Stump, David M. 190
substitute soldier 36, 39–41, 44
suicide 162
Sullivan, Patrick 161–62
Sullivan, Timothy 183
surgeons
    as court-martial member 15
    dual agency 142
    veterinary 190
USS *Susquehanna* 139–40
sutlers 68, 72, 78, 100, 195
Sweeney, Hugh 188
swindling 190

Tampa Bay, Florida 218
tapeworm 163–64
Taylor, Albert 48
Taylor, Alfred W. 91
Taylor, Charles 146
Taylor, George W. 112
Taylor, William B. 122
tea 71, 73, 157, 215
Temperance Movement 70–71
Tepley, William 56
testimony
    black women 174
    contradictory 59, 172
    medical 105, 142, 162, 164, 198, 203
    procedure 20
Tevis, Charles Carroll 210
Thanksgiving 161
theft
    ammunition 191
    birds 114
    petty 187
Thistleton, George 179
Thompson, Edward R. 73
Thornton, James S. 94–97
Tighe, Richard F. 47
tobacco 74–75, 96, 204–5
Train, Samuel F. 97
Treadwell, Joshua B. 217

Trenchard, Stephen D. 48
Trickey, William H. 41
Trout, Jacob 31
Tullahoma, Tennessee 178
Turner, Thomas E. 167
Turner, Thomas J. 123, 142
typhoid fever 14, 83, 85, 104, 193

Union Navy
  executions 65
  rebel joins 42
United States
  Colored Cavalry 149
  Colored Infantry 145, 170, 178
  Colored Troops 54, 66
  Infantry 31, 106, 137, 167
  Sanitary Commission 70, 216
  Supreme Court 13, 158
Urann, William D. 193

Vail, Abram L. 98
Van Wyck, Charles H. 199
verdicts, valid 21
Vermont Infantry 52
Vicksburg, Mississippi 57, 140
Victoria, Abraham 146
violence
  domestic 169
  seasonality, database 130

Waddle, George 41
Wade, Eugene J. 72
Walker, James 190
Wallace, John 139, 229
Walton, Oliver 203
Ward, James 139
Warren, Oliver B. 143
Waters, Henry 182
Weiderhold, Louis 198
Weidner, Charles 208

Welles, Gideon 24, 60–61, 109–10, 151, 154, 156
Wells, Philip 110
Wenthorn, William 99
West Gulf Blockading Squadron 76, 96, 122, 203
West Point Military Academy 18, 23
Weston, George M. 113, 151
Wharton, Franklin 77
Whipple, Edward A. 92
Whipple, John P. 83
whiskey
  medicinal 69, 71, 73, 96
  ration 68
  riots 106
White, Richard 177
Whitehead, Paul 39
Whitehouse, Edward N. 98, 119
Whittier, Andrew J. 149
Wild, Edward A. 66, 223
Wild's African Brigade 66
USS *William G. Anderson* 42, 184
Williams, Harry 146
Williams, Jackson 138
Wills, William 101
Wilson, Joseph 73
USS *Winono* 94, 96
Wisconsin
  artillery 191
  infantry 208
witnesses
  character 74, 92, 167
  prohibited 21
Wolf, Frank 168
Wood, William M. 71
Woodbury, Jesse P. 83
Wright, John 69

Young, Jonathan 180

www.ingramcontent.com/pod-product-compliance
Lightning Source LLC
Chambersburg PA
CBHW032037300426
44117CB00009B/1088